A Longman Cultural Edition

D0706415

William Shakespeare's

ANTONY AND CLEOPATRA

Edited by

David Quint
Yale University

PEARSON
Longman

New York   Boston   San Francisco
London   Toronto   Sydney   Tokyo   Singapore   Madrid
Mexico City   Munich   Paris   Cape Town   Hong Kong   Montreal

Editor-in-Chief: Joseph P. Terry
Executive Marketing Manager: Ann Stypuloski
Production Coordinator: Scarlett Lindsay
Project Coordination, Text Design, and Electronic Page Makeup:
  Grapevine Publishing Services, Inc.
Cover Design Manager: Wendy Ann Fredericks
Cover Art: Sebastien Bourdon (1616–1671 French), "The Meeting of Anthony
  and Cleopatra," ca. 1645. Oil on canvas; Musée du Louvre, Paris. Peter
  Willi/Superstock.
Senior Manufacturing Buyer: Al Dorsey
Printer and Binder: R. R. Donnelly & Sons Company / Harrisonburg
Cover Printer: Coral Graphics Services, Inc.

Library of Congress Cataloging-in-Publication Data

Shakespeare, William, 1564–1616.
   [Antony and Cleopatra]
   William Shakespeare's Antony and Cleopatra / edited by David Quint.
      p. cm. — (A Longman cultural edition)
   Includes bibliographical references.
   ISBN 0-321-19874-3
   1. Antonius, Marcus, 83?–30 B.C.—Drama. 2. Cleopatra, Queen of Egypt, d. 30
B.C.—Drama. 3. Rome—History—Civil War, 43–31 B.C.—Drama. 4. Egypt—
History—332–30 B.C.—Drama. 5. Romans—Egypt—Drama. I. Quint, David,
1950– II. Title.

PR2802.A2Q8 2007
822.3'3—dc22

                                                                    2007016816

Visit us at www.ablongman.com

ISBN-13: 978-0-321-19874-7
ISBN-10:   0-321-19874-3

1 2 3 4 5 6 7 8 9 10—DOH—10 09 08 07

Contents

Antony and Cleopatra on the Sixteenth- and Seventeenth-Century Stage 204

The Great Critics on Antony and Cleopatra: *Schlegel to Bradley* 235

Further Reading 271

List of Illustrations

Cover: Sebastien Bourdon (1616–1671 French), "The Meeting of Anthony and Cleopatra," ca. 1645. Oil on canvas; Musée du Louvre, Paris. Peter Willi/Superstock.

p. xii. Mark Antony, portrait bust. Vatican Museums, Vatican State. By permission of Alinari/Art Resource, NY.

p. xiii. Cleopatra VII, Queen of Egypt, portrait bust. Antikensammlung, Staaliche Museen, Berlin. By permission of Bildarchiv Preussischer Kulturbesitz/Art Resource, NY.

p. xxx. Map of the Eastern Mediterranean world in 31 BCE.

p. 140. Octavius Caesar (Augustus), the statue of Prima Porta. Vatican Museums, Vatican State. By permission of Alinari/Art Resource, NY.

p. 145. Octavia Minor, sister of Octavius Caesar, coin portrait. Muenzkabinett, Staatliche Museen, Berlin. By permission of Bildarchiv Preussischer Kulturbesitz/Art Resource, NY.

p. 150. Mark Antony and Cleopatra, coin portraits. By permission of Yale University Art Gallery.

p. 205. Mark Antony and Cleopatra, engraved images drawn from ancient gems collected by Fulvio Orsini, in Théodore Galle, *Illustrium imagines*, Antwerp, Plantin, 1606. By permission of Beinecke Rare Book and Manuscript Library, Yale University.

About Longman Cultural Editions

Reading always vibrates with the transformations of the day—now, yesterday, and centuries ago, when presses first put printed language into circulation. So, too, literary culture is always open to change, with new pulses of imagination confronting older practices, texts transforming under new ways of reading and new perspectives of understanding, canons shifting and expanding, traditions reviewed and renewed, recast and reformed. Inspired by the innovative *Longman Anthology of British Literature*, Longman Cultural Editions present key texts in contexts that illuminate the lively intersections of literature, tradition, and culture. In each volume, a principal work gains new dimensions from materials that relate it to its past, present, and future: to informing traditions and debates, to the conversations and controversies of its own historical moment, to later eras of reading and reaction.

The series is designed for several kinds of readers and several situations of reading: The cultural editions offer appealing complements to the *Anthology*, as well as attractive resources for a variety of coursework, or for independent encounters. First-time readers will find productive paths to investigate, while more seasoned readers will enjoy the fresh perspectives and provocative juxtapositions. The contexts for adventure vary from volume to volume, but the constants (in addition to handsome production and affordable pricing) are an important literary work, expertly edited and helpfully annotated; an inviting introduction; a table of dates to track its composition, publication, and reception in relation to biographical, cultural, and historical events; and a guide for further study. To these common measures and uncommon enhancements, we invite your attention and curiosity.

Susan J. Wolfson
General Editor
Professor of English
Princeton University

About This Edition

To Samuel Taylor Coleridge, *Antony and Cleopatra* was the "most wonderful" of Shakespeare's plays. Nowhere else does Shakespeare write so evidently as the product of the Renaissance and its infatuation with classical antiquity. In bringing to life one of the greatest love affairs of the ancient world, Shakespeare conveys an era grander, sexier, more diverse than his own. In the play itself, he reflects this fascination in the appeal that ancient Egypt and the "infinite variety" of Cleopatra hold for imperial Rome, the latecoming, narrower culture that will conquer and replace them. *Antony and Cleopatra* expresses, with a mixture of nostalgia and irony, that sense of historical distance from the past that arose with the Renaissance rediscovery of antiquity and has come to define "modernity." As he stages a world-historical event and turning point (the conquest of Egypt and the consolidation of Rome's power under Augustus Caesar, her first emperor), Shakespeare also meditates on history itself as theater: as a war of public relations and image making that his Antony and Cleopatra ultimately win, even if they lose the battle of Actium together with their own lives. Yet *Antony and Cleopatra* is a tragedy with a difference: our sense that death has not and cannot extinguish the fully lived and fully imagined lives and love of the Roman general and his Egyptian queen.

The text of the play in this edition is that established by David Bevington for *The Complete Works of Shakespeare*, fifth edition (Longman, 2004), itself based on the First Folio published in 1623. The explanatory notes are also Bevington's, used with my gratitude and appreciation.

The Contexts materials invite readers to assess Shakespeare's imagination of Antony and Cleopatra in relation to the historical record, classical sources, and dramatic tradition. The historical background is provided by an overview of events and key figures in Roman history from 60 to 30 BCE—the action of the play properly begins in 40 BCE. The map displays its amazing geographical sweep; illustrations provide portraits of its lead characters from antiquity and in the Renaissance imagination. The next section offers samples from the ancient authors who wrote about and commented on the play's events. Shakespeare's primary source is Plutarch's *Life of Marcus Antonius*, from which I supply a generous extract; the bracketed act, scene, and line numbers indicate the relevant passages in *Antony and Cleopatra*. I also include a passage from Dio Cassius's *Roman History* that bears on 3.13, the pivotal encounter of Cleopatra with Thidias, the emissary of Octavius. Three passages of Roman poetry from the play's historical era follow: Virgil's depiction of the battle of Actium on the shield of Aeneas in Book 8 of the *Aeneid*, Horace's famous drinking ode on the death of Cleopatra, and, perhaps more unusual, Propertius's love poem comparing himself to Antony. All this poetry, probably familiar to Shakespeare and certainly to his culture, testifies to the varying degrees of sympathy elicited by the doomed lovers.

This sympathy is more fully felt in the tragedies produced in the sixteenth and seventeenth centuries in different national languages and theatrical traditions. Dryden's title, *All for Love or The World Well Lost*, is iconic. At the same time, these more classically minded playwrights tried to observe rigid decorum and the unities of time, place, and action. Sampling these plays with different versions of Cleopatra's death by Giraldi Cinzio, Jodelle, Sidney, and Daniel, the third Contexts section illuminates just how daring was Shakespeare's departure from neoclassical norms. The further extracts from Sedley and Dryden show these Restoration playwrights wrestling to reinstate those norms without sacrificing Shakespeare's dazzling complexity and dramatic energy.

Nineteenth-century Romantic criticism, in self-conscious disdain of neoclassical taste and rules, engendered a modern appreciation of Shakespeare and of *Antony and Cleopatra* in particular, its extravagant, sprawling structure an emblem of his challenging modernity. The final Contexts section traces the growth of this new understanding through the great critics, Schlegel, Hazlitt, and Jameson, up to Bradley's landmark essay at the beginning of the twentieth century. While these essays are clearly of their age, their broad reassessments and remarkable insights are still compelling and continue to set the terms of critical discussions today, including views on the nature of theatrical performance itself.

It is my pleasure here to acknowledge and thank the friendship, wit, and hard work of Susan Wolfson, whose expert editing has helped to shape and sharpen this volume and to make it more reader-friendly. I am also deeply grateful to Chrysta Meadowbrooke and Dianne Hall for the great skill and care with which they have prepared this volume for press.

DAVID QUINT
Yale University

Introduction

Antony and Cleopatra depends upon a mood of nostalgia and ret-
rospection. Through its "fall of princes" plot, in the medieval tradition of Boccaccio's *De Casibus*, where the proud and mighty are
overturned by Fortune's wheel, Shakespeare's play makes us feel
that an era is ending, that something great has passed from the
earth. This feeling may be common to the genre of tragedy: A com-
munity (including the audience) is left to wonder at the catastrophe
that has struck the titanic and individualized tragic protagonist.
But in *Antony and Cleopatra* the fall is especially alluring and, par-
adoxically, less tragic: Who would not want to be an Antony or a
Cleopatra?

With strange music heard beneath the stage, the spirit of Hercules leaves Antony in 4.3 and seems to take with it that magnificence and charisma that made Antony, like Hercules, a kind of
demigod on earth. Even Cleopatra, who did not shrink to present
herself at Cydnus as the goddess Venus, and later at Alexandria "In
th' habiliments of the goddess Isis" (3.6.17), laments at the moment
of his death,

> Young boys and girls
> Are level now with men. The odds is gone,
> And there is nothing left remarkable
> Beneath the visiting moon. (4.15.67–70)

Larger than life, these lovers open up a larger vision of life and way
of experiencing it. At the same time, the play is full of irony and
downright cynicism about Antony and Cleopatra and their nostal-
gic yearning for an age of everything great and remarkable. This is
a nostalgia not least for the world of classical antiquity itself. Of all
Shakespeare's plays, *Antony and Cleopatra* most vividly conveys

Mark Antony (82–30 BCE), ancient portrait bust.
By permission of Alinari/Art Resource, NY.

Cleopatra VII, Queen of Egypt (70/69–30 BCE), ancient portrait bust.
By permission of Bildarchiv Preussischer Kulturbesitz/Art Resource, NY.

the Renaissance fascination with classical culture and its expansive, heroic view of the human individual. Set in the ancient world, it realizes a dream of Renaissance humanism and brings classical heroes back to life on stage.

This "renaissance" happens, however, in a modern perspective that the characters themselves could not possess (the source of the play's most pervasive irony): Classical antiquity was dead and had come to an end. Such modernism, the discovery of history itself, was the other side of the humanists' veneration of the ancients. Classical culture could be resuscitated only with ironic awareness of the distance and difference of the past from the present Renaissance world.

What constitutes this awareness for Shakespeare? The play suggests five key, overlapping historical scenarios that measure the similarities and differences between antiquity and his modern world.

1. Octavius Caesar, ending the long era of civil wars, establishes one-man rule over Rome.
2. Cleopatra, the last Egyptian pharaoh, dies, "a princess / Descended of so many royal kings" (5.2.323–24), and Egypt succumbs to a narrower Roman culture.
3. Classical culture is about to be superseded by Christianity.
4. In Shakespeare's Europe, feudal arrangements of independent noblemen and petty states are succumbing to strong, centralized monarchies and nation states.
5. The Renaissance culture of individual aggrandizement is developing into a narrower, less aristocratic, more mercenary, and more puritanical culture.

In Shakespeare's hands, these developments are no smooth progress and may cross purposes. When, for instance, the Roman civil wars seem to settle into Octavius Caesar's victorious pronouncement, "The time of universal peace is near" (4.6.5), his language speaks past his intent to point—as do the play's repeated references to Herod of Jewry and to the child to which Herod may do homage (1.2.26–28; 3.6.75; 4.6.12–15)—to a Christian era offstage, waiting to be born. Inaugurating one-man imperial rule in Rome, Caesar may himself be part of another historical scheme, and Shakespeare reminds us of a whole new culture of Christianity that will challenge and supplant classical antiquity itself.

This double advent spells the end for the magnificent individuality of Antony and Cleopatra. It is not just the ethos of Christianity that runs counter to their self-glorification; so does the ethos of political absolutism. Power centralized under one ruler leaves no room for other self-aggrandizers. The great individuality of an Antony or a Cleopatra is possible only in competition and collision with other great individuals—a virtually constant state of war. It was in the competition of the Italian despots of the fourteenth and fifteenth centuries that the great historian Jakob Burckhardt identified the political roots of Renaissance individualism, wrested from and tested in struggles for power. So Octavius Caesar, shrewd Machiavellian analyst of power, weeps crocodile tears (2.7.49; 3.2.51–60) over the dead Antony: "I must perforce / Have shown to thee such a declining day, / Or look on thine" (5.1.37–39).

Closer to Shakespeare's home and history, this political struggle and its consequences took shape in the decline of a feudal nobility fighting both among themselves and against their king in order to retain local prerogatives and power. The Wars of the Roses (chronicled in Shakespeare's history plays) led to a strong central monarchy under the Tudors. The resulting "crisis of the aristocracy" found a belated, if spectacular expression in the failed revolt of the Earl of Essex in 1601, some half dozen years before the first performance of *Antony and Cleopatra*. The Essex conspirators paid Shakespeare's company to revive a play about an infamously weak king: It may have been Shakespeare's own *Richard II*. But the next play of Shakespeare's tetralogy, *Henry IV, Part One*, depicted the new monarchical order defeating its fractious nobles. Like the Roman order that supplants Cleopatra's Egypt, it is victorious, but far less grand. King Henry and his son Prince Hal bring peace and order to the realm, but with a death knell on the chivalry incarnated by the rebel magnate Hotspur, the soldier who would pluck bright honor from the pale-faced moon and who is full of scorn for the popingay courtier, that royal creature into which a formerly proud nobility has been reduced.

In *Antony and Cleopatra*, the struggle between monarch and nobility is projected historically backward into the conflict between Octavius Caesar, the "universal landlord" (3.13.72), and Antony and Cleopatra. In a key scene at the center of the play, Antony sees Caesar's emissary Thidias kiss Cleopatra's hand and feels doubly displaced: by Caesar, and by this mere courtier, "a fellow that will take rewards / And say 'God quit you!'" (3.13.125–26). Antony's inability to hold the "visible shape" (4.14.14) of his own character registers the identity crisis of an entire noble caste. At his death, Cleopatra laments a lost dream: "His face was as the heavens, and therein stuck / A sun and moon, which kept their course and lighted / The little O, the earth" (5.2.78–80). Shakespeare used almost the same language for Lady Percy's eulogy on Hotspur in *Henry IV, Part Two*: His honor "stuck upon him as the sun / In the grey vault of heaven, and by his light / Did all the chivalry of England move" (*2 Henry 4* 2.3.18–20). In the fall of charismatic Antony and Cleopatra, Shakespeare chronicles again the demise of an aristocracy and its grand style.

This style is epitomized in the title pair, Antony and Cleopatra, especially in contrast to Caesar. Their greatness shuns all measurement and rational calculation: to make a high-stakes gamble and fight by sea at Actium, to seek honor rather than expedience, to lavish gifts without thought for the cost, to surrender to drunkenness and gluttony, above all to love one another in spite of public opinion and political consequences. Their love is as reckless as it is grand. As if responding to the opening complaint of Philo that "this dotage of our general's / O'erflows the measure," Antony asserts, "There's beggary in the love that can be reckoned" (1.1.15). This is what (a few lines on) he will call the "nobleness of life," the exaltation of being seen through the eyes of one's lover. In its mutual flattery and self-aggrandizement, this regard is perilously close to a *folie à deux*. Yet this is no folly of youth: These lovers are middle-aged, with gray hair and wrinkles. Antony may echo Shakespeare's teenaged Juliet—"They are but beggars that can count their worth" (*Romeo and Juliet* 2.6.32)—but he and his queen know the illusions and costs of love. Their extravagant valentines to each other brave all censure.

Antony achieves this nobleness of life not in Rome, but in Egypt. This Eastern world, so much older and culturally richer, is itself a realm of excess—feasting, drinking, gaming, sex—and nowhere more so than in the superabundance of the Nile. "The higher Nilus swells," says Antony, "The more it promises; as it ebbs, the seedsman / Upon the slime and ooze scatters his grain, / And shortly comes to harvest" (2.7.20–23). This overflowing of the measure is life-giving; the more the Nile floods, the better the harvest. "Egypt" herself (so Antony calls Cleopatra) is generative. She has been "plowed" by both Julius Caesar and Antony and has "cropped" with children (2.2.237), while her attendants Charmian and Iras banter about future offspring with the soothsayer (1.2.25–72).

At the same time, this fertility brings human beings into contact with the body and its messy elemental appetites, where fertility cannot be separated from waste, the dung that is "The beggar's nurse and Caesar's" (5.2.8). Sexual pleasure pushes to excess that familiar equation of orgasm and death. Cleopatra is good at dying—"I have seen her die twenty times upon far poorer moment . . . she hath such a celerity in dying," jokes Enobarbus (1.2.140–42)—and the joke will play even in her suicide as she experiences for one last time the "joy o'th' worm" (5.2.276). This link of Egypt to the lower appetites parallels the pleasures of slumming. Cleopatra can "Hop forty paces through the public street" (2.2.238) and, to Caesar's dismay, Antony is wont to "keep the turn of tippling with a slave, / To reel the streets at noon, and stand the buffet / With knaves that smells of sweat" (1.4.19–21). Gender is just as malleable, exchangeable. Caesar again complains that Antony "is not more manlike / Than Cleopatra, nor the queen of Ptolemy / More womanly than he" (1.4.5–7). Cleopatra laughs to recall how she "put my tires and mantles on him, whilst / I wore his sword Philippan" (2.5.22–23). Commenting on the street scene of Alexandria, Caesar sounds like a Puritan critic of Shakespeare's theater, appalled by the mingling of classes in the playhouse and the transvestism of the stage (where boys played all the female parts).

Egypt and its queen radiate theatrical artistry. Shakespeare is shrewd to have her first meeting with Antony, a pageant of Venus on the river Cydnus, reported to us by the normally practical-minded soldier, Enobarbus. An already magical passage in Plutarch's *Life* of Antony becomes something extraordinary in Shakespeare's overflowing measures.[1]

---

[1] See North's translation of Plutarch's *Life of Marcus Antonius* (Contexts, pp. 158–59).

> The barge she sat in, like a burnished throne
> Burnt on the water. The poop was beaten gold;
> Purple the sails, and so perfumèd that
> The winds were lovesick with them. The oars were silver,
> Which to the tune of flutes kept stroke, and made
> The water which they beat to follow faster,
> As amorous of their strokes. For her own person,
> It beggared all description: she did lie
> In her pavilion—cloth-of-gold of tissue—
> O'erpicturing that Venus where we see
> The fancy outwork nature. On each side her
> Stood pretty dimpled boys, like smiling Cupids,
> With divers-colored fans, whose wind did seem
> To glow the delicate cheeks which they did cool,
> And what they undid did. (2.2.200–14)

The poetry adds its alliterative sound effects—consonance of the *p* and *b*, assonance of *u*—to the flute accompaniment it describes. The winds seem lovesick not only with the perfume from the sails but with the sails themselves. Appealing to all the senses, the whole tableau is redolent of sexual excitement, and the accompanying mermaids add to the effect: "The silken tackle / Swell with the touches of those flower-soft hands, / That yarely frame the office" (2.2.218–20). The fans that make Cleopatra's face glow even as they cool transvalues Philo's initial disapproving description of Antony, whose heart had "become the bellows and the fan / To cool a gypsy's lust" (1.1.9–10). It is not just the sexual aura that empowers her *coup de theatre* but also its dazzling luxury: gold throne, purple sails, silver oars, cloth-of-gold pavilion. She has turned herself into a work of art, with a hint of eternity in her charm: both doing and undoing at the same time, sex that can go on forever. As if he were experiencing the wonder all over again in his report, Enobarbus comments,

> Age cannot wither her, nor custom stale
> Her infinite variety. Other women cloy
> The appetites they feed, but she makes hungry
> Where most she satisfies; (2.2.244–47)

Through her artifice, Cleopatra makes life a never-ending feast.

These theatrics of greatness register what the play's train of events will strip away. Over the course of the five acts, Antony and Cleopatra seem to lose everything. Followers, pomp, jewels flow away from them, and Antony, when he thinks he has been betrayed by Cleopatra herself, feels he cannot even keep his own "visible shape," which dissolves like a cloud. Yet Cleopatra never loses her power to reshape, to recast their greatness: She dresses Antony up as a soldier just after his highest desertion of all, by the heroic spirit of Hercules. She, too, will don her finery, her robe and crown, before she plays for the last time.

Roman Antony can take a Roman's view of Egyptian "idleness" and see the perverse side to its fertility: "Ten thousand harms, more than the ills I know / My idleness doth hatch" (1.2.128–29), knowing "we bring forth weeds / When our quick winds lie still" (1.2.107–8). Caesar, by contrast, is all business: "Our graver business / Frowns at this levity" (2.7.120–21), he says as he breaks up the drinking party on Pompey's galley. To Antony's invitation, "Be a child o'th' time," the abstemious Caesar snaps, "Possess it, I'll make answer" (2.7.99–100). He will indeed be the universal landlord, giving nothing away: "Caesar gets money where / He loses hearts" (2.1.13–14). Antony is generous to a fault and is loved by his soldiers for it: He breaks the deserter Enobarbus's heart by sending his treasure after him.

The "boy" Caesar is a politician, but no soldier. As Antony bitterly recalls, he "kept / His sword e'en like a dancer" at Philippi (3.11.35–36)—the crucial battle for which Antony named his favorite sword. How futile it is to challenge this unchivalric dancer to fight "sword against sword, / Ourselves alone" (3.13.27–28). Caesar dismisses him as an "old ruffian" (4.1.4), not just old in years and a whoremonger with Cleopatra but an old-style swaggering soldier unequipped for the new political world. A more pragmatic Enobarbus has to spell out to Antony, who has fought at sea at Actium as a point of honor because Caesar "dares us to't" (3.7.30), that Caesar, with twenty men to their one, calculates the odds and does not respond to dares. So, too, Caesar's calculation even of the traditionally lavish victory feast: "we have store to do't, / And they have earned the waste" (4.1.16–17). Antony (compare 4.8.32–35) would never consider a feast a "waste," nor a measured expense, nor as something to be "earned."

Caesar's is the small-minded, narrower style of centralized power. In its calculation, its getting of money instead of hearts, its insistence on measuring everything—even love—the era ushered in by Caesar predicts the rationality of the modern political state and the reckoning of an entrepreneurial middle class, tightfisted and self-denying. It would be an age distrustful of pleasure, including the pleasures of the theater. On the advent of this new era of calculation and efficiency, Shakespeare looks back, even as his Antony and Cleopatra do at the end of their lives, on a world of greatness that now seems to be a dream of the larger possibilities of human experience. We might call this dream-world what Shakespeare's play does: "Egypt," its ancient culture now subsumed as a province of homogenizing Rome. Or we might call it what Shakespeare's day did: the outmoded ethos of an old aristocracy, the bearer of the magnificent individualism of the Renaissance, yielding before the new political and cultural arrangements of the nation-state and its new ally, the bourgeoisie. Or we might call it classical antiquity itself in the dreams of the Renaissance.

* * *

Even as *Antony and Cleopatra* makes us feel the pathos of historical change, the play calls into question the very category of "history." Basing his play on history, particularly Plutarch's *Life of Marcus Antonius*, Shakespeare not only refracts his source but nearly defeats the possibility of a coherent historical story in the theatrical world, and whirl, he puts on stage. The play's master image, the Nile, suggests the river of time, ever flowing and impervious to human meaning. The play closely relates it to another watery figure, the sea of chance, to which Antony and Cleopatra commit their military fortunes. Caesar's success, according to the Soothsayer, is due to a special luck that causes him to defeat Antony in all games of hazard, including the supreme cast of the dice at Actium. Key events seem governed by sheer chance. Vanquished Cleopatra bitterly calls Caesar "Fortune's knave" (5.2.3), even as Philo had introduced Antony as a "strumpet's fool" (1.1.13). The echo is telling: Lady Fortune (Hamlet tells us) is a fickle strumpet (*Hamlet* 2.2.238–39). There is a sense in which Cleopatra is an alter ego of Fortune, of contingency itself. Her infinite variety, her quicksilver changeability and possible treachery, can seem a product of and perfect adaptation to mutable time and chance.

The Nile's association both with flux and with a constant process of birth flows into the play's human, political world, where messengers continuously appear with the latest news. "With news the time's with labor, and throws forth / Each minute some," Canidius says just before Actium (3.7.82–83). "Much is breeding," says Antony earlier (1.2.188). "Every time / Serves for the matter that is then born in't" (2.2.9–10), says Enobarbus. Events overtake events—Eros says he has strange news, Enobarbus tells him it is already old (3.5.1–5)—and the play's world seems too busy, too multiple for the characters or the audience to take it all in.

This dizzying sense is aggravated by the breathtaking structure of *Antony and Cleopatra*, an array of scenes and events crisscrossing the Mediterranean world over some ten years. No play of Shakespeare more extravagantly flouts the classical unities of time, place, and action. Modern editions define some forty-two scenes, a constant sequence of entrances and exits. We continuously have to fix our bearings, switch our perspective. In an insistent pattern, choral characters (Philo, Enobarbus, Menas, Charmian) comment on the action we have just observed, yet they can report only from personal bias and limited information. Shakespeare thwarts our full grasp, any clear comprehension of characters and actions—as if to convey the impossibility of fully understanding these world-changing events. In this way *Antony and Cleopatra* dramatizes and makes part of its formal plan the Renaissance discovery of the contingency of human experience, of time liberated from the closed schemes of both Christian history and the political histories of nations.

Shakespeare's switching of scene reflects not only the intense creativity and diversity of experience in the flux of time but also fragmentation and dissolution:

> Let Rome in Tiber melt and the wide arch
> Of the ranged empire fall! (1.1.35–36)

> Melt Egypt into Nile, and kindly creatures
> Turn all to serpents! (2.5.79–80)

> So half my Egypt were submerged and made
> A cistern for scaled snakes! (2.5.96–97)

> Sink Rome, and their tongues rot
> That speak against us! (3.7.15–16)

> The hearts
> That spanieled me at heels, to whom I gave
> Their wishes, do discandy, melt their sweets
> On blossoming Caesar; (4.12.20–23)

> That which is now a horse, even with a thought
> The rack dislimns and makes it indistinct
> As water is in water. (4.14.9–11)

> The crown o'th'earth doth melt. (4.15.65)

> Dissolve, thick cloud, and rain, that I may say
> The gods themselves do weep! (5.2.296–97)

The sense of a world that liquefies or dissolves is the backwash of the overflowing, teeming Nile. Cleopatra voices the starkest version of this idea: Before she will let herself be led in triumph in Rome, she'd

> Rather a ditch in Egypt
> Be gentle grave unto me! Rather on Nilus' mud
> Lay me stark nak'd and let the waterflies
> Blow me into abhorring! (5.2.56–59)

The asp with its Nile slime might seem to grant her wish. But Cleopatra has other ideas, and through the design of her last, greatest work of art, she can proclaim: "I am fire and air; my other elements / I give to baser life" (5.2.286–87). She escapes water and earth, that is, the elemental mud of the Nile.

This is Cleopatra's solution. But how are *we* to make sense of this world of time constantly in motion, ever creating and dissolving itself? Should we follow Caesar and "possess" it, by turning it into "History"? Shakespeare thwarts that hope by confronting us with histories within history. Take, for example, a little passage at the beginning of 2.2. With their common enemy Pompey still to be dealt with, the third triumvir Lepidus thinks that this is no time for allies to quarrel:

LEPIDUS   'Tis not a time for private stomaching.
ENOBARBUS   Every time
  Serves for the matter that is then born in't.
LEPIDUS   But small to greater matters must give way.
ENOBARBUS   Not if the small come first. (2.2.9–12)

Enobarbus is saying something more than "we won't let an insult pass unchallenged," though that is the immediate idea. Time comes to us in discrete moments, each with its own set of circumstances. One must focus on what comes first, even if it is a small matter— and there really are no small matters. Similarly, there are no small scenes in this play. Each has it own weight, much compressed into little; each possesses value in and of itself.

To feel the play in this way, as a series of moments, each capable of lyrical expansion, within "History," places a premium not so much on what happens but on *how* it happens, on style. In a world of perpetual becoming, one of the play's running puns insists, it may be a matter of being becoming. This is what Antony and Cleopatra do best. In the first scene, Antony addresses his lover:

                      Fie wrangling queen!
  Whom everything becomes—to chide, to laugh,
  To weep; whose every passion fully strives
  To make itself, in thee, fair and admired! (1.1.50–53)

Two scenes later, Cleopatra responds in kind, teasing Antony into anger.

                Look, prithee, Charmian
  How this Herculean Roman does become
  The carriage of his chafe. (1.3.83–85)

And so she addresses Antony, even absent:

                Be'st thou sad or merry,
  The violence of either thee becomes,
  So does it no man else. (1.5.62–64)

She is the queen of this art of the moment: "vilest things / Become themselves in her, that the holy priests / Bless her when she is riggish,"

Enobarbus reports (2.2.247–49). Things, emotions, actions become themselves, are most fully realized in Antony and Cleopatra. And this dazzling pair, too, are represented not as one thing or another—sad or merry, Roman or Egyptian—but as all at once and in dynamic tension and movement: "painted one way like a Gorgon, / The other way's a Mars" (2.5.118–19), says Cleopatra of the Antony she thinks has betrayed *her* by marrying Octavia. The larger sense of life that is associated with them is an all-inclusive one, faults and all.

If style cannot save Antony and Cleopatra, it can make their deaths pale before their large lives. In staging her own death, Cleopatra challenges the "History" Caesar is trying to make. He has writings in his tent to prove his version of events and polish his image and place in history. With Cleopatra as a mere prop, a trophy from a victorious campaign, "her life in Rome / Would be eternal in our triumph" (5.1.65–66). Shakespeare makes us think hard here about "History": about how much of what we take to be the transparent record of events is a scenario scripted by those in power—with the documents already prepared for later historians. "History" gets written by the victors. He also makes us think hard about how his own play transmits and changes these events.

Antony and Cleopatra ends in a contest of would-be historians. In its most daring metadramatic moment, Cleopatra imagines Caesar's version of her and Egypt, the eternal life he has in mind for her in the eyes of posterity.

> The quick comedians
> Extemporally will stage us and present
> Our Alexandrian revels; Antony
> Shall be brought drunken forth, and I shall see
> Some squeaking Cleopatra boy my greatness
> I'th' posture of a whore. (5.2.216–21)

On Shakespeare's stage, these lines *were* recited by a boy actor playing the role of Cleopatra—and earlier the play *has* portrayed Antony getting himself drunk (2.7). It is a highly risky moment, for the audience has to ask itself what it is seeing. Inside the world of the play, Cleopatra imagines the degraded plays that enemy propaganda will stage about her. And she answers by preempting Caesar with her own version of her (historically unwitnessed) death, the image of her in the very play that we are watching:

> Give me my robe. Put on my crown. I have
> Immortal longings in me. (5.2.277–78)

Even here we cannot quite tell whether Cleopatra is making a last joke. The clown who brought the asps has made the malapropism about the bite of the worm being immortal, and she may be picking it up with a wink or roll of her eye: "I have immortal longings in me." Yes, she is playing in the mode of high camp that is her signature, and perhaps we should not take an overly solemn view of this death scene. But the phrase also speaks both of possible immortality beyond this "wild world" and, even more extravagantly, of the immortality of desire itself: "The stroke of death is as a lover's pinch, / Which hurts, and is desired" (5.2.292–93). Cleopatra casts death as a final erotic release, a "dying" in dying. And she reaffirms her and Antony's love, the love that unites the play—"Husband, I come!" (5.2.284)—one last time and for all time.

But, just as naturally, sex is a prelude to birth:

> Peace, peace!
> Dost thou not see my baby at my breast,
> That sucks the nurse asleep? (5.2.305–7)

The sublime tenderness and acceptance in her words remind us that Cleopatra is a mother. They recall all of the images of fertility and birth in the play, and their association with female experience, dramatically staged in this final scene of the queen and her women. Her evocation of the experience of nursing that men can never know, life-giving and pleasurable, suggests a "knot intrinsicate" (5.2.301) that cannot be untied in the natural cycle between death and generation. Is Cleopatra also giving birth to the soul that leaves her body? Having lived larger than life, she even succeeds, through imagination, through stagecraft, in expanding the moment of her extinction to its fullest.

Cleopatra gives birth, above all, to her own fame and myth, to the "Cleopatra" whom Shakespeare's play places before us, with all the self-consciousness of the modern Renaissance writer recreating the classical past—partly in the image of his own times, partly in imagination of how its own historical actors self-consciously staged history. And he closes the play with the victory of this "lass unparalleled" (5.2.313) over Caesar, the "ass / Unpolicied" (5.2.304–5). Faced with defeat, Caesar tries to appropriate Cleopatra's performance for his own narrative:

> High events as these
> Strike those that make them; and their story is
> No less in pity than his glory which
> Brought them to be lamented. (5.2.357–60)

I made their "story," Caesar insists, and it's my "glory." But the rhyme is muted by Shakespeare, who calls his play not "The Famous Victories of Octavius Caesar" but *Antony and Cleopatra*.

Table of Dates

82 BCE	Birth of Mark Antony.
70–69	Birth of Cleopatra.
63	Birth of Octavius Caesar.
60	First Triumvirate: Pompey the Great, Julius Caesar, and Marcus Licinius Crassus.
53	Defeat and death of Crassus at Carrhae.
49	Visit of Gnaeus Pompey, son of Pompey the Great, to Egypt.
48	Julius Caesar defeats Pompey the Great at Pharsalia; murder of Pompey in Egypt. Julius Caesar meets Cleopatra in Alexandria.
47	Cleopatra named Queen of Egypt; birth of Caesarion (Ptolemy Caesar).
44	Assassination of Julius Caesar.
43	War at Mutina. Second Triumvirate: Mark Antony, Octavius Caesar (Octavian), and Marcus Lepidus. Proscriptions, murder of Cicero.
42	Antony and Octavius Caesar defeat Brutus and Cassius at Philippi.
41	Antony summons Cleopatra to meet him at Tarsus; Antony spends winter with Cleopatra in Alexandria.

xxviii • Table of Dates

40	Rebellion and death of Fulvia, wife of Mark Antony; reconciliation of Antony and Octavius at Brundisium; Antony marries Octavia, sister of Octavius.
	Birth of Cleopatra's twin children by Antony, Alexander Helios and Cleopatra Selene.
39	Treaty at Misenum between triumvirs and Sextus Pompey, son of Pompey the Great.
39–38	Parthians driven beyond Rome's frontiers.
37	Antony sends Octavia to Rome and rejoins Cleopatra.
36	Birth of Cleopatra's son by Antony, Ptolemy Philadelphus.
	Forces of Octavius defeat Sextus Pompey.
	Octavius deposes Lepidus from Second Triumvirate.
35	Sextus Pompey killed in Asia Minor by one of Antony's generals.
34	Antony confers titles and territories on Cleopatra's children in the public "Donations of Alexandria."
32	Antony divorces Octavia.
31	Octavius defeats Antony and Cleopatra at Battle of Actium.
30	Octavius conquers Egypt; suicides of Antony and Cleopatra.
27	Roman senate confers title of Augustus on Octavius Caesar.
14 CE	Death of Augustus Caesar.

* * *

1558	Elizabeth I becomes Queen of England.
1564	Birth of William Shakespeare at Stratford-upon-Avon.
1574	Estienne Jodelle, *Cléopatre captive* (written in 1553).

1579	Sir Thomas North, *The Life of Marcus Antonius*, in his translation of Plutarch's *Lives of the noble Grecians and Romans*.
1582	Shakespeare marries Anne Hathaway.
1583	Shakespeare's first daughter, Susannah, is born six months after his marriage.
	Giovan Battista Cinzio, *Cleopatra* (written 1541–43).
1592	Mary Sidney-Robert Garnier, *The Tragedie of Antonie*.
1594	Shakespeare's acting company, The Lord Chamberlain's Men, is formed.
	Samuel Daniel, *Tragedy of Cleopatra*.
1596–98	Shakespeare's *Henry IV, Parts One and Two*, are performed.
1601	Revolt, trial, and execution of Earl of Essex.
1603	Death of Elizabeth I; accession of King James I (James VI of Scotland); Shakespeare's company now becomes The King's Men.
1607	Samuel Daniel, *Tragedy of Cleopatra*, revised.
1607–08	Shakespeare's *Antony and Cleopatra* is performed.
1616	Death of Shakespeare at Stratford-upon-Avon.
1623	*Mr. William Shakespeares Comedies, Histories, & Tragedies* (now called the First Folio) is published; first edition of *Antony and Cleopatra* is listed among the tragedies as *Anthony and Cleopater*.
1642–60	Theaters closed during the Commonwealth.
1677	Sir Charles Sedley, *Antony and Cleopatra*.
1678	John Dryden, *All for Love*.

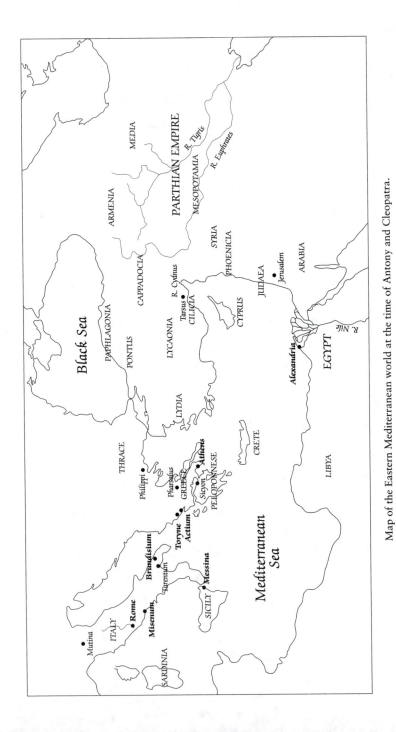

Map of the Eastern Mediterranean world at the time of Antony and Cleopatra.

Antony and Cleopatra

by William Shakespeare

Antony and Cleopatra

[*Dramatis Personae*

MARK ANTONY,
OCTAVIUS CAESAR, } *triumvirs*
LEPIDUS,

CLEOPATRA,
CHARMIAN,
IRAS,
ALEXAS, } *Cleopatra's attendants*
MARDIAN, *a eunuch,*
DIOMEDES,
SELEUCUS, *Cleopatra's treasurer,*

OCTAVIA, *sister of Octavius Caesar and wife of Antony*

DEMETRIUS,
PHILO,
DOMITIUS ENOBARBUS,
VENTIDIUS,
SILIUS, } *Antony's friends and followers*
EROS,
CANIDIUS,
SCARUS,
DERCETUS,
A SCHOOLMASTER, *Antony's* AMBASSADOR *to Caesar*

MAECENAS,
AGRIPPA,
TAURUS,
THIDIAS,   } *Octavius Caesar's friends and followers*
DOLABELLA,
GALLUS,
PROCULEIUS,

SEXTUS POMPEIUS *or* POMPEY
MENAS,
MENECRATES,   } *Pompey's friends*
VARRIUS,

MESSENGERS *to Antony, Octavius, Caesar, and Cleopatra*
A SOOTHSAYER
Two SERVANTS *of Pompey*
SERVANTS *of Antony and Cleopatra*
A BOY
SOLDIERS, SENTRIES, GUARDSMEN *of Antony and Octavius Caesar*
A CAPTAIN *in Antony's army*
An EGYPTIAN
A CLOWN *with figs*

Ladies attending Cleopatra, Eunuchs, Servants, Soldiers, Captains, Officers, silent named characters (Rannius, Lucillius, Lamprius)

SCENE: *In several parts of the Roman Empire*]

ACT 1
SCENE 1

Location: Alexandria. Cleopatra's palace.

Enter Demetrius and Philo

PHILO Nay, but this dotage° of our general's
O'erflows the measure.° Those his goodly eyes,
That o'er the files and musters° of the war
Have glowed like plated° Mars, now bend, now turn
The office° and devotion of their view   5
Upon a tawny front.° His captain's heart,
Which in the scuffles of great fights hath burst
The buckles on his breast, reneges all temper°
And is become the bellows and the fan
To cool a gypsy's° lust.

Flourish°
Enter Antony, Cleopatra, her ladies,
the train,° with eunuchs fanning her

Look, where they come.   10
Take but good note, and you shall see in him
The triple° pillar of the world transformed
Into a strumpet's fool.° Behold and see.
CLEOPATRA   If it be love indeed, tell me how much.
ANTONY   There's beggary in the love that can be reckoned.°   15
CLEOPATRA   I'll set a bourn° how far to be beloved.
ANTONY   Then must thou needs find out new heaven, new earth.°

Enter a Messenger

1 **dotage** foolish affection, sometimes associated with old age   2 **O'erflows the measure** exceeds moderation, exceeds the means of measuring it   3 **files and musters** orderly formations   4 **plated** clothed in armor   5 **office** function   6 **tawny front** dark face (literally, forehead)   8 **reneges all temper** renounces all moderation   10 **gypsy's** (gypsies were widely believed to have come from Egypt, to enjoy magical powers, and to be lustful and cunning) | s.d. *Flourish* trumpet fanfare announcing the arrival or departure of important person | *train* retinue   12 **triple** one of three (alludes to the triumvirate of Antony, Lepidus, and Octavius Caesar; also to tripartite division of the world into Asia, Africa, and Europe)   13 **fool** plaything   15 **There's . . . reckoned** love that can be quantified is paltry; ours is infinite   16 **bourn** boundary, limit   17 **Then . . . earth** only in some new universe could you find a limit to my love (the language echoes Revelation 21.1 and other biblical passages)

MESSENGER News, my good lord, from Rome.
ANTONY Grates me! The sum.°
CLEOPATRA Nay, hear them,° Antony.   20
  Fulvia° perchance is angry, or who knows
  If the scarce-bearded Caesar° have not sent
  His powerful mandate to you, "Do this, or this;
  Take in° that kingdom, and enfranchise° that;
  Perform't, or else we damn° thee."   25
ANTONY How,° my love?
CLEOPATRA Perchance?° Nay, and most like.°
  You must not stay here longer; your dismission°
  Is come from Caesar. Therefore hear it, Antony.
  Where's Fulvia's process?° Caesar's, I would say. Both?   30
  Call in the messengers. As I am Egypt's queen,
  Thou blushest, Antony, and that blood of thine
  Is Caesar's homager; else so thy cheek pays shame°
  When shrill-tongued Fulvia scolds. The messengers!
ANTONY Let Rome in Tiber melt and the wide arch   35
  Of the ranged° empire fall! Here is my space.
  Kingdoms are clay; our dungy earth alike
  Feeds beast as man. The nobleness of life
  Is to do thus;° when such a mutual pair
  And such a twain can do't, in which I bind,   40
  On pain of punishment, the world to weet
  We stand up peerless.°
CLEOPATRA   Excellent falsehood!
  Why did he marry Fulvia, and not° love her?

---

19 **Grates . . . sum** it annoys me! be brief   20 **them** the news   21 **Fulvia** Antony's wife   22 **scarce-bearded Caesar** (Octavius Caesar was 23 in 40 BCE, at the time of the play's opening; Antony was 43)   24 **Take in** conquer | **enfranchise** set free   25 **damn** condemn to death   26 **How** what's that you say?   27 **Perchance** (Cleopatra reconsiders what she has said in line 21) | **like** likely   28 **dismission** order to depart   30 **process** writ to appear in court   33 **Is . . . shame** is Caesar's vassal, doing homage to him; or else your blushing pays the tribute of shame   36 **ranged** well ordered and far-extending   39 **thus** (may indicate an embrace, or Antony may refer more generally to their way of life)   40–2 **in which . . . peerless** with respect to which I insist that the world, under penalty of punishment if it fails to do so, acknowledge us to be peerless   43 **and not** if he did not

I'll seem the fool I am not.° Antony
Will be himself.°

ANTONY   But stirred° by Cleopatra.   45
Now, for the love of Love and her soft hours,
Let's not confound° the time with conference° harsh.
There's not a minute of our lives should stretch°
Without some pleasure now. What sport tonight?

CLEOPATRA   Hear the ambassadors.

ANTONY   Fie, wrangling queen!   50
Whom everything becomes—to chide, to laugh,
To weep; whose every passion fully strives
To make itself, in thee, fair and admired!
No messenger but thine; and all alone
Tonight we'll wander through the streets and note   55
The qualities of people. Come, my queen,
Last night you did desire it.—Speak not to us.

         Exeunt [Antony and Cleopatra] with the train

DEMETRIUS   Is Caesar with Antonius prized° so slight?

PHILO   Sir, sometimes when he is not Antony
He comes too short of that great property°   60
Which still° should go with Antony.

DEMETRIUS   I am full sorry
That he approves° the common liar, who
Thus speaks of him at Rome; but I will hope
Of° better deeds tomorrow. Rest you happy!

                              Exeunt

♣

---

44 I'll . . . not I'll pretend to be gullible and believe him, though I know better
45 be himself be the Roman Antony, be the fool and deceiver he always is, etc. |
stirred (1) prompted to noble deeds (2) moved to folly (3) sexually stirred
47 confound ruin, waste | **conference** conversation   **48 should stretch** that should
be prolonged   **58 prized** valued   **60 property** quality, distinction   **61 still** always
62 approves corroborates   **64 Of** for

ACT 1
SCENE 2

Location: Alexandria. Cleopatra's palace.

Enter Enobarbus, Lamprius, a Soothsayer, Rannius,
Lucillius,° Charmian, Iras, Mardian the eunuch, and Alexas

CHARMIAN Lord Alexas, sweet Alexas, most anything Alexas,
almost most absolute° Alexas, where's the soothsayer that
you praised so to th' Queen? Oh, that I knew this husband,°
which, you say, must charge his horns with garlands!°

ALEXAS Soothsayer! 5

SOOTHSAYER Your will?

CHARMIAN Is this the man?—Is't you, sir, that know things?

SOOTHSAYER In nature's infinite book of secrecy
A little I can read.

ALEXAS [*to Charmian*] Show him your hand. 10

ENOBARBUS [*to servants within*]
Bring in the banquet° quickly; wine enough
Cleopatra's health to drink.

CHARMIAN [*giving her hand to the Soothsayer*]
Good sir, give me good fortune.

SOOTHSAYER I make not, but foresee.

CHARMIAN Pray, then, foresee me one. 15

SOOTHSAYER You shall be yet far fairer than you are.

CHARMIAN He means in flesh.°

IRAS No, you shall paint° when you are old.

CHARMIAN Wrinkles forbid!

ALEXAS Vex not his prescience. Be attentive. 20

CHARMIAN Hush!

SOOTHSAYER You shall be more beloving than beloved.

CHARMIAN I had rather heat my liver with drinking.°

0.1–2 *Lamprius . . . Lucillius* (Lamprius may possibly be the Soothsayer, but
Rannius and Lucillius have no speaking parts here and do not appear again in the
play; Mardian is mute here but does speak in later scenes) **2 absolute** perfect
4 this husband (evidently Alexas has told Charmian that the Soothsayer will
prophesy a husband for her) **4 must . . . garlands** must decorate his cuckold's
horns with a garland of flowers, like a sacrificial beast (cuckolded men were
derisively thought of as growing horns, as a badge of their infamy) **11 banquet**
light repast, dessert **17 in flesh** by putting on weight **18 paint** use makeup **23 heat
. . . drinking** heat my liver with wine rather than with unrequited love (the liver was
believed to be the seat of sexual desire)

ALEXAS Nay, hear him.

CHARMIAN Good now,° some excellent fortune! Let me be mar-   25
ried to three kings in a forenoon and widow them all. Let
me have a child at fifty, to whom Herod of Jewry° may do
homage. Find me° to marry me with Octavius Caesar, and
companion me with my mistress.°

SOOTHSAYER You shall outlive the lady whom you serve.   30

CHARMIAN Oh, excellent! I love long life better than figs.°

SOOTHSAYER You have seen and proved° a fairer former fortune
Than that which is to approach.

CHARMIAN Then belike° my children shall have no names.°
Prithee, how many boys and wenches° must I have?°   35

SOOTHSAYER If every of your wishes had a womb,
And fertile every wish, a million.

CHARMIAN Out, fool! I forgive thee for a witch.°

ALEXAS You think none but your sheets are privy to° your
wishes.   40

CHARMIAN Nay, come, tell Iras hers.

ALEXAS We'll know all our fortunes.

ENOBARBUS Mine, and most of our fortunes tonight, shall be—
drunk to bed.

IRAS [*giving her hand to the Soothsayer*]
There's a palm presages chastity, if nothing else.   45

CHARMIAN E'en as the o'erflowing Nilus presageth famine.°

IRAS Go, you wild° bedfellow, you cannot soothsay.

CHARMIAN Nay, if an oily palm° be not a fruitful prognostication,° I cannot scratch mine ear. Prithee, tell her but a
workaday° fortune.   50

SOOTHSAYER Your fortunes are alike.

IRAS But how, but how? Give me particulars.

25 Good now come on, now   **27 Herod of Jewry** even the blustering tyrant who
massacred the children of Judea   **28 Find me** find in my palm   **29 companion . . .
mistress** give me equal fortune with Cleopatra; or, perhaps, let Cleopatra become
my "companion" or attendant   **31 better than figs** (probably a proverbial
expression; with genital suggestion)   **32 proved** experienced   **34 belike** probably |
have no names be illegitimate   **35 wenches** girls | **must I have** am I to have
38 Out . . . witch (Charmian jokingly says that, since soothsayers, like fools, are
allowed to speak freely without penalty, she will forgive him for slander)   **39 privy
to** in on the secret of   **46 E'en . . . famine** (Charmian speaks ironically; the
overflowing Nile presages abundance; see 2.7.17–23)   **47 wild** wanton   **48 oily
palm** sweaty or moist palm (indicating a sensual disposition)   **48–9 fruitful
prognostication** omen of fertility   **50 workaday** ordinary

SOOTHSAYER I have said.°

IRAS Am I not an inch of fortune better than she?

CHARMIAN Well, if you were but an inch of fortune better than   55
I, where would you choose it?

IRAS Not in my husband's nose.°

CHARMIAN Our worser thoughts heavens mend!° Alexas—
come, his fortune, his fortune! Oh, let him marry a woman
that cannot go,° sweet Isis,° I beseech thee, and let her die   60
too, and give him a worse, and let worse follow worse till
the worst of all follow him laughing to his grave, fiftyfold a
cuckold! Good Isis, hear me° this prayer, though thou deny
me a matter of more weight; good Isis, I beseech thee!

IRAS Amen, dear goddess, hear that prayer of the people! For,   65
as it is a heart-breaking to see a handsome man loose-
wived,° so it is a deadly sorrow to behold a foul° knave un-
cuckolded. Therefore, dear Isis, keep decorum,° and fortune him° accordingly!

CHARMIAN Amen.   70

ALEXAS Lo now, if it lay in their hands to make me a cuckold,
they would make themselves whores but they'd do't.°

Enter Cleopatra

ENOBARBUS Hush! Here comes Antony.

CHARMIAN Not he. The Queen.

CLEOPATRA Saw you my lord?   75

ENOBARBUS No, lady.

CLEOPATRA Was he not here?

CHARMIAN No, madam.

CLEOPATRA He was disposed to mirth, but on the sudden
A Roman thought hath struck him. Enobarbus!   80

ENOBARBUS Madam?

---

53 I have said I have no more to say   **57 Not . . . nose** (Iras bawdily hints at some
place other than in the nose where she would prefer to see her husband well
endowed)   **58 Our . . . mend!** (Charmian pretends to be shocked: may heaven
improve our dirty minds!)   **60 cannot go** (1) is lame (2) cannot make love
satisfactorily or cannot bear children | **Isis** Egyptian goddess usually identified
with fertility and the moon   **63 hear me** hear (on my behalf)   **66–7 loose-wived**
with an unfaithful wife   **67 foul** ugly   **68 keep decorum** deal suitably with the case
68–9 fortune him grant him fortune   **72 they . . . do't** they would stop at nothing,
even becoming whores, to cuckold me

CLEOPATRA   Seek him and bring him hither. Where's Alexas?

ALEXAS   Here at your service.—My lord approaches.

Enter Antony with a Messenger

CLEOPATRA   We will not look upon him. Go with us.

Exeunt [all but Antony and the Messenger]

FIRST MESSENGER   Fulvia thy wife first came into the field.°   85

ANTONY   Against my brother Lucius?

FIRST MESSENGER   Ay.

But soon that war had end, and the time's state°
Made friends of them, jointing° their force 'gainst Caesar,
Whose better issue in the war from Italy   90
Upon the first encounter drave them.°

ANTONY   Well, what worst?

FIRST MESSENGER   The nature of bad news infects the teller.°

ANTONY   When it concerns the fool or coward. On.

Things that are past are done with me. 'Tis thus: 95
Who tells me true, though in his tale lie death,
I hear him as° he flattered.

FIRST MESSENGER   Labienus—°

This is stiff news—hath with his Parthian force
Extended° Asia; from Euphrates
His conquering banner shook, from Syria   100
To Lydia and to Ionia,
Whilst—

ANTONY   Antony, thou wouldst say.

FIRST MESSENGER   Oh, my lord!

ANTONY   Speak to me home; mince not the general tongue.°

Name Cleopatra as she is called in Rome;
Rail thou in Fulvia's phrase,° and taunt my faults   105
With such full license as both truth and malice
Have power to utter. Oh, then we bring forth weeds

---

85 **field** battlefield   88 **time's state** circumstances prevailing at the moment   89 **jointing** uniting   90–1 **Whose . . . them** whose better military success drove them from Italy upon the very first encounter   93 **infects the teller** makes the teller seem unwelcome   97 **as** as if | **Labienus** (Brutus and Cassius had sent Quintus Labienus to Orodes, King of Parthia, to seek aid against Antony and Octavius Caesar; with a force thus obtained, he is now overrunning the Roman provinces in the Middle East)   99 **Extended** seized upon (a legal phrase)   103 **Speak . . . tongue** speak bluntly; don't minimize the common report   105 **Rail . . . phrase** scold me as Fulvia would

When our quick° winds lie still, and our ills told us
Is as our earing.° Fare thee well awhile.
FIRST MESSENGER At your noble pleasure.   110

Exit [First] Messenger

Enter another Messenger

ANTONY From Sicyon, ho, the news! Speak there.
SECOND MESSENGER The man from Sicyon°—is there such an one?
THIRD MESSENGER He stays upon° your will.   *at the door*
ANTONY   Let him appear.—
[Exeunt Second and Third Messengers]
These strong Egyptian fetters I must break,
Or lose myself in dotage.

Enter another Messenger, with a letter

What are you?   115
FOURTH MESSENGER Fulvia thy wife is dead.
ANTONY Where died she?
FOURTH MESSENGER In Sicyon.
Her length of sickness, with what else more serious
Importeth° thee to know, this bears.   *[He gives a letter]*
ANTONY   Forbear° me.   120
[Exit Fourth Messenger]
There's a great spirit gone! Thus did I desire it.
What our contempts doth often hurl from us
We wish it ours again. The present pleasure,
By revolution lowering,° does become
The opposite of itself. She's good, being gone;   125
The hand could° pluck her back that shoved her on.
I must from this enchanting queen break off.
Ten thousand harms more than the ills I know

108 **quick** alive, inventive   108–9 **our ills . . . earing** hearing our faults told to us improves us, as plowing *(earing)* improves land by rooting out the weeds   112 **The man from Sicyon** (the messenger who has just entered, not being from Sicyon, realizes in some confusion that Antony wants to hear the news from Sicyon; this second messenger therefore calls out to ask if the messenger from Sicyon is to be found; another messenger at the door replies that such a man is indeed waiting, and in a moment that messenger from Sicyon enters with his report; some editors change the second and third messengers into attendants) *Sicyon* is an ancient city in Greece, where Antony left Fulvia   113 **stays upon** awaits   120 **Importeth** concerns | **forbear** leave   124 **By revolution lowering** sinking in our estimation in the course of time and Fortune's turning wheel   126 **could** would be willing to

My idleness doth hatch.—How now, Enobarbus!

Enter Enobarbus

ENOBARBUS   What's your pleasure, sir?   130

ANTONY   I must with haste from hence.

ENOBARBUS   Why, then, we kill all our women. We see how
mortal an unkindness is to them; if they suffer our departure, death's the word.

ANTONY   I must be gone.   135

ENOBARBUS   Under a compelling occasion, let women die. It
were pity to cast them away for nothing, though between
them and a great cause they should be esteemed nothing.
Cleopatra, catching but the least noise° of this, dies instantly;
I have seen her die° twenty times upon far poorer moment.°   140
I do think there is mettle° in death, which commits some
loving act upon her, she hath such a celerity in dying.

ANTONY   She is cunning past man's thought.

ENOBARBUS   Alack, sir, no, her passions are made of nothing
but the finest part of pure love. We cannot call her winds   145
and waters sighs° and tears; they are greater storms and
tempests than almanacs can report. This cannot be cunning
in her; if it be, she makes a shower of rain as well as Jove.

ANTONY   Would I had never seen her!

ENOBARBUS   Oh, sir, you had then left unseen a wonderful piece   150
of work, which not to have been blessed withal would have
discredited your travel.

ANTONY   Fulvia is dead.

ENOBARBUS   Sir?

ANTONY   Fulvia is dead.   155

ENOBARBUS   Fulvia?

ANTONY   Dead.

ENOBARBUS   Why, sir, give the gods a thankful sacrifice.
When it pleaseth their deities to take the wife of a man
from him, it shows to man the tailors° of the earth; com-   160
forting therein, that when old robes are worn out, there

---

139 **noise** hint, rumor   140 **die** (playing on a common second meaning of "achieve
sexual orgasm") | **poorer moment** lesser cause   141 **mettle** sexual vigor
146 **sighs** mere sighs   160 **tailors** (the gods can fashion a new wife for a man, much
as a tailor can mend or replace a worn-out garment)

are members° to make new. If there were no more women
but Fulvia, then had you indeed a cut, and the case to be
lamented. This grief is crowned with consolation; your old
smock° brings forth a new petticoat, and indeed the tears   165
live in an onion that should water this sorrow.°

ANTONY   The business she hath broachèd° in the state
Cannot endure my absence.

ENOBARBUS   And the business you have broached here cannot
be without you, especially that of Cleopatra's, which wholly   170
depends on your abode.°

ANTONY   No more light° answers. Let our officers
Have notice what we purpose. I shall break°
The cause of our expedience° to the Queen
And get her leave° to part. For not alone   175
The death of Fulvia, with more urgent touches,°
Do strongly speak to us, but the letters too
Of many our contriving friends° in Rome
Petition us at home.° Sextus Pompeius°
Hath given the dare to Caesar and commands   180
The empire of the sea. Our slippery° people,
Whose love is never linked to the deserver
Till his deserts are past, begin to throw°
Pompey the Great° and all his dignities
Upon his son, who—high in name and power,   185
Higher than both in blood and life°—stands up
For the main soldier;° whose quality, going on,
The sides o'th' world may danger.° Much is breeding,

---

162 **members** (the word has a bawdy suggestion, pursued in ll. 173–4 and 180 in *cut,
case, business,* and *broached; cut* and *case* suggest the female sexual organs; *broached*
suggests something that is stabbed, pricked, opened)   165 **smock** undergarment (also
used defamatorily of women)   165–6 **the tears . . . sorrow** only an onion could produce
tears on this occasion of Fulvia's death   167 **broachèd** opened up (but see the note for
l. 162)   171 **abode** staying   172 **light** frivolous, indelicate   173 **break** break the news
of   174 **expedience** haste   175 **leave** consent   176 **urgent touches** pressing matters
178 **Of . . . friends** from many friends working in our interest   179 **at home** to come
home | **Sextus Pompeius** son of Pompey the Great, who, though outlawed, has
been able to exploit the division between Antony and Octavius and thereby gain
command of Sicily and the sea; he appears in Act 2   181 **slippery** fickle   183 **throw**
bestow   184 **Pompey the Great** the title and honored status of "Pompey the Great"
186 **blood and life** mettle and vitality   186–7 **stands . . . soldier** lays claim to being the
greatest soldier   187–8 **whose . . . danger** whose aspiring character and situation, if
allowed to continue unchecked, may endanger the frame of the Roman world

Which, like the courser's hair,° hath yet but life,
And not a serpent's poison.° Say our pleasure,   190
To such whose place is under us, requires
Our quick remove from hence.°
ENOBARBUS   I shall do't.

[Exeunt separately]

✤

ACT 1
SCENE 3

Location: Alexandria. Cleopatra's palace.

Enter Cleopatra, Charmian, Alexas, and Iras

CLEOPATRA   Where is he?
CHARMIAN   I did not see him since.°
CLEOPATRA *[to Alexas]*
  See where he is, who's with him, what he does.
  I did not send you.° If you find him sad,°
  Say I am dancing; if in mirth, report
  That I am sudden° sick. Quick, and return.   5

[Exit Alexas]

CHARMIAN   Madam, methinks, if you did love him dearly,
  You do not hold the method° to enforce
  The like from him.
CLEOPATRA   What should I do I do not?°
CHARMIAN   In each thing give him way. Cross him in nothing.
CLEOPATRA   Thou teachest like a fool: the way to lose him.   10
CHARMIAN   Tempt° him not so too far. I wish,° forbear;
  In time we hate that which we often fear.

Enter Antony

---

189 **like . . . hair** (allusion to the popular belief that a horsehair put into water
would turn to a snake)   189–90 **hath . . . poison** is alive at this point but not yet a
poisonous full-grown serpent   190–92 **Say . . . hence** tell those who serve me that
my wish is to depart quickly

1 **since** lately   3 **I did . . . you** do not let him know I sent you | **sad** serious
5 **sudden** suddenly taken   7 **hold the method** follow the right course   8 **I do not**
that I am not doing   11 **Tempt** try | **I wish** I wish you would

But here comes Antony.
CLEOPATRA   I am sick and sullen.°
ANTONY   I am sorry to give breathing° to my purpose—
CLEOPATRA   Help me away, dear Charmian! I shall fall.   15
  It cannot be thus long;° the sides of nature°
  Will not sustain it.
ANTONY   Now, my dearest queen—
CLEOPATRA
  Pray you, stand farther from me.°
ANTONY   What's the matter?
CLEOPATRA   I know by that same eye there's some good news.
  What, says the married woman° you may go?   20
  Would she had never given you leave to come!
  Let her not say 'tis I that keep you here.
  I have no power upon you; hers you are.
ANTONY   The gods best know—
CLEOPATRA   Oh, never was there queen
  So mightily betrayed! Yet at the first   25
  I saw the treasons planted.
ANTONY   Cleopatra—
CLEOPATRA   Why should I think you can be mine, and true—
  Though you in swearing shake the thronèd gods—
  Who° have been false to Fulvia? Riotous madness,°
  To be entangled with those mouth-made° vows   30
  Which break themselves in swearing!°
ANTONY   Most sweet queen—
CLEOPATRA   Nay, pray you, seek no color° for your going,
  But bid farewell and go. When you sued staying,°
  Then was the time for words. No going then.
  Eternity was in our° lips and eyes,   35
  Bliss in our brows' bent;° none our parts so poor°
  But was a race of heaven.° They are so still,

---

13 **sullen** depressed, melancholy 14 **breathing** utterance 16 **It . . . long** I can't last
long at this rate | **sides of nature** human body, frame 18 **stand farther from me**
give me air 20 **the married woman** Fulvia 29 **Who** you who | **Riotous madness**
what folly on my part 30 **mouth-made** insincerely spoken 31 **in swearing** even
while they are being sworn 32 **color** pretext 33 **sued staying** begged to stay
35 **our** my (the royal plural) 36 **bent** arch, curve | **none . . . poor** none of my
features, however poor 37 **race of heaven** of heavenly origin, or, possibly, of the
flavor of heaven

Or thou, the greatest soldier of the world,
Art turned the greatest liar.

ANTONY   How now, lady?

CLEOPATRA   I would I had thy inches.° Thou shouldst know   40
There were a heart in Egypt.°

ANTONY   Hear me, Queen:
The strong necessity of time commands
Our services awhile, but my full heart
Remains in use with you.° Our Italy
Shines o'er with civil swords;° Sextus Pompeius   45
Makes his approaches to the port of Rome;
Equality of two domestic powers
Breed scrupulous faction;° the hated, grown to strength,
Are newly grown to love;° the condemned Pompey,
Rich in his father's honor, creeps apace°   50
Into the hearts of such as have not thrived
Upon the present state,° whose° numbers threaten;
And quietness, grown sick of rest, would purge
By any desperate change.° My more particular,°
And that which most with you should safe° my going,   55
Is Fulvia's death.

CLEOPATRA   Though age from folly could not give me freedom,
It does from childishness. Can Fulvia die?

ANTONY   She's dead, my queen.   [*He offers letters*]
Look here, and at thy sovereign leisure read   60
The garboils° she awaked, at the last, best,°
See when and where she died.

CLEOPATRA   Oh, most false love!

---

40 inches (1) height (2) manly strength (with perhaps a bawdy suggestion)   **41 a heart in Egypt** a mighty courage in the Queen of Egypt   **44 in use with you** for your use   **45 Shines . . . swords** glitters everywhere with weapons of civil war   **47–8 Equality . . . faction** the equal splitting of domestic power between two (Antony and Caesar) breeds petty bickering   **48–9 the hated . . . love** those (like Pompey) who were out of favor, being now strong, have recently come back into popular favor   **49–50 Pompey . . . apace** Sextus Pompeius, richly inheriting the honor once accorded Pompey the Great, quickly insinuates himself   **52 state** government (of the triumvirate) | **whose** those supporting Pompey   **53–4 And quietness . . . change** and peace, bored with its own long continuance, longs to purge itself by the violence of war (medically speaking, by vomiting, bowel evacuation, or bloodletting)   **54 particular** personal concern   **55 safe** make safe   **61 garboils** disturbances, commotions | **best** best of all

Where be the sacred vials° thou shouldst fill
With sorrowful water? Now I see, I see,
In Fulvia's death how mine received shall be.   65
ANTONY   Quarrel no more, but be prepared to know
The purposes I bear, which are° or cease
As you shall give th'advice. By the fire°
That quickens Nilus' slime,° I go from hence
Thy soldier, servant, making peace or war   70
As thou affects.°
CLEOPATRA   Cut my lace,° Charmian, come!
But let it be; I am quickly ill, and well,
So° Antony loves.
ANTONY   My precious queen, forbear,
And give true evidence to his love which stands
An honorable trial.°
CLEOPATRA   So Fulvia told me.°   75
I prithee, turn aside and weep for her;
Then bid adieu to me, and say the tears
Belong to Egypt.° Good now,° play one scene
Of excellent dissembling, and let it look
Like perfect honor.
ANTONY   You'll heat my blood.° No more.   80
CLEOPATRA   You can do better yet; but this is meetly.°
ANTONY   Now, by my sword—
CLEOPATRA   And target.° Still he mends.°
But this is not the best. Look, prithee, Charmian,
How this Herculean Roman does become
The carriage of his chafe.°   85
ANTONY   I'll leave you, lady.

63 **sacred vials** (alludes to the supposed Roman custom of putting bottles filled with
tears in the tombs of the departed)   67 **which are** which will proceed   68 **fire** sun
69 **quickens . . . slime** brings to life the mud left by the overflow of the Nile
71 **thou affects** you desire | **lace** cord or laces fastening the bodice (Cleopatra
pretends she is fainting)   73 **So** provided that, or, possibly, "in the same way, with
changes as sudden as my own"   74–5 **And . . . trial** and bear true witness to the
love of one who withstands any honorable test   75 **So . . . me** so Fulvia would have
said, no doubt (said as a taunt)   78 **Belong to Egypt** are shed for the Queen of Egypt
| **Good now** (an expression of entreaty)   80 **heat my blood** anger me   81 **meetly**
fairly well acted (said mockingly)   82 **target** shield | **mends** improves (in his
"scene / Of excellent dissembling")   84–5 **How . . . chafe** how Antony, who claims
descent from Hercules, plays the role of his enraged ancestor well (Hercules had
become a stock figure of the enraged hero or tyrant) | **chafe** rage

CLEOPATRA   Courteous lord, one word.
  Sir, you and I must part, but that's not it;
  Sir, you and I have loved, but there's not it;
  That you know well. Something it is I would°—   90
  Oh, my oblivion is a very Antony,°
  And I am all forgotten.°
ANTONY   But that your royalty
  Holds idleness your subject, I should take you
  For idleness itself.°
CLEOPATRA   'Tis sweating labor
  To bear such idleness so near the heart   95
  As Cleopatra this.° But sir, forgive me,
  Since my becomings° kill me when they do not
  Eye° well to you. Your honor calls you hence;
  Therefore be deaf to my unpitied folly,
  And all the gods go with you! Upon your sword   100
  Sit laurel° victory, and smooth success
  Be strewed before your feet!
ANTONY   Let us go. Come;
  Our separation so abides and flies°
  That thou, residing here, goes yet with me,
  And I, hence fleeting, here remain with thee.   105
  Away!

Exeunt

❖

90 would wished to say **91 my . . . Antony** my forgetful memory is like Antony (who is now leaving and thus forgetting me) **92 I . . . forgotten** (1) I have forgotten what I was going to say (2) I am entirely forgotten (by Antony) **92–4 But . . . itself** since you are a queen, your frivolousness must be your subject (ruled by you); otherwise, I'd think you were frivolousness itself **94–6 'Tis . . . this** I am not being frivolous; this is hard for me to bear (*sweating, labor*, and *bear* are all associated with pregnancy) **97 my becomings** (1) those qualities that become me (2) the various roles that I adopt **98 Eye** appear **101 laurel** wreathed with laurel **103 so abides and flies** mingles remaining and going in such a paradoxical fashion

ACT 1
SCENE 4

Location: Rome

Enter Octavius [Caesar], reading a
letter, Lepidus, and their train

CAESAR   You may see, Lepidus, and henceforth know,
It is not Caesar's natural vice to hate
Our great competitor.° From Alexandria
This is the news: he fishes, drinks, and wastes
The lamps of night in revel; is not more manlike   5
Than Cleopatra, nor the queen of Ptolemy°
More womanly than he; hardly gave audience,° or
Vouchsafed to think he had partners. You shall find there
A man who is the abstract° of all faults
That all men follow.

LEPIDUS   I must not think there are   10
Evils enough to darken all his goodness.
His faults in him seem as the spots of heaven,
More fiery by night's blackness,° hereditary
Rather than purchased,° what he cannot change
Than what he chooses.   15

CAESAR   You are too indulgent. Let's grant° it is not
Amiss to tumble on the bed of Ptolemy,
To give a kingdom for a mirth,° to sit
And keep the turn of° tippling with a slave,
To reel the streets at noon, and stand the buffet°   20
With knaves that smells of sweat. Say this becomes him—
As his composure° must be rare indeed
Whom these things cannot blemish—yet must Antony

---

3 **competitor** partner (with a suggestion also of "rival")   6 **Ptolemy** (Cleopatra's royal brother, to whom she had been married according to Egyptian custom)   7 **gave audience** received messengers   9 **abstract** epitome   12–13 **His . . . blackness** his faults are enhanced by contrast with his virtues, just as the stars in the sky stand out from the darkness   14 **purchased** acquired   16 **Let's grant** even if we were to grant   18 **mirth** jest, diversion   19 **keep . . . of** take turns   20 **stand the buffet** exchange blows   22 **As his composure** and a man's composition or temperament

No way excuse his foils° when we do bear
So great weight in his lightness.° If he filled   25
His vacancy° with his voluptuousness,
Full surfeits and the dryness of his bones
Call on him for't.° But to confound° such time
That drums° him from his sport° and speaks as loud
As his own state and ours,° 'tis to be chid°   30
As we rate° boys who, being mature in knowledge,°
Pawn their experience to their present pleasure°
And so rebel to judgment.°

                                        Enter a Messenger

LEPIDUS   Here's more news.

FIRST MESSENGER   Thy biddings have been done, and every hour,
Most noble Caesar, shalt thou have report   35
How 'tis abroad. Pompey is strong at sea,
And it appears he is beloved of° those
That only have feared Caesar.° To the ports
The discontents° repair, and men's reports
Give him much° wronged.   [*Exit*]

CAESAR   I should have known no less.   40
It hath been taught us from the primal state
That he which is was wished until he were;
And the ebbed man, ne'er loved till ne'er worth love,
Comes deared by being lacked.° This common body,°
Like to a vagabond flag° upon the stream,   45

---

24 foils blemishes **24–5 when . . . lightness** when we have to carry the heavy burden imposed by his levity **26 His vacancy** his leisure time **27–8 Full . . . for't** the physical disabilities resulting from such voluptuousness (such as venereal disease) would call him to account and would be adequate punishment **28 confound** waste **29 drums** summons (as by a military drum) | **sport** amorous pastime **29–30 speaks . . . ours** summons him urgently in view of his political position and ours as well **30 chid** chided, reprimanded **31 rate** berate | **mature in knowledge** old enough to know better **32 Pawn . . . pleasure** risk for the sake of immediate gratification what experience tells them will be ultimately painful **33 to judgment** against better judgment **37 of** by **38 That . . . Caesar** that have obeyed Caesar only through fear **39 discontents** discontented (see 1.3.48–52) **40 Give him** represent him as **41–4 It . . . lacked** it is an ironic lesson of history from the earliest times that the man currently in the public eye is avidly sought after only until he becomes ruler, whereas the public figure whose fortunes have decayed, sought after only when he is no longer worthy of love, becomes loved once he is gone **44 common body** populace **45 vagabond flag** shifting and undependable weeds

Goes to and back, lackeying° the varying tide
To rot itself with motion.

[*Enter a Second Messenger*]

SECOND MESSENGER   Caesar, I bring thee word
    Menecrates and Menas, famous° pirates,
    Makes the sea serve them, which they ear° and wound   50
    With keels of every kind. Many hot inroads
    They make in Italy. The borders maritime°
    Lack blood° to think on't, and flush° youth revolt.
    No vessel can peep forth but 'tis as soon
    Taken as seen; for Pompey's name strikes more   55
    Than could his war resisted.°   [*Exit*]
CAESAR   Antony,
    Leave thy lascivious wassails.° When thou once
    Was beaten from Modena, where thou slew'st
    Hirtius and Pansa, consuls, at thy heel
    Did famine follow, whom° thou fought'st against,   60
    Though daintily brought up, with patience more
    Than savages could suffer.° Thou didst drink
    The stale° of horses and the gilded° puddle
    Which beasts would cough at. Thy palate then did deign°
    The roughest berry on the rudest hedge.   65
    Yea, like the stag, when snow the pasture sheets,°
    The barks of trees thou browsèd.° On the Alps
    It is reported thou didst eat strange flesh,
    Which some did die to look on. And all this—
    It wounds thine honor that I speak it now—   70
    Was borne so like a soldier that thy cheek
    So much as lanked not.°
LEPIDUS   'Tis pity of° him.

---

46 lackeying following in servile fashion, like a lackey **49 famous** notorious
50 ear plow **52 borders maritime** coastal territories **53 Lack blood** turn pale |
flush vigorous; flushed, ruddy (contrasted with those who *Lack blood*) **55–6 strikes
. . . resisted** inflicts more damage than his forces could against our resistance
57 wassails carousals **60 whom** famine **62 suffer** show in suffering **63 stale**
urine | **gilded** covered with iridescent slime **64 deign** not disdain **66 sheets**
covers **67 browsèd** fed upon **72 lanked not** did not become thin **73 of** about

CAESAR   Let his shames quickly
    Drive him to Rome. 'Tis time we twain   75
    Did show ourselves i'th' field, and to that end
    Assemble we immediate council. Pompey
    Thrives in our idleness.
LEPIDUS   Tomorrow, Caesar,
    I shall be furnished to inform you rightly
    Both what by sea and land I can be able°   80
    To front° this present time.
CAESAR   Till which encounter
    It is my business too. Farewell.
LEPIDUS   Farewell, my lord. What you shall know meantime
    Of stirs° abroad, I shall beseech you, sir,
    To let me be partaker.   85
CAESAR   Doubt not, sir, I knew° it for my bond.°

                         Exeunt [separately]

❖

ACT 1
SCENE 5

Location: Egypt. Cleopatra's palace.

Enter Cleopatra, Charmian, Iras, and Mardian

CLEOPATRA   Charmian!
CHARMIAN   Madam?
CLEOPATRA   Ha, ha! Give me to drink mandragora.°
CHARMIAN   Why, madam?
CLEOPATRA   That I might sleep out this great gap of time   5
    My Antony is away.
CHARMIAN   You think of him too much.
CLEOPATRA   Oh, 'tis treason!
CHARMIAN   Madam, I trust not so.

---

80 be able be capable of mustering **81 front** confront, deal with **84 stirs** commotions **86 knew** already knew | **bond** duty, obligation
3 mandragora juice of the mandrake (a narcotic)

CLEOPATRA
Thou, eunuch Mardian!
MARDIAN   What's Your Highness' pleasure?
CLEOPATRA   Not now to hear thee sing. I take no pleasure   10
In aught° an eunuch has. 'Tis well for thee
That, being unseminared,° thy freer thoughts
May not fly forth of° Egypt. Hast thou affections?°
MARDIAN   Yes, gracious madam.
CLEOPATRA   Indeed?   15
MARDIAN   Not in deed,° madam, for I can do° nothing
But what indeed is honest° to be done.
Yet have I fierce affections, and think
What Venus did with Mars.
CLEOPATRA   Oh, Charmian,
Where think'st thou he is now? Stands he or sits he?   20
Or does he walk? Or is he on his horse?
Oh, happy horse, to bear the weight of Antony!
Do° bravely, horse, for wot'st thou° whom thou mov'st?
The demi-Atlas° of this earth, the arm°
And burgonet° of men. He's speaking now,   25
Or murmuring, "Where's my serpent of old Nile?"
For so he calls me. Now I feed myself
With most delicious poison. Think on me,
That am with Phoebus'° amorous pinches black
And wrinkled deep in time.° Broad-fronted Caesar,°   30
When thou wast here above the ground, I was
A morsel for a monarch. And great Pompey°
Would stand and make his eyes grow in my brow;°

---

11 **aught** (with bawdy suggestion)   12 **unseminared** castrated   13 **of** from |
affections passions   16 **Not in deed** (Mardian punningly takes the *deed* of *Indeed*
in l. 15 to mean "physical act") | **do** (with suggestion of sexual intercourse)
17 **honest** chaste   23 **Do** (with sexual suggestion, as in l. 16) | **wot'st thou** do
you know   24 **demi-Atlas** one who (together with Caesar) supports the weight of
the whole world, as Atlas did (Cleopatra disregards Lepidus as a triumvir) | **arm**
strong right arm or weapon   25 **burgonet** light helmet or steel cap, protector
28–30 **Think . . . time** (Cleopatra reflects on her ability to attract Antony, given the
fact that she is dark-skinned [as from the amorous pinches of her lover, the sun] and
increasingly wrinkled with age)   29 **Phoebus'** the sun's   30 **Broad-fronted Caesar**
broad-foreheaded Julius Caesar   32 **great Pompey** Gnaeus Pompey, oldest son of
Pompey the Great (Shakespeare may conflate the two)   33 **make . . . brow** rivet his
eyes on my face

There would he anchor his aspect,° and die°
With looking on his life.°   35

                                        Enter Alexas

ALEXAS   Sovereign of Egypt, hail!
CLEOPATRA   How much unlike art thou Mark Antony!
    Yet, coming from him, that great med'cine° hath
    With his tinct° gilded thee.
    How goes it with my brave° Mark Antony?   40
ALEXAS   Last thing he did, dear Queen,
    He kissed—the last of many doubled kisses—
    This orient° pearl. [*He gives a pearl*] His speech sticks in my
        heart.
CLEOPATRA
    Mine ear must pluck it thence.
ALEXAS   "Good friend," quoth he,
    "Say the firm° Roman to great Egypt° sends   45
    This treasure of an oyster; at whose foot,
    To mend the petty present, I will piece°
    Her opulent throne with kingdoms. All the East,
    Say thou, shall call her mistress." So he nodded,
    And soberly did mount an arm-gaunt° steed,   50
    Who neighed so high that what I would have spoke
    Was beastly dumbed° by him.
CLEOPATRA   What, was he sad, or merry?
ALEXAS   Like to the time o'th' year between the extremes
    Of hot and cold, he was nor sad° nor merry.   55
CLEOPATRA   Oh, well-divided disposition!° Note him,
    Note him, good Charmian, 'tis the man;° but° note him.
    He was not sad, for he would° shine on those

---

34 aspect look, gaze | **die** suffer the extremity of love (and with suggestion of orgasm, as at 1.2.140)   **35 his life** that which he lived for   **38 great med'cine** the philosopher's stone, the supposed substance by which alchemists hoped to turn all baser metals into gold   **39 his tinct** its alchemical potency; also, its color   **40 brave** splendid   **43 orient** shining, bright (the best pearls were from the East or Orient)   **45 firm** constant, true | **Egypt** the Queen of Egypt   **47 piece** augment   **50 arm-gaunt** made trim and hard by warlike service, or hungry for battle   **52 dumbed** drowned out, made inaudible   **55 nor sad** neither sad   **56 well-divided disposition** well-balanced temperament   **57 the man** perfectly characteristic of him | **but** do but, only   **58 would** wished to

That make their looks by his;° he was not merry,
Which seemed to tell them his remembrance lay   60
In Egypt with his joy; but between both.
Oh, heavenly mingle! Be'st thou sad or merry,
The violence of either thee becomes,°
So does it no man else.—Met'st thou my posts?°
ALEXAS Ay, madam, twenty several° messengers.   65
Why do you send so thick?
CLEOPATRA   Who's° born that day
When I forget to send to Antony
Shall die a beggar.° Ink and paper, Charmian.
Welcome, my good Alexas. Did I, Charmian,
Ever love Caesar so?
CHARMIAN   Oh, that brave Caesar!   70
CLEOPATRA Be choked with such another emphasis!°
Say, "the brave Antony."
CHARMIAN   The valiant Caesar!
CLEOPATRA By Isis, I will give thee bloody teeth
If thou with Caesar paragon° again
My man of men.
CHARMIAN   By your most gracious pardon,   75
I sing but after you.
CLEOPATRA   My salad days,
When I was green° in judgment, cold in blood,
To say as I said then. But, come, away,
Get me ink and paper.
He shall have every day a several greeting,   80
Or I'll unpeople Egypt.°

                                                  Exeunt

❖

---

59 **make . . . his** model their demeanor on his look   63 **thee becomes** is becoming
to you   64 **posts** messengers   65 **several** separate, distinct (also in l. 80)
66 **Who's** anyone who is   68 **Shall . . . beggar** (since that day, sure never to come,
would be ill-omened)   71 **emphasis** emphatic expression   74 **paragon** match or
compare   77 **green** immature   81 **Or . . . Egypt** or I will send so many messengers
that Egypt will be unpeopled (perhaps too with a darker threat of violence)

ACT 2
SCENE 1

Location: Pompey's camp, probably at Messina, Sicily

Enter Pompey, Menecrates, and Menas, in warlike manner

POMPEY   If the great gods be just, they shall assist
The deeds of justest men.
MENAS°   Know, worthy Pompey,
That what they do delay they not deny.°
POMPEY   Whiles we are suitors to their throne, decays
The thing we sue for.°
MENAS   We, ignorant of ourselves,   5
Beg often our own harms, which the wise powers
Deny us for our good; so find we profit
By losing of our prayers.
POMPEY   I shall do well.
The people love me, and the sea is mine;
My powers are crescent,° and my auguring° hope   10
Says it° will come to th' full. Mark Antony
In Egypt sits at dinner, and will make
No wars without doors.° Caesar gets money where
He loses hearts. Lepidus flatters both,
Of° both is flattered; but he neither loves,°   15
Nor either cares for him.
MENAS   Caesar and Lepidus
Are in the field. A mighty strength they carry.°
POMPEY   Where have you this? 'Tis false.
MENAS   From Silvius, sir.
POMPEY   He dreams. I know they are in Rome together
Looking° for Antony. But all the charms° of love,   20

---

2 MENAS (the Folio assigns the speeches in this scene to "*Mene.*"; some could be for
Menecrates, but Pompey ignores him entirely at ll. 43–53, and Menecrates never
reappears in the play)   3 **not deny** do not necessarily deny   4–5 **Whiles . . . for**
while we are praying, that for which we pray is being destroyed   10 **My . . . crescent**
my armed forces are on the increase | **auguring** prophesying   11 **it** my powers or
fortune (seen as a crescent moon, becoming full)   13 **without doors** outdoors, in the
battlefield, rather than in the bedroom   15 **Of** by | **neither loves** loves neither
17 **A . . . carry** they command a mighty army   20 **Looking for** awaiting | **charms**
spells

Salt° Cleopatra, soften thy waned° lip!
Let witchcraft joined with beauty, lust with both,
Tie up the libertine in a field of feasts,°
Keep his brain fuming. Epicurean° cooks,
Sharpen with cloyless° sauce his appetite,   25
That sleep and feeding may prorogue° his honor
Even till a Lethe'd° dullness—

Enter Varrius

How now, Varrius?
VARRIUS   This is most certain that I shall deliver:°
Mark Antony is every hour in Rome
Expected. Since he went from Egypt 'tis   30
A space for further travel.°
POMPEY   I could have given less° matter
A better ear. Menas, I did not think
This amorous surfeiter would have donned his helm°
For such a petty war. His soldiership   35
Is twice the other twain. But let us rear°
The higher our opinion,° that our stirring
Can from the lap of Egypt's widow° pluck
The ne'er-lust-wearied Antony.
MENAS   I cannot hope°
Caesar and Antony shall well greet° together.   40
His wife that's dead did trespasses to° Caesar;
His brother° warred upon him, although, I think,
Not moved° by Antony.
POMPEY   I know not, Menas,
How lesser enmities may give way to greater.
Were 't not that we stand up against them all,   45
'Twere pregnant° they should square° between themselves,

---

21 Salt lustful | **waned** faded, withered   **23 Tie . . . feasts** tether him like an animal in a rich pasture   **24 Epicurean** let epicurean   **25 cloyless** which will not satiate   **26 prorogue** defer the operation of   **27 Lethe'd** oblivious (from the river of the underworld whose waters cause forgetfulness in those who drink)   **28 deliver** report   **31 space . . . travel** time enough for an even longer journey and labor (travail)   **32 less** less important   **34 helm** helmet   **36 rear** raise   **37 opinion** of ourselves   **38 Egypt's widow** Cleopatra, widow of the young King Ptolemy   **39 hope** expect   **40 well greet** greet one another kindly   **41 did trespasses to** wronged   **42 brother** Lucius Antonius (see 1.2.86ff)   **43 moved** provoked, incited   **46 pregnant** clear, obvious | **square** quarrel

For they have entertainèd° cause enough
To draw their swords. But how the fear of us
May cement their divisions and bind up
The petty difference, we yet not know. 50
Be't as our gods will have't! It only stands
Our lives upon to use our strongest hands.°
Come, Menas.

Exeunt

❖

ACT 2
SCENE 2

*Location: Rome. Furniture is put out
on which Antony and Caesar are to sit.*

Enter Enobarbus and Lepidus

LEPIDUS Good Enobarbus, 'tis a worthy deed,
And shall become you well, to entreat your captain
To soft and gentle speech.
ENOBARBUS   I shall entreat him
To answer like himself.° If Caesar move him,°
Let Antony look over Caesar's head° 5
And speak as loud as Mars. By Jupiter,
Were I the wearer of Antonio's beard,
I would not shave't° today.
LEPIDUS 'Tis not a time for private stomaching.°
ENOBARBUS   Every time
Serves for the matter that is then born in't. 10
LEPIDUS But small to greater matters must give way.
ENOBARBUS
Not if the small come first.
LEPIDUS   Your speech is passion;

---

47 **entertainèd** maintained 51–2 **It . . . hands** our very lives depend upon our using
our greatest strength
4 **like himself** in a way befitting his greatness | **move him** to anger 5 **look . . .
head** condescend to Caesar as a smaller man 8 **I . . . shave't** I would continue to
wear it and thereby dare Caesar to pluck it (in a symbolic gesture for starting a fight)
9 **private stomaching** personal resentment

But pray you stir no embers up. Here comes
The noble Antony.

Enter Antony and Ventidius [in conversation]

ENOBARBUS   And yonder, Caesar.

Enter Caesar, Maecenas, and Agrippa,
[also in conversation, by another door]

ANTONY   If we compose° well here, to Parthia.   15
Hark, Ventidius.   [*They confer apart*]
CAESAR   I do not know, Maecenas, ask Agrippa.
LEPIDUS   Noble friends,
That which combined us was most great, and let not
A leaner° action rend° us. What's° amiss,   20
May it be gently heard. When we debate
Our trivial difference loud, we do commit
Murder in healing° wounds. Then, noble partners,
The rather for° I earnestly beseech,
Touch you the sourest points with sweetest terms,   25
Nor curstness grow° to th' matter.
ANTONY   'Tis spoken well.
Were we before our armies, and to° fight,
I should do thus.   *Flourish*
CAESAR   Welcome to Rome.
ANTONY   Thank you.   30
CAESAR   Sit.
ANTONY   Sit, sir.
CAESAR   Nay, then.   [*They sit*]
ANTONY   I learn you take things ill which are not so,
Or being,° concern you not.
CAESAR   I must be laughed at   35
If, or for nothing or° a little, I
Should say myself offended, and with you
Chiefly i'th' world;° more laughed at that I should

---

15 **compose** come to an agreement 20 **leaner** lesser, more trivial | **rend** divide | **What's** whatever is 23 **healing** attempting to heal 24 **The rather for** all the more because 26 **Nor . . . grow** nor let ill humor be added 27 **to** about to 35 **being** being so, even if they are amiss 36 **or . . . or** either . . . or 38 **i'th' world** of all people

Once° name you derogately,° when to sound your name
It not concerned me.°   40
ANTONY   My being in Egypt, Caesar, what was't to you?
CAESAR   No more than my residing here at Rome
Might be to you in Egypt. Yet if you there
Did practice on my state,° your being in Egypt
Might be my question.°
ANTONY   How intend you° "practiced"?   45
CAESAR   You may be pleased to catch at° mine intent
By what did here befall me. Your wife and brother
Made wars upon me, and their contestation
Was theme for you. You were the word of war.°
ANTONY   You do mistake your business. My brother never   50
Did urge me in his act.° I did inquire° it,
And have my learning from some true reports°
That drew their swords with you.° Did he not rather
Discredit° my authority with° yours,
And make the wars alike against my stomach,°   55
Having alike your cause?° Of this my letters
Before did satisfy you. If you'll patch a quarrel,
As matter whole you have to make it with,
It must not be with this.°
CAESAR   You praise yourself
By laying defects of judgment to me, but   60
You patched up your excuses.
ANTONY   Not so, not so.
I know you could not lack—I am certain on't—
Very necessity of this thought,° that I,
Your partner in the cause 'gainst which he° fought,

---

39 **Once** under any circumstances | **derogately** disparagingly **39–40 when . . .
concerned me** if, as you say, it were none of my business **44 practice on my state**
plot against my position **45 question** business | **How intend you** what do you
mean **46 catch at** infer **49 Was . . . war** had you for its theme; they made war in
your name (*word* here means "watchword") **51 urge . . . act** claim that he was
fighting in my behalf | **inquire** inquire into **52 reports** reporters **53 That . . . you**
that fought in your army **54 Discredit** injure | **with** along with **55 stomach** desire
56 Having . . . cause I having just as much reason as you to deplore Lucius's action
57–9 If . . . this if you insist on manufacturing a quarrel out of shreds and patches, as
if you had substantial material to make it with, you've chosen a weak matter to use
62–3 I know . . . thought I'm certain you must have realized **64 he** Lucius

Could not with graceful eyes attend° those wars 65
Which fronted° mine own peace. As for my wife,
I would you had her spirit in such another.°
The third o'th' world is yours, which with a snaffle°
You may pace° easy, but not such a wife.

ENOBARBUS   Would we had all such wives, that the men 70
might go to wars with the women!

ANTONY   So much uncurbable, her garboils, Caesar,
Made out of her impatience—which not wanted
Shrewdness of policy too—I grieving grant
Did you too much disquiet.° For that you must 75
But say° I could not help it.

CAESAR   I wrote to you
When° rioting in Alexandria; you
Did pocket up my letters and with taunts
Did gibe my missive out of audience.°

ANTONY   Sir,
He fell° upon me ere admitted, then. 80
Three kings I had newly feasted, and did want
Of what I was i'th' morning.° But next day
I told him of myself,° which was as much
As to have asked him pardon. Let this fellow
Be nothing of° our strife; if we contend, 85
Out of our question° wipe him.

CAESAR   You have broken
The article° of your oath, which you shall never
Have tongue to charge me with.

LEPIDUS   Soft,° Caesar!

ANTONY   No, Lepidus, let him speak. 90
The honor is sacred which he talks on now,

---

65 with . . . attend regard favorably   66 fronted confronted, opposed   67 her . . .
another a wife such as she was   68 snaffle bridle bit   69 pace put through its paces,
manage   72–5 So . . . disquiet I unhappily concede that her unmanageable
commotions, caused by her impatience (at my being in Egypt) but not lacking in
keenness of stratagem, did much to disquiet you, Caesar   76 But say concede that
77 When while you were   79 Did . . . audience taunted my messenger out of your
presence   80 fell burst in   81–2 did want . . . morning was not at my best as I had
been earlier in the day   83 of myself of my having had a lot to drink   85 Be . . . of
have no part in   86 question contention   87 article terms   89 Soft gently, go easy

Supposing° that I lacked it. But, on, Caesar:
The article of my oath—

CAESAR   To lend me arms and aid when I required° them,
The which you both denied.

ANTONY   Neglected, rather;   95
And then when poisoned hours had bound me up
From mine own knowledge.° As nearly as I may
I'll play the penitent to you, but mine honesty
Shall not make poor my greatness, nor my power
Work without it.° Truth is that Fulvia,   100
To have me out of Egypt, made wars here,
For which myself, the ignorant motive,° do
So far ask pardon as befits mine honor
To stoop in such a case.

LEPIDUS   'Tis noble° spoken.

MAECENAS   If it might please you to enforce no further   105
The griefs° between ye; to forget them quite
Were to remember that the present need
Speaks to atone° you.

LEPIDUS   Worthily spoken, Maecenas.

ENOBARBUS   Or, if you borrow one another's love for the
instant, you may, when you hear no more words of Pompey,   110
return it again. You shall have time to wrangle in when you
have nothing else to do.

ANTONY   Thou art a soldier only. Speak no more.

ENOBARBUS   That truth should be silent I had almost forgot.

ANTONY   You wrong this presence.° Therefore speak no more.   115

ENOBARBUS   Go to, then; your considerate stone.°

CAESAR   I do not much dislike the matter, but
The manner of his speech; for't cannot be
We shall remain in friendship, our conditions°
So diff'ring in their acts. Yet, if I knew   120

---

92 **Supposing** implying   94 **required** requested   97 **From . . . knowledge** from
knowing myself   98–100 **mine . . . it** my honesty (in admitting my overindulgence)
will not go so far as to dishonor my greatness, nor, conversely, will my authority be
used in a dishonorable way   102 **motive** moving or inciting cause   104 **noble**
nobly   106 **griefs** grievances   108 **atone** reconcile   115 **presence** company
116 **Go . . . stone** all right, all right; I'll keep my thoughts to myself   119 **conditions**
temperaments, dispositions

What hoop° should hold us staunch,° from edge to edge
O'th' world I would pursue it.
AGRIPPA   Give me leave, Caesar.
CAESAR   Speak, Agrippa.
AGRIPPA   Thou hast a sister by the mother's side,   125
   Admired Octavia. Great Mark Antony
   Is now a widower.
CAESAR   Say not so, Agrippa.
   If Cleopatra heard you, your reproof
   Were well deserved of rashness.°
ANTONY   I am not married, Caesar. Let me hear   130
   Agrippa further speak.
AGRIPPA   To hold you in perpetual amity,
   To make you brothers, and to knit your hearts
   With an unslipping knot, take Antony
   Octavia to his wife, whose beauty claims   135
   No worse a husband than the best of men,
   Whose virtue and whose general graces speak
   That which none else can utter.° By this marriage
   All little jealousies,° which now seem great,
   And all great fears, which now import° their dangers,   140
   Would then be nothing. Truths would be tales,
   Where now half tales be truths.° Her love to both
   Would each to other and all loves to both
   Draw after her. Pardon what I have spoke,
   For 'tis a studied, not a present thought,   145
   By duty ruminated.
ANTONY   Will Caesar speak?
CAESAR   Not till he hears how Antony is touched
   With° what is spoke already.
ANTONY   What power is in Agrippa
   If I would say, "Agrippa, be it so,"   150

---

121 hoop barrel hoop | **staunch** firm, watertight   **129 Were . . . rashness** would
richly deserve the rebuke it would get for such rashness   **137–8 Whose . . . utter**
whose virtues declare themselves better than any words about them could do
139 jealousies misunderstandings, suspicions   **140 import** imply; carry with them
141–2 Truths . . . truths true reports (no matter how distressing) would then be
discounted as mere rumors, whereas at present half-true reports are taken for the
whole truth   **147–8 touched With** affected by

To make this good?

CAESAR   The power of Caesar and
His power unto° Octavia.

ANTONY   May I never
To this good purpose, that so fairly shows,°
Dream of impediment! Let me have thy hand
Further° this act of grace, and from this hour   155
The heart of brothers govern in our loves
And sway our great designs!

CAESAR   There's my hand.

                              [*They clasp hands*]

A sister I bequeath you whom no brother
Did ever love so dearly. Let her live
To join our kingdoms and our hearts; and never   160
Fly off our loves again!°

LEPIDUS   Happily, amen!

ANTONY   I did not think to draw my sword 'gainst Pompey,
For he hath laid strange° courtesies and great
Of late upon me. I must thank him only,°
Lest my remembrance suffer ill report;°   165
At heel of° that, defy him.

LEPIDUS   Time calls upon 's.
Of° us must Pompey presently° be sought,
Or else he seeks out us.

ANTONY   Where lies he?

CAESAR   About the mount Misena.°

ANTONY   What is his strength   170
By land?

CAESAR   Great and increasing; but by sea
He is an absolute master.

ANTONY   So is the fame.°
Would we had spoke together!° Haste we for it.

---

152 **unto** over   153 **so fairly shows** looks so promising   155 **Further** in furtherance of   160–1 **never . . . again** may our amity never desert us again   163 **strange** remarkable   164 **only** at least   165 **Lest . . . report** lest I be accused of ingratitude   166 **At heel of** immediately after   167 **Of** by | **presently** at once   170 **Misena** Misenum, in southern Italy (not in Sicily, where 2.1 perhaps takes place)   172 **So is the fame** so it is reported   173 **Would . . . together!** would that we had had a chance to parley before battle!

Yet, ere we put ourselves in arms, dispatch we
The business we have talked of.

CAESAR   With most° gladness,   175
And do invite you to my sister's view,°
Whither straight° I'll lead you.

ANTONY   Let us, Lepidus, not lack your company.

LEPIDUS   Noble Antony, not sickness should detain me.

Flourish. Exeunt. Manent° Enobarbus, Agrippa, Maecenas

MAECENAS   Welcome from Egypt, sir.   180

ENOBARBUS   Half the heart of Caesar,° worthy Maecenas! My
honorable friend, Agrippa!

AGRIPPA   Good Enobarbus!

MAECENAS   We have cause to be glad that matters are so well
digested.° You stayed well by't° in Egypt.   185

ENOBARBUS   Ay, sir, we did sleep day out of countenance° and
made the night light° with drinking.

MAECENAS   Eight wild boars roasted whole at a breakfast, and
but twelve persons there; is this true?

ENOBARBUS   This was but as a fly by an eagle.° We had much   190
more monstrous matter of feast, which worthily deserved
noting.

MAECENAS   She's a most triumphant° lady, if report be square°
to her.

ENOBARBUS   When she first met Mark Antony, she pursed up°   195
his heart upon the river of Cydnus.

AGRIPPA   There she appeared indeed, or my reporter devised°
well for her.

ENOBARBUS   I will tell you.
The barge she sat in, like a burnished° throne   200
Burnt on the water. The poop° was beaten gold;
Purple the sails, and so perfumèd that

---

175 **most** the greatest   176 **to my sister's view** to see my sister   177 **straight** straightway   179.1 *Manent* they remain onstage   181 **Half . . . Caesar** you who are very close to Caesar, one of his closest advisers   185 **digested** disposed | **stayed well by't** kept at it   186 **we . . . countenance** we insulted day by sleeping right through it   187 **light** (1) brightly lit (2) debauched and giddy   190 **This . . . eagle** this was nothing compared with greater feasting   193 **triumphant** magnificent | **square** just   195 **pursed up** pocketed up, put in her purse   197 **devised** invented   200 **burnished** lustrous, shiny   201 **poop** a short deck built over the main deck at the stern of the vessel

The winds were lovesick with them. The oars were silver,
Which to the tune of flutes kept stroke, and made
The water which they beat to follow faster,   205
As° amorous of their strokes. For° her own person,
It beggared all description: she did lie
In her pavilion—cloth-of-gold of tissue°—
O'erpicturing that Venus where we see
The fancy° outwork nature. On each side her   210
Stood pretty dimpled boys, like smiling Cupids,
With divers-colored° fans, whose wind did seem
To glow° the delicate cheeks which they did cool,
And what they undid did.

AGRIPPA   Oh, rare for Antony!

ENOBARBUS   Her gentlewomen, like the Nereides,°   215
So many mermaids, tended her i'th'eyes°
And made their bends adornings.° At the helm
A seeming mermaid steers. The silken tackle
Swell with the touches of those flower-soft hands,
That yarely frame the office.° From the barge   220
A strange invisible perfume hits the sense
Of the adjacent wharfs.° The city cast
Her people out upon her; and Antony,
Enthroned i'th' marketplace, did sit alone,
Whistling to th'air, which, but for vacancy,°   225
Had gone to gaze on Cleopatra too,
And made a gap in nature.

AGRIPPA   Rare Egyptian!

ENOBARBUS   Upon her landing, Antony sent to her,
Invited her to supper. She replied
It should be better he became her guest,   230
Which she entreated. Our courteous Antony,
Whom ne'er the word of "No" woman heard speak,
Being barbered ten times o'er, goes to the feast,

---

206 As as if | **For** as for   **208 cloth-of-gold of tissue** cloth made of gold thread and silk woven together   **210 fancy** imagination   **212 divers-colored** multicolored **213 glow** cause to glow   **215 Nereides** sea nymphs   **216 So . . . i'th'eyes** as if they were so many mermaids, attended to her every glance or nod   **217 made . . . adornings** made their graceful bowings beautiful   **220 yarely . . . office** nimbly perform their function   **222 wharfs** banks   **225 but for vacancy** except that it would have created a vacuum

And for his ordinary° pays his heart
For what his eyes eat° only.
AGRIPPA   Royal wench!   235
She made great Caesar° lay his sword to bed;
He plowed her, and she cropped.°
ENOBARBUS   I saw her once
Hop forty paces through the public street,
And having lost her breath, she spoke and panted,
That° she did make defect perfection,   240
And, breathless, power breathe forth.
MAECENAS Now Antony must leave her utterly.
ENOBARBUS Never. He will not.
Age cannot wither her, nor custom stale°
Her infinite variety. Other women cloy   245
The appetites they feed, but she makes hungry
Where most she satisfies; for vilest things
Become themselves° in her, that° the holy priests
Bless her when she is riggish.°
MAECENAS If beauty, wisdom, modesty can settle   250
The heart of Antony, Octavia is
A blessèd lottery° to him.
AGRIPPA   Let us go.
Good Enobarbus, make yourself my guest
Whilst you abide here.
ENOBARBUS   Humbly, sir, I thank you.
                              Exeunt

❧

234 **ordinary** meal, supper (such as one might obtain at a public table in a tavern) 235 **eat** ate (pronounced *et*) 236 **Caesar** Julius Caesar, by whom Cleopatra had a son named Caesarion 237 **cropped** bore fruit (a son) 240 **That** so that 244 **custom stale** repeated experience make stale 248 **Become themselves** are becoming, attractive | **that** so that 249 **riggish** lustful 252 **lottery** prize, gift of fortune

ACT 2
SCENE 3

Location: Rome

Enter Antony, Caesar, Octavia between them

ANTONY   The world and my great office will sometimes
Divide me from your bosom.

OCTAVIA   All which time
Before the gods my knee shall bow my prayers
To them for you.

ANTONY   Good night, sir. My Octavia,
Read° not my blemishes in° the world's report.   5
I have not kept my square,° but that° to come
Shall all be done by th' rule. Good night, dear lady.
Good night, sir.

CAESAR   Good night.   *Exit [with Octavia]*

Enter Soothsayer

ANTONY   Now, sirrah:° you do wish yourself in Egypt?   10

SOOTHSAYER   Would I had never come from thence, nor you
thither!°

ANTONY   If you can, your reason?

SOOTHSAYER   I see it in my motion,° have it not in my tongue;
but yet hie° you to Egypt again.   15

ANTONY   Say to me, whose fortunes shall rise higher,
Caesar's or mine?

SOOTHSAYER   Caesar's.
Therefore, O Antony, stay not by his side.
Thy daemon—that thy spirit which keeps thee°—is   20
Noble, courageous, high unmatchable,°
Where Caesar's is not;° but near him thy angel

---

5 **Read** interpret | **in** according to   6 **kept my square** kept to a straight course (as guided by a carpenter's square; with pun on *rule,* "ruler" in next line) | **that** that which is   10 **sirrah** (a form of address to a social inferior)   12 **thither** to that place   14 **in my motion** intuitively, by inward prompting   15 **hie** hasten   20 **Thy . . . thee** your guardian spirit, the spirit that protects you   21 **high unmatchable** unmatchable in the extreme   22 **Where . . . not** wherever Caesar's spirit is not present (to daunt yours)

Becomes afeard, as being o'erpowered. Therefore
Make space enough between you.

ANTONY   Speak this no more.

SOOTHSAYER   To none but thee; no more but when° to thee.   25
    If thou dost play with him at any game,
    Thou art sure to lose; and of° that natural luck
    He beats thee 'gainst the odds. Thy luster thickens°
    When he shines by.° I say again, thy spirit
    Is all afraid to govern thee near him;   30
    But, he away, 'tis noble.

ANTONY   Get thee gone.
    Say to Ventidius I would speak with him.

Exit [Soothsayer]

    He shall to Parthia.—Be it art or hap,°
    He hath spoken true. The very dice obey him,
    And in our sports my better cunning° faints   35
    Under his chance.° If we draw lots, he speeds;°
    His cocks do win the battle still of° mine
    When it is all to naught,° and his quails ever
    Beat mine, inhooped,° at odds.° I will to Egypt;
    And though I make this marriage for my peace,   40
    I'th'East my pleasure lies.

Enter Ventidius

                      Oh, come, Ventidius.
    You must to Parthia. Your commission's ready;
    Follow me, and receive't.

Exeunt

❖

---

25 **no more but when** only when   27 **of** by   28 **thickens** grows dim   29 **by** nearby
33 **art or hap** skill or luck   35 **cunning** skill   36 **chance** luck | **speeds** wins
37 **still of** always from   38 **When . . . naught** when the odds are everything to
nothing (in my favor)   39 **inhooped** (the birds were enclosed in hoops to make
them fight) | **at odds** against the odds

ACT 2
SCENE 4

Location: Rome

Enter Lepidus, Maecenas, and Agrippa

LEPIDUS   Trouble yourselves no further. Pray you, hasten
Your generals after.°

AGRIPPA   Sir, Mark Antony
Will e'en but° kiss Octavia, and we'll follow.

LEPIDUS   Till I shall see you in your soldier's dress,°
Which will become° you both, farewell.

MAECENAS   We shall,   5
As I conceive° the journey, be at th' Mount°
Before you, Lepidus.

LEPIDUS   Your way is shorter;
My purposes do draw me much about.°
You'll win two days upon me.

MAECENAS, AGRIPPA   Sir, good success!

LEPIDUS   Farewell.   10

Exeunt

❖

ACT 2
SCENE 5

Location: Alexandria. Cleopatra's palace.

Enter Cleopatra, Charmian, Iras, and Alexas

CLEOPATRA   Give me some music; music, moody food
Of us that trade in love.

ALL   The music, ho!

Enter Mardian the eunuch

---

2 **Your generals after** after your generals   3 **e'en but** only, just   4 **dress** garb, apparel   5 **become** suit   6 **conceive** understand | **th' Mount** Mount Misenum   8 **about** roundabout

CLEOPATRA   Let it alone. Let's to billiards. Come, Charmian.

CHARMIAN   My arm is sore. Best play with Mardian.

CLEOPATRA   As well a woman with an eunuch played   5
As with a woman. Come, you'll play with me, sir?

MARDIAN   As well as I can, madam.

CLEOPATRA
And when good will is showed, though 't come too short,°
The actor may plead pardon. I'll none now.°
Give me mine angle;° we'll to th' river. There,   10
My music playing far off, I will betray
Tawny-finned fishes. My bended hook shall pierce
Their slimy jaws, and as I draw them up
I'll think them every one an Antony,
And say, "Aha! You're caught."

CHARMIAN   'Twas merry when   15
You wagered on your angling, when your diver
Did hang a salt° fish on his hook, which he
With fervency drew up.

CLEOPATRA   That time—oh, times!—
I laughed him out of patience; and that night
I laughed him into patience. And next morn,   20
Ere the ninth hour,° I drunk° him to his bed,
Then put my tires° and mantles° on him, whilst
I wore his sword Philippan.°

Enter a Messenger

                 Oh, from Italy!
Ram thou thy fruitful tidings in mine ears,
That long time have been barren.

MESSENGER   Madam, madam—   25

CLEOPATRA   Antonio's dead! If thou say so, villain,
Thou kill'st thy mistress; but well and free,

---

8 too short (a bawdy joke on Mardian's being castrated; *will* suggests "sexual desire"; *come* suggests "reach orgasm")   **9 I'll none now** I won't play billiards after all   **10 angle** rod and line   **17 salt** dried, preserved in salt   **21 ninth hour** 9 A.M. **drunk** drank   **22 tires** headdresses, or perhaps attire | **mantles** garments **23 Philippan** (named for Antony's victory over Brutus and Cassius at Philippi)

If thou so yield° him, there is gold, and here
My bluest veins to kiss—a hand that kings
Have lipped, and trembled kissing.   30
               [*She offers him gold, and her hand to kiss*]
MESSENGER   First, madam, he is well.
CLEOPATRA   Why, there's more gold. But, sirrah, mark, we use
To say the dead are well.° Bring it to that,°
The gold I give thee will I melt and pour
Down thy ill-uttering throat.   35
MESSENGER   Good madam, hear me.
CLEOPATRA   Well, go to,° I will.
But there's no goodness in thy face, if Antony
Be free and healthful—so tart a favor°
To trumpet such good tidings! If not well,   40
Thou shouldst come like a Fury° crowned with snakes,
Not like a formal man.°
MESSENGER   Will't please you hear me?
CLEOPATRA   I have a mind to strike thee ere thou speak'st.
Yet, if thou say Antony lives, is well,
Or friends with Caesar, or not captive to him,   45
I'll set thee in a shower of gold and hail
Rich pearls upon thee.
MESSENGER   Madam, he's well.
CLEOPATRA   Well said.
MESSENGER   And friends with Caesar.
CLEOPATRA   Thou'rt an honest° man.
MESSENGER   Caesar and he are greater friends than ever.
CLEOPATRA   Make thee a fortune from me.
MESSENGER   But yet, madam—   50
CLEOPATRA   I do not like "But yet"; it does allay
The good precedence.° Fie upon "But yet"!
"But yet" is as a jailer to bring forth
Some monstrous malefactor. Prithee, friend,
Pour out the pack of matter° to mine ear,   55

---

28 yield (1) grant (2) report   **33 well** well out of it, in heaven | **Bring it to that** if that is your meaning   **37 go to** all right, then (said remonstratingly)   **39 tart a favor** sour a face   **41 Fury** avenging goddess of classical mythology   **42 like . . . man** in ordinary human form   **48 honest** worthy   **51–2 allay . . . precedence** annul the good news that preceded it   **55 pack of matter** entire contents (as of a peddler's pack)

The good and bad together. He's friends with Caesar,
In state of health, thou say'st, and, thou say'st, free.
MESSENGER   Free, madam? No, I made no such report.
He's bound unto Octavia.
CLEOPATRA   For what good turn?°
MESSENGER   For the best turn i'th' bed.
CLEOPATRA   I am pale, Charmian.   60
MESSENGER   Madam, he's married to Octavia.
CLEOPATRA   The most infectious pestilence upon thee!
                                              Strikes him down

MESSENGER
Good madam, patience.
CLEOPATRA   What say you?   *Strikes him*
                                              Hence,
Horrible villain, or I'll spurn° thine eyes
Like balls before me! I'll unhair thy head!   65
                    She hales° him up and down
Thou shalt be whipped with wire and stewed in brine,
Smarting in ling'ring pickle!°
MESSENGER   Gracious madam,
I that do bring the news made not the match.
CLEOPATRA   Say 'tis not so, a province I will give thee
And make thy fortunes proud. The blow thou hadst   70
Shall make thy peace° for moving me to rage,
And I will boot thee with° what° gift beside
Thy modesty° can beg.
MESSENGER   He's married, madam.
CLEOPATRA   Rogue, thou hast lived too long!   *Draw[s] a knife*
MESSENGER   Nay then, I'll run.
What mean you, madam? I have made no fault.   *Exit* 75
CHARMIAN   Good madam, keep yourself° within yourself.
The man is innocent.

---

59 turn favor, purpose (but the messenger replies in the sense of "feat, bout," with sexual suggestion)   **64 spurn** kick   **65.1** *hales* drags   **67 pickle** pickling solution   **71 make thy peace** compensate, mollify me   **72 boot thee with** give you into the bargain, or, make amends with | **what** whatever   **73 Thy modesty** one of your modest expectations   **76 keep . . . yourself** control yourself

CLEOPATRA   Some innocents scape not the thunderbolt.
Melt Egypt into Nile, and kindly° creatures
Turn all to serpents! Call the slave again.   80
Though I am mad,° I will not bite him. Call!
CHARMIAN   He is afeard to come.
CLEOPATRA   I will not hurt him.

                        [*The Messenger is sent for*]

These hands do lack nobility, that they strike
A meaner° than myself, since I myself
Have given myself the cause.°

                            Enter the Messenger again

                            Come hither, sir.   85
Though it be honest, it is never good
To bring bad news. Give to a gracious message
An host° of tongues, but let ill tidings tell
Themselves when they be felt.°
MESSENGER   I have done my duty.   90
CLEOPATRA   Is he married?
I cannot hate thee worser than I do
If thou again say "Yes."
MESSENGER   He's married, madam.
CLEOPATRA   The gods confound° thee! Dost thou hold there still?°
MESSENGER   Should I lie, madam?
CLEOPATRA   Oh, I would thou didst,   95
So° half my Egypt were submerged and made
A cistern° for scaled° snakes! Go, get thee hence.
Hadst thou Narcissus° in thy face, to me
Thou wouldst appear most ugly. He is married?
MESSENGER   I crave Your Highness' pardon.
CLEOPATRA   He is married?   100

---

79 **kindly** endowed with innately good qualities   81 **mad** (1) angry (2) insane, and
so apt to bite   84 **A meaner** one of lower social station   84–5 **since . . . cause** since
I am the one I ought to blame   85 **the cause** by loving Antony   88 **host** multitude
89 **when . . . felt** by being felt rather than spoken aloud; let bad tidings announce
themselves   94 **confound** destroy | **hold there still** stick to your story   96 **So** even
if   97 **cistern** tank | **scaled** scaly   98 **Narcissus** beautiful youth of Greek
mythology who fell in love with his own reflected image

MESSENGER   Take no offense that I would not offend you.°
  To punish me for what you make me do
  Seems much unequal.° He's married to Octavia.
CLEOPATRA   Oh, that his fault should make a knave of thee,
  That art not what thou'rt sure of!° Get thee hence.   105
  The merchandise which thou hast brought from Rome
  Are all too dear° for me. Lie they upon thy hand,
  And be undone by 'em!°   [Exit Messenger]
CHARMIAN   Good Your Highness, patience.
CLEOPATRA   In praising Antony, I have dispraised Caesar.
CHARMIAN   Many times, madam.   110
CLEOPATRA   I am paid for't now. Lead me from hence;
  I faint. Oh, Iras, Charmian! 'Tis no matter.
  Go to the fellow, good Alexas. Bid him
  Report the feature of Octavia: her years,
  Her inclination.° Let him not leave out   115
  The color of her hair. Bring me word quickly.
                          [Exit Alexas]
  Let him forever go!—Let him° not, Charmian.
  Though he be painted one way like a Gorgon,
  The other way's a Mars.° [To Mardian] Bid you Alexas
  Bring me word how tall she is.—Pity me, Charmian,   120
  But do not speak to me. Lead me to my chamber.
                          Exeunt

❖

101 Take . . . offend you don't be offended that I hesitate to offend you (by telling bad news), or, don't interpret as offense what is not meant to offend   103 much unequal most unjust   104–5 Oh, that . . . sure of! how regrettable that Antony's fault puts you in the wrong, you who are not yourself hateful even if you have had to report hateful news as a certain fact!   107 dear (1) expensive (2) emotionally precious   107–8 Lie . . . by 'em! may they remain in your possession unsold, and may you be bankrupt, financially ruined! (may you never profit from your bad tidings!)   115 inclination disposition   117 him Antony   118–19 Though . . . Mars (alludes to a type of picture known as a perspective, which shows different images when looked at from different angles of vision; a Gorgon is a female monster with serpents in her hair, capable of turning to stone anything that meets her gaze)

ACT 2
SCENE 6

*Location: Near Misenum, in southern Italy near modern
Naples. (But 2.1 perhaps took place in Messina, Sicily.)*

> *Flourish. Enter Pompey [and] Menas at one door, with
> drum and trumpet; at another, Caesar, Lepidus, Antony,
> Enobarbus, Maecenas, Agrippa, with soldiers marching*

POMPEY   Your hostages I have, so have you mine,
And we shall talk before we fight.

CAESAR   Most meet°
That first we come to words; and therefore have we
Our written purposes° before us sent,
Which if thou hast considered, let us know   5
If 'twill tie up thy discontented sword°
And carry back to Sicily much tall° youth
That else must perish here.

POMPEY   To you all three,
The senators alone° of this great world,
Chief factors° for the gods: I do not know   10
Wherefore my father should revengers want,°
Having a son and friends, since Julius Caesar,
Who at Philippi the good Brutus ghosted,°
There saw you laboring for him.° What was't
That moved pale Cassius to conspire? And what   15
Made th'all-honored, honest° Roman Brutus,
With the armed rest,° courtiers of beauteous freedom,°
To drench° the Capitol, but that they would

---

2 meet fitting   **4 purposes** propositions   **6 tie . . . sword** satisfy your concerns and
allow you to forgo a fight   **7 tall** brave   **9 senators alone** sole rulers of the state
(who have thus supplanted the Senate)   **10 factors** agents   **10–14 I do . . . for him**
(Julius Caesar defeated Pompey's father, Pompey the Great, and was subsequently
assassinated by Brutus and Cassius, among others; Caesar's ghost appeared to
Brutus at Philippi, where the combined forces of Antony, Octavius, and Lepidus
defeated Brutus and Cassius; since Antony, Octavius, and Lepidus thus defeated
the avengers of Pompey the Great's death, Pompey the Great's sons and friends
should become his avengers by continuing to war on Antony, Octavius, and
Lepidus)   **11 want** lack   **13 ghosted** haunted   **16 honest** honorable   **17 the
armed rest** the rest of those who were armed | **courtiers . . . freedom** those who
serve freedom only   **18 drench** bathe in blood

Have one man but a man?° And that is it
Hath made me rig my navy, at whose burden   20
The angered ocean foams, with which I meant
To scourge th'ingratitude that despiteful Rome
Cast on my noble father.

CAESAR   Take your time.

ANTONY   Thou canst not fear° us, Pompey, with thy sails;
We'll speak with° thee at sea. At land thou know'st   25
How much we do o'ercount° thee.

POMPEY   At land indeed
Thou dost o'ercount me of my father's house;
But since the cuckoo° builds not for himself,
Remain in't as thou mayst.°

LEPIDUS   Be pleased to tell us—
For this is from the present°—how you take   30
The offers we have sent you.

CAESAR   There's the point.

ANTONY   Which do not be entreated to,° but weigh
What it is worth embraced.°

CAESAR   And what may follow,
To try a larger fortune.°

POMPEY   You have made me offer
Of Sicily, Sardinia; and I must   35
Rid all the sea of pirates; then, to send°
Measures of wheat to Rome. This 'greed upon,
To part° with unhacked edges° and bear back
Our targes° undinted.

CAESAR, ANTONY, LEPIDUS   That's our offer.

POMPEY   Know then

---

19 Have . . . a man (the republican conspirators acted to keep Julius Caesar from accepting the crown)   **24 fear** frighten   **25 speak with** confront   **26 o'ercount** outnumber (but Pompey's use of the word in the next line implies that Antony has cheated him; Plutarch informs us that Antony bought the elder Pompey's house at auction and later refused to pay for it)   **28 cuckoo** a bird that builds no nest for itself but lays its eggs in other birds' nests   **29 as thou mayst** as long as you can, or, since you can   **30 from the present** digressing from the business at hand   **32 do . . . to** do not accept merely because we ask   **33 embraced** if accepted by you   **34 To . . . fortune** if you decide to risk war with the triumvirs, or, if you join with us to share a greater fortune   **36 to send** I am to send   **38 To part** we are to part company |
edges swords   **39 targes** shields

I came before you here a man prepared 40
To take this offer, but Mark Antony
Put me to some impatience. Though I lose
The praise of it by telling,° you must know,
When Caesar and your brother were at blows,
Your mother came to Sicily and did find 45
Her welcome friendly.

ANTONY   I have heard it, Pompey,
And am well studied for° a liberal thanks
Which I do owe you.

POMPEY   Let me have your hand.

                                        [*They shake hands*]
I did not think, sir, to have met you here.

ANTONY   The beds i'th'East are soft; and thanks to you, 50
That called me timelier° than my purpose hither,
For I have gained by't.

CAESAR   Since I saw you last
There's a change upon you.

POMPEY   Well, I know not
What counts° harsh Fortune casts° upon my face,
But in my bosom shall she never come 55
To make my heart her vassal.

LEPIDUS   Well met here.

POMPEY   I hope so, Lepidus. Thus we are agreed.
I crave our composition° may be written
And sealed between us.°

CAESAR   That's the next to do.

POMPEY   We'll feast each other ere we part, and let's 60
Draw lots who shall begin.

ANTONY   That will I,° Pompey.

POMPEY   No, Antony, take the lot.° But, first or last,°
Your fine Egyptian cookery shall have

42–3 **Though . . . telling** though I forfeit praise from others by praising myself
47 **well studied for** well prepared to deliver   51 **timelier** earlier   54 **counts** tally
marks (from the practice of casting accounts or reckonings by means of marks or
notches on tallies) | **casts** calculates   58 **composition** agreement   59 **sealed
between us** stamped with the official seal of each co-signer   61 **That will I** I will
begin   62 **take the lot** draw lots with the rest of us, accept the results of the lottery |
first or last whether you win the lottery to go first or last

The fame. I have heard that Julius Caesar
Grew fat with feasting there.   65
ANTONY   You have heard much.
POMPEY   I have fair° meanings, sir.
ANTONY   And fair° words to them.
POMPEY   Then so much have I heard.°
And I have heard Apollodorus carried—   70
ENOBARBUS   No more of that. He did so.
POMPEY   What, I pray you?
ENOBARBUS   A certain queen to Caesar in a mattress.°
POMPEY   I know thee now. How far'st thou, soldier?
ENOBARBUS   Well,
And well am like° to do, for I perceive
Four feasts are toward.°
POMPEY   Let me shake thy hand.   75

                            [*They shake hands*]

I never hated thee. I have seen thee fight
When I have envied thy behavior.
ENOBARBUS   Sir,
I never loved you much, but I ha' praised ye
When you have well deserved ten times as much
As I have said you did.
POMPEY   Enjoy thy plainness;°   80
It nothing ill becomes thee.°
Aboard my galley I invite you all.
Will you lead, lords?
CAESAR, ANTONY, LEPIDUS   Show 's the way, sir.
POMPEY   Come.

                    Exeunt. Manent° *Enobarbus and Menas*

MENAS [*aside*]   Thy father, Pompey, would ne'er have made this
treaty.—You and I have known,° sir.   85
ENOBARBUS   At sea, I think.
MENAS   We have, sir.

---

67 fair friendly   **68 fair** well-chosen   **69 Then . . . heard** I am not implying more
about Antony in Egypt than my words honestly mean   **70–2 Apollodorus . . .
mattress** (alludes to a tale told by Plutarch according to which Cleopatra had herself
rolled up in a mattress and carried secretly by Apollodorus to meet Julius Caesar)
74 like likely   **75 toward** coming up   **80 Enjoy thy plainness** give free rein to your
bluntness   **81 nothing . . . thee** suits you not at all badly   **83.1 Manent** they remain
onstage   **85 known** known each other

ENOBARBUS   You have done well by water.

MENAS   And you by land.

ENOBARBUS   I will praise any man that will praise me, though it   90
cannot be denied what I have done by land.

MENAS   Nor what I have done by water.

ENOBARBUS   Yes, something you can deny for your own safety:
you have been a great thief by sea.

MENAS   And you by land.   95

ENOBARBUS   There° I deny my land service. But give me your
hand, Menas. [*They shake hands*] If our eyes had authority,°
here they might take° two thieves kissing.°

MENAS   All men's faces are true, whatsome'er their hands are.

ENOBARBUS   But there is never a fair woman has a true° face.   100

MENAS   No slander; they steal hearts.°

ENOBARBUS   We came hither to fight with you.

MENAS   For my part, I am sorry it is turned to a drinking.°
Pompey doth this day laugh away his fortune.

ENOBARBUS   If he do, sure he cannot weep't back again.   105

MENAS   You've said,° sir. We looked not for Mark Antony here.
Pray you, is he married to Cleopatra?

ENOBARBUS   Caesar's sister is called Octavia.

MENAS   True, sir. She was the wife of Caius Marcellus.

ENOBARBUS   But she is now the wife of Marcus Antonius.   110

MENAS   Pray ye, sir?°

ENOBARBUS   'Tis true.

MENAS   Then is Caesar and he forever knit together.

ENOBARBUS   If I were bound to divine of° this unity, I would not
prophesy so.   115

MENAS   I think the policy of that purpose made more° in the
marriage than the love of the parties.

ENOBARBUS   I think so too. But you shall find the band that
seems to tie their friendship together will be the very stran-

---

96 There in respect to that   **97 authority** to make arrests, like a constable   **98 take**
arrest | **two thieves kissing** (1) our two thieving hands shaking (2) two thieves
greeting each other   **100 true** honest (because women use cosmetic art to conceal
defects)   **101 No . . . hearts** you speak true, since women in their own way are thieves,
stealing men's affections   **103 a drinking** an occasion for drinking   **106 You've said**
you've spoken truly   **111 Pray ye, sir?** are you in earnest?   **114 divine of** prophesy
about   **116 made more** played more of a role

gler of their amity. Octavia is of a holy, cold, and still con- 120
versation.°

MENAS Who would not have his wife so?

ENOBARBUS Not he that himself is not so, which is Mark
Antony. He will to his Egyptian dish again. Then shall the
sighs of Octavia blow the fire up in Caesar, and, as I said be- 125
fore, that which is the strength of their amity shall prove the
immediate author of their variance.° Antony will use his affection where it is;° he married but his occasion° here.

MENAS And thus it may be. Come, sir, will you aboard? I have
a health° for you. 130

ENOBARBUS I shall take it, sir. We have used our throats in
Egypt.

MENAS Come, let's away.

Exeunt

❧

ACT 2
SCENE 7

*Location: On board Pompey's galley, off Misenum
in southern Italy. A table and stools are brought on.*

Music plays. Enter two or three Servants with a banquet°

FIRST SERVANT Here they'll be, man. Some o' their plants° are
ill-rooted already; the least wind i'th' world will blow them
down.

SECOND SERVANT Lepidus is high-colored.°

FIRST SERVANT They have made him drink alms-drink.° 5

SECOND SERVANT As they pinch one another by the disposition,
he cries out, "No more," reconciles them to his entreaty,
and himself to th' drink.°

120–1 **conversation** demeanor 127 **author . . . variance** cause of their falling out
127–8 **use . . . it is** satisfy his passion in Egypt 128 **his occasion** what his interests
demanded 130 **health** toast

0.1 *banquet* a course of the feast, probably dessert 1 **plants** (1) planted trees (2) soles
of the feet 4 **high-colored** flushed 5 **alms-drink** drink charitably consumed in the
furtherance of reconciliation (see next speech and note) 6–8 **As . . . drink** as they
chafe one another, prompted by their various temperaments, Lepidus entreats them
to stop quarreling, and reconciles himself to the peacemaking business of downing
one drink after another in response to their toasts

FIRST SERVANT   But it raises the greater war between him and his
    discretion.   10

SECOND SERVANT   Why, this it is to have a name° in great men's
    fellowship. I had as lief° have a reed that will do me no ser-
    vice as a partisan° I could not heave.

FIRST SERVANT   To be called into a huge sphere, and not to be
    seen to move in't, are the holes where eyes should be, which   15
    pitifully disaster the cheeks.°

> *A sennet° sounded. Enter Caesar, Antony, Pompey,*
> *Lepidus, Agrippa, Maecenas, Enobarbus,*
> *Menas, with other captains [and a Boy]*

ANTONY   Thus do they, sir:° they take° the flow o'th' Nile
    By certain scales° i'th' pyramid. They know
    By th' height, the lowness, or the mean° if dearth
    Or foison° follow. The higher Nilus swells   20
    The more it promises; as it ebbs, the seedsman
    Upon the slime and ooze scatters his grain,
    And shortly comes to harvest.

LEPIDUS   You've strange serpents there.

ANTONY   Ay, Lepidus.   25

LEPIDUS   Your serpent° of Egypt is bred now of your mud by
    the operation of your sun; so is your crocodile.

ANTONY   They are so.

POMPEY   Sit—and some wine. A health° to Lepidus!
                                          [They sit and drink]

LEPIDUS   I am not so well as I should be, but I'll ne'er out.°   30

---

11 **a name** a name only   12 **had as lief** would just as soon   13 **partisan** long-bladed
spear (here, metaphorically, too large a weapon for Lepidus to wield)   **14–16 To . . .
cheeks** to be summoned by fortune to greatness and yet not be able to fulfill the role
greatly is like having eye sockets with no eyes in them, a defect that will disfigure
(*disaster*) the cheeks (the underlying image is of a heavenly body that cannot move
properly in its sphere, causing *disaster*, meaning both disfigurement and the evil
effects of unfavorable aspect of a planet)   **16.1 *sennet*** trumpet call signaling the
approach of a procession   17 **sir** (usually thought to refer to Caesar, but the matter
is uncertain) | **take** measure   18 **scales** graduated markings   19 **mean** middle
20 **foison** plenty   26 **Your serpent** this serpent that people talk about (the colloquial
indefinite *your*)   29 **health** toast (Lepidus is obliged to drink up every time a toast
is proposed to him)   30 **I'll ne'er out** I'll never refuse a toast, never quit

ENOBARBUS   Not till you have slept; I fear me you'll be in° till
then.

LEPIDUS   Nay, certainly, I have heard the Ptolemies' pyramises°
are very goodly things; without contradiction I have heard
that.   35

MENAS [aside to Pompey]   Pompey, a word.

POMPEY [to Menas]   Say in mine ear. What is't?

MENAS (whispers in 's ear)
Forsake thy seat, I do beseech thee, captain,
And hear me speak a word.

POMPEY [to Menas]
Forbear me till anon.°—This wine for Lepidus!   40

LEPIDUS   What manner o' thing is your crocodile?

ANTONY   It is shaped, sir, like itself, and it is as broad as it hath
breadth. It is just so high as it is, and moves with it own° organs. It lives by that which nourisheth it, and, the elements°
once out of it, it transmigrates.   45

LEPIDUS   What color is it of?

ANTONY   Of it own color too.

LEPIDUS   'Tis a strange serpent.

ANTONY   'Tis so. And the tears° of it are wet.

CAESAR   Will this description satisfy him?   50

ANTONY   With the health that Pompey gives him, else he is a
very epicure.°   [Menas whispers again]

POMPEY [aside to Menas]
Go hang, sir, hang! Tell me of that? Away!
Do as I bid you.—Where's this cup I called for?

MENAS [aside to Pompey]
If for the sake of merit° thou wilt hear me,   55
Rise from thy stool.

POMPEY [rising]   I think thou'rt mad. The matter?
                                                                     [They walk aside]

31 **in** in drink, in your cups (with a play of antitheses between *in* and *out* in l. 30)
33 **pyramises** (Lepidus's drunken error for *pyramides*, plural of *pyramis* or *pyramid*)
40 **Forbear . . . anon** excuse me for a moment   43 **it own** its own (also in l. 47)
44 **elements** vital elements   49 **tears** (alludes to the ancient belief that the crocodile
wept insincere "crocodile tears" over its victim before devouring it)   52 **epicure**
(1) glutton (2) atheist (the Epicureans did not believe in an afterlife; Antony's jesting
point is that only an atheist or epicure would be skeptical of such a satisfying
description as Antony has just given of the crocodile)   55 **merit** my merits as a loyal
follower, or, the merit of my ideas

MENAS   I have ever held my cap off° to thy fortunes.

POMPEY

Thou hast served me with much faith.° What's else to say?—
Be jolly, lords.

ANTONY   These quicksands, Lepidus,
Keep off them, for you sink.   60

                    [*Menas and Pompey speak aside*]

MENAS   Wilt thou be lord of all the world?

POMPEY   What say'st thou?

MENAS   Wilt thou be lord of the whole world? That's twice.

POMPEY   How should that be?

MENAS   But entertain it,°
And, though thou think me poor, I am the man
Will give thee all the world.

POMPEY   Hast thou drunk well?   65

MENAS   No, Pompey, I have kept me from the cup.
Thou art, if thou dar'st be, the earthly Jove.
Whate'er the ocean pales or sky inclips°
Is thine, if thou wilt ha 't.

POMPEY   Show me which way.

MENAS   These three world-sharers, these competitors,°   70
Are in thy vessel. Let me cut the cable,
And, when we are put off,° fall to their throats.
All there is thine.

POMPEY   Ah, this thou shouldst have done
And not have spoke on't!° In me 'tis villainy;
In thee 't had been good service. Thou must know,°   75
'Tis not my profit that does lead mine honor;
Mine honor, it.° Repent° that e'er thy tongue
Hath so betrayed thine act. Being done unknown,°
I should have found it afterwards well done,
But must condemn it now. Desist, and drink.   80

                            [*He returns to the feast*]

---

57 **held . . . off** been a respectful and faithful servant   58 **faith** faithfulness   63 **But entertain it** only accept the possibility   68 **pales** impales, fences in   68 **inclips** embraces   70 **competitors** partners (with secondary sense of "rivals")   72 **are put off** have put to sea   74 **on't** of it   75 **Thou must know** I must inform you that   77 **Mine honor, it** my honor comes before my personal profit | **Repent** regret   78 **unknown** without my knowledge

MENAS [*aside*]　For this,
I'll never follow thy palled° fortunes more.
Who° seeks and will not take when once 'tis offered
Shall never find it more.
POMPEY　　　　　　　This health to Lepidus!
ANTONY　Bear him ashore. I'll pledge it° for him, Pompey.　　85
ENOBARBUS　Here's to thee, Menas!　　　　[*They drink*]
MENAS　　　　　　　　Enobarbus, welcome!
POMPEY　Fill till the cup be hid.
ENOBARBUS　There's a strong fellow, Menas.
　　　　　　[*Pointing to one who carries off Lepidus*]
MENAS　Why?
ENOBARBUS　'A° bears the third part of the world, man; see'st not?　90
MENAS　The third part, then, is drunk. Would it were all,
That it might go on wheels!°
ENOBARBUS　Drink thou; increase the reels.°
MENAS　Come.
POMPEY　This is not yet an Alexandrian feast.　　　　95
ANTONY　It ripens towards it. Strike the vessels,° ho!
Here's to Caesar!
CAESAR　　　　　　I could well forbear't.
It's monstrous labor when I wash my brain
And it grows fouler.
ANTONY　　　　　　Be a child o'th' time.
CAESAR　Possess it, I'll make answer.°　　　　100
But I had rather fast from all° four days
Than drink so much in one.
ENOBARBUS [*to Antony*]　　　　Ha, my brave° emperor!
Shall we dance now the Egyptian Bacchanals°
And celebrate° our drink?
POMPEY　Let's ha 't, good soldier.　　　　105

---

82 palled decayed, darkened　**83 Who** he who　**85 pledge it** drink the toast (since
Lepidus is too far gone to drink)　**90 'A** he　**92 go on wheels** go fast or easily
(proverbial)　**93 reels** (1) revels (2) reeling and whirling of drunkenness　**96 Strike
the vessels** broach or tap the casks　**100 Possess . . . answer** my answer is, be master
of the time; or, possibly, drink it off, I'll drink in return　**101 all** all nourishment
102 brave splendid　**103 Bacchanals** drunken dance to Bacchus, god of wine
104 celebrate consecrate with observances

ANTONY   Come, let's all take hands
  Till that° the conquering wine hath steeped our sense
  In soft and delicate Lethe.°
ENOBARBUS   All take hands.
  Make battery to° our ears with the loud music,
  The while I'll place you; then the boy shall sing.   110
  The holding° every man shall bear° as loud
  As his strong sides can volley.°

     Music plays. Enobarbus places them hand in hand

        The Song

BOY [*sings*]
     Come, thou monarch of the vine,
     Plumpy Bacchus with pink eyne!°
     In thy fats° our cares be drowned,   115
     With thy grapes our hairs be crowned.
ALL   Cup° us till the world go round,
     Cup us till the world go round!
CAESAR   What would you more? Pompey, good night.—Good
  brother,
  Let me request you off.° Our graver business   120
  Frowns at this levity. Gentle lords, let's part;
  You see we have burnt our cheeks.° Strong Enobarb
  Is weaker than the wine, and mine own tongue
  Splits what it speaks. The wild disguise° hath almost
  Anticked us° all. What needs more words? Good night. 125
  Good Antony, your hand.
POMPEY   I'll try you° on the shore.
ANTONY   And shall, sir. Give 's your hand.
POMPEY   Oh, Antony,
  You have my father's house. But what? We are friends.
  Come down into the boat.°
ENOBARBUS   Take heed you fall not.

107 **Till that** until   108 **Lethe** forgetfulness (literally, the river of oblivion in Hades)   109 **make battery to** assault   111 **holding** refrain | **bear** carry, sing   112 **volley** sing in return, answering the stanza with the refrain   114 **pink eyne** eyes half-shut, from drinking   115 **fats** vats, vessels   117 **Cup** intoxicate   120 **off** to disembark   122 **we . . . cheeks** our complexions are flushed with drinking   124 **disguise** (1) masque (2) transforming drunkenness   125 **Anticked us** (1) made dancers of us in a masque (2) made buffoons or fools of us   126 **try you** take you on in a drinking contest   129 **boat** small boat for taking the party ashore

[*Exeunt all but Enobarbus and Menas*]
Menas, I'll not on shore.

MENAS   No, to my cabin.   130

These drums, these trumpets, flutes! What!
Let Neptune hear we bid a loud farewell
To these great fellows. Sound and be hanged, sound out!

Sound a flourish, with drums

ENOBARBUS   Hoo! says 'a. There's my cap.

[*He flings it in the air*]

MENAS   Hoo! Noble captain, come.   135

Exeunt

❖

ACT 3
SCENE 1

Location: The Middle East

*Enter Ventidius as it were in triumph [with
Silius, and other Romans, officers, and soldiers],
the dead body of Pacorus borne before him*

VENTIDIUS   Now, darting° Parthia,° art thou struck, and now
Pleased fortune does of Marcus Crassus' death°
Make me revenger. Bear the King's son's body
Before our army. Thy Pacorus, Orodes,°
Pays this for Marcus Crassus.

SILIUS   Noble Ventidius,   5

Whilst yet with Parthian blood thy sword is warm,
The fugitive Parthians follow.° Spur through Media,
Mesopotamia, and the shelters whither
The routed fly. So thy grand captain, Antony,

---

1 darting (the Parthians were famous for archery and for the Parthian dart, which they discharged as they fled) | **Parthia** Orodes, King of Parthia **2 Crassus' death** (Crassus, member of the first triumvirate with Pompey the Great and Julius Caesar, was overthrown and treacherously murdered by Orodes in 53 BCE) **4 Pacorus, Orodes** (Pacorus was the son of Orodes) **7 The . . . follow** follow the fleeing Parthians

Shall set thee on triumphant° chariots and   10
Put garlands on thy head.
VENTIDIUS   Oh, Silius, Silius,
    I have done enough. A lower place,° note well,
    May make too great an act. For learn this, Silius:
    Better to leave undone than by our deed
    Acquire too high a fame when him we serve's away.   15
    Caesar and Antony have ever won
    More in their officer than person.° Sossius,
    One of my place° in Syria, his lieutenant,°
    For quick accumulation of renown,
    Which he achieved by th' minute,° lost his favor.   20
    Who° does i'th' wars more than his captain can
    Becomes his captain's captain; and ambition,
    The soldier's virtue, rather makes choice of loss
    Than gain which darkens him.°
    I could do more to do Antonius good,   25
    But 'twould offend him, and in his offense°
    Should my performance perish.
SILIUS   Thou hast, Ventidius, that
    Without the which a soldier and his sword
    Grants scarce distinction.° Thou wilt write to Antony?   30
VENTIDIUS   I'll humbly signify what in his name,
    That magical word° of war, we have effected:°
    How with his banners and his well-paid ranks
    The ne'er-yet-beaten horse° of Parthia
    We have jaded° out o'th' field.
SILIUS   Where is he now?   35
VENTIDIUS   He purposeth to Athens, whither, with what haste
    The weight we must convey with 's° will permit,
    We shall appear before him.—On, there. Pass along!
                                        Exeunt

---

10 **triumphant** triumphal   12 **A lower place** one of lower rank   17 **More . . . person**
more through the actions of their lieutenants than by their own efforts   18 **of my
place** of the same rank as I | **his lieutenant** the commanding officer acting for
Antony   20 **by th' minute** minute by minute, continually   21 **Who** he who
23–4 **rather . . . him** prefers to lose rather than gain in such a way as to darken his
reputation   26 **offense** taking offense   28–30 **that . . . distinction** discretion,
without which a soldier can scarcely be distinguished from the sword he uses   32 **word**
watchword | **effected** achieved   34 **horse** cavalry   35 **jaded** driven exhausted like
jades, inferior horses   37 **with 's** with us

❖

ACT 3
SCENE 2

Location: Rome

Enter Agrippa at one door, Enobarbus at another

AGRIPPA What, are the brothers parted?°

ENOBARBUS They have dispatched° with Pompey; he is gone.
The other three are sealing.° Octavia weeps
To part from Rome; Caesar is sad;° and Lepidus,
Since Pompey's feast, as Menas says, is troubled   5
With the greensickness.°

AGRIPPA   'Tis a noble Lepidus.

ENOBARBUS A very fine° one. Oh, how he loves Caesar!

AGRIPPA Nay, but how dearly he adores Mark Antony!

ENOBARBUS Caesar? Why, he's the Jupiter of men.

AGRIPPA What's Antony? The god of Jupiter.   10

ENOBARBUS Spake you of Caesar? How, the nonpareil!

AGRIPPA O Antony, O thou Arabian bird!°

ENOBARBUS
Would you praise Caesar, say "Caesar"; go no further.

AGRIPPA Indeed, he plied them both with excellent praises.

ENOBARBUS
But he loves Caesar best; yet he loves Antony.   15
Hoo! Hearts, tongues, figures,° scribes, bards, poets, cannot
Think, speak, cast,° write, sing, number,° hoo!
His love to Antony. But as for Caesar,
Kneel down, kneel down, and wonder.

AGRIPPA   Both he loves.

---

1 brothers parted brothers-in-law departed   **2 dispatched** concluded the business
3 sealing affixing seals to their agreements, settling matters   **4 sad** sober
6 greensickness a kind of anemia supposed to affect young women, especially those
afflicted with love-longing (used ironically here to refer to Lepidus's hangover and
to his love for Antony and Caesar)   **7 fine** (*lepidus* in Latin means "fine,"
"elegant")   **12 Arabian bird** the fabled phoenix (only one existed at a time; it re-
created itself by arising from its ashes)   **16 figures** figures of speech   **17 cast**
calculate | **number** write verses

ENOBARBUS   They are his shards,° and he their beetle. So;   20
                            [*Trumpets within*]
  This is to horse.° Adieu, noble Agrippa.
AGRIPPA   Good fortune, worthy soldier, and farewell.

              Enter Caesar, Antony, Lepidus, and Octavia

ANTONY   No further,° sir.
CAESAR   You take from me a great part of myself;
  Use me well in't.—Sister, prove such a wife   25
  As my thoughts make thee, and as my farthest bond
  Shall pass on thy approof.°—Most noble Antony,
  Let not the piece° of virtue which is set
  Betwixt us as the cement of our love
  To keep it builded be the ram to batter   30
  The fortress of it; for better might we
  Have loved without this mean,° if on both parts
  This be not cherished.
ANTONY   Make me not offended
  In° your distrust.
CAESAR   I have said.°
ANTONY   You shall not find,
  Though you be therein curious,° the least cause   35
  For what you seem to fear. So the gods keep you,
  And make the hearts of Romans serve your ends!
  We will here part.
CAESAR   Farewell, my dearest sister, fare thee well.
  The elements° be kind to thee, and make   40
  Thy spirits all of comfort! Fare thee well.
OCTAVIA [*weeping*]   My noble brother!
ANTONY   The April's in her eyes; it is love's spring,
  And these the showers to bring it on.—Be cheerful.
OCTAVIA [*to Caesar*]
  Sir, look well to my husband's house;° and—   45

---

20 shards patches of dung, or, perhaps, wings or wing-cases, protectors, patrons
21 This is to horse the trumpet call gives the signal to depart   **23 No further** you
need not go on urging your point, or, you need accompany me no further   **26–7 as
. . . approof** such that my utmost bond shall be justified in certifying what you will
prove to be   **28 piece** masterpiece   **32 mean** intermediary, or means   **34 In** by |
I have said I stand by what I've said   **35 curious** overly inquisitive or touchy
40 elements heavens   **45 husband's house** Antony's house, as at 2.7.128, though
Octavia is also a widow; see 3.3.29

CAESAR   What, Octavia?

OCTAVIA   I'll tell you in your ear.

                              [*She whispers to Caesar*]

ANTONY   Her tongue will not obey her heart, nor can
  Her heart inform her tongue—the swan's down feather,
  That stands upon the swell at full of tide,
  And neither way inclines.°   50

ENOBARBUS [*aside to Agrippa*]   Will Caesar weep?

AGRIPPA [*aside to Enobarbus*]   He has a cloud in 's face.

ENOBARBUS [*aside to Agrippa*]
  He were the worse for that, were he a horse;°
  So is he, being a man.

AGRIPPA [*aside to Enobarbus*]   Why, Enobarbus,
  When Antony found Julius Caesar dead,   55
  He cried almost to roaring; and he wept
  When at Philippi he found Brutus slain.

ENOBARBUS [*aside to Agrippa*]
  That year indeed he was troubled with a rheum.°
  What willingly he did confound he wailed,°
  Believe't, till I wept too.

CAESAR   No, sweet Octavia,   60
  You shall hear from me still.° The time shall not
  Outgo my thinking on you.°

ANTONY   Come, sir, come,
  I'll wrestle with you in my strength of love.
  Look, here I have you [*embracing him*]; thus I let you go,
  And give you to the gods.

CAESAR   Adieu. Be happy!   65

LEPIDUS
  Let all the number of the stars give light
  To thy fair way!

CAESAR   Farewell, farewell!   *Kisses Octavia*

ANTONY   Farewell!

                    Trumpets sound. Exeunt [in separate groups]

47–50 Her . . . inclines her conflicting emotions make her unable to speak aloud, like
a swan's down feather floating at full tide, moving neither up nor down stream
53 He . . . horse (alludes to the belief that a horse with a dark spot on its face was
apt to be bad-tempered)   58 rheum running at the eyes (said of any discharge of
secretion from the head)   59 What . . . bewailed he bewailed what he intentionally
destroyed   61 still regularly   61–2 The time . . . you time itself will not outlast my
thinking of you

❖

ACT 3
SCENE 3

Location: Alexandria. Cleopatra's palace.

Enter Cleopatra, Charmian, Iras, and Alexas

CLEOPATRA Where is the fellow?

ALEXAS   Half afeard to come.

CLEOPATRA Go to,° go to.

Enter the Messenger as before

Come hither, sir.

ALEXAS   Good Majesty,
   Herod of Jewry° dare not look upon you
   But when you are well pleased.

CLEOPATRA   That Herod's head
   I'll have; but how, when Antony is gone,   5
   Through whom I might command it?—Come thou near.

MESSENGER Most gracious Majesty!

CLEOPATRA Didst thou behold Octavia?

MESSENGER Ay, dread Queen.

CLEOPATRA   Where?

MESSENGER   Madam, in Rome.
   I looked her in the face, and saw her led   10
   Between her brother and Mark Antony.

CLEOPATRA Is she as tall as me?

MESSENGER   She is not, madam.

CLEOPATRA Didst hear her speak? Is she shrill-tongued or low?

MESSENGER Madam, I heard her speak. She is low-voiced.

CLEOPATRA That's not so good.° He cannot like her long.   15

CHARMIAN Like her! Oh, Isis, 'tis impossible.

CLEOPATRA
   I think so, Charmian. Dull of tongue, and dwarfish.—
   What majesty is in her gait? Remember,

---

2 Go to (an expression of impatience)   **3 Herod of Jewry** even the famous tyrant
who slaughtered the children (see 1.2.27)   **15 not so good** not so good for her

If e'er thou looked'st on majesty.

MESSENGER   She creeps:
Her motion and her station are as one.°   20
She shows° a body rather than a life,
A statue than a breather.°

CLEOPATRA   Is this certain?

MESSENGER   Or I have no observance.

CHARMIAN   Three in Egypt
Cannot make better note.°

CLEOPATRA   He's very knowing,
I do perceive't. There's nothing in her yet.   25
The fellow has good judgment.

CHARMIAN   Excellent.

CLEOPATRA   Guess at her years, I prithee.

MESSENGER   Madam,
She was a widow—

CLEOPATRA   Widow? Charmian, hark.

MESSENGER   And I do think she's thirty.   30

CLEOPATRA   Bear'st thou her face in mind? Is't long or round?

MESSENGER   Round, even to faultiness.

CLEOPATRA
For the most part, too, they are foolish that are so.—
Her hair, what color?

MESSENGER   Brown, madam; and her forehead   35
As low as she would wish it.°

CLEOPATRA [*giving money*]   There's gold for thee.
Thou must not take my former sharpness ill.
I will employ thee back again;° I find thee
Most fit for business. Go make thee ready;   40
Our letters are prepared.   [*Exit Messenger*]

CHARMIAN   A proper° man.

CLEOPATRA   Indeed, he is so. I repent me much
That so I harried° him. Why, methinks, by° him,

---

20 Her . . . one she moves with so little animation that it's all the same whether she's moving or standing   **21 shows** appears as   **22 breather** living being   **23–4 Three . . . note** there are not three people in Egypt who are better observers   **36 As . . . it** such that she wouldn't wish it to be any lower (a colloquial way of suggesting she is ugly; high foreheads were thought more beautiful)   **39 employ . . . again** send you back with a message   **41 proper** good   **43 harried** maltreated I **by** according to

This creature's no such thing.°

CHARMIAN   Nothing, madam.

CLEOPATRA The man hath seen some majesty, and should know.   45

CHARMIAN Hath he seen majesty? Isis else defend,°
And serving° you so long!

CLEOPATRA
I have one thing more to ask him yet, good Charmian—
But 'tis no matter; thou shalt bring him to me
Where I will write. All may be well enough.   50

CHARMIAN I warrant° you, madam.

Exeunt

❖

ACT 3
SCENE 4

Location: Athens

Enter Antony and Octavia

ANTONY Nay, nay, Octavia, not only that—
That were excusable, that and thousands more
Of semblable° import—but he hath waged
New wars 'gainst Pompey; made his will, and read it°
To public ear;   5
Spoke scantly° of me; when perforce he could not
But pay me terms of honor, cold and sickly
He vented° them, most narrow measure lent me;°
When the best hint° was given him, he not took't,
Or did it from his teeth.°

OCTAVIA   Oh, my good lord,   10
Believe not all, or, if you must believe,
Stomach° not all. A more unhappy lady,

---

44 **no such thing** nothing much   46 **else defend** forbid that it be otherwise (an interjection)   47 **serving** he having served   51 **warrant** assure

3 **semblable** similar   4 **read it** (in order to win the populace by showing them what benefits they might expect from him)   6 **scantly** slightingly   8 **vented** gave vent to, expressed | **narrow measure lent me** gave me minimal praise   9 **hint** occasion (to praise Antony)   10 **from his teeth** between clenched teeth, not from the heart   12 **Stomach** resent

If this division chance,° ne'er stood between,
Praying for both parts.
The good gods will mock me presently   15
When I shall pray, "Oh, bless my lord and husband!"
Undo° that prayer by crying out as loud,
"Oh, bless my brother!" Husband win, win brother,
Prays and destroys the prayer; no midway
Twixt these extremes at all.

ANTONY   Gentle Octavia,   20
Let your best love draw to that point which seeks
Best to preserve it.° If I lose mine honor,
I lose myself; better I were not yours
Than yours so branchless.° But, as you requested,
Yourself shall go between 's. The meantime,° lady,   25
I'll raise the preparation of a war
Shall stain your brother.° Make your soonest haste;
So your desires are yours.°

OCTAVIA   Thanks to my lord.
The Jove of power make me, most weak, most weak,
Your reconciler! Wars twixt you twain would be   30
As if the world should cleave,° and that slain men
Should° solder up the rift.

ANTONY   When it appears to you where this begins,°
Turn your displeasure that way, for our° faults
Can never be so equal that your love   35
Can equally move with them.° Provide° your going;
Choose your own company and command what cost
Your heart has mind to.

                                           Exeunt

                              ❧

13 chance occur   17 Undo and then undo, or, I shall undo   21–2 Let . . . it let your
warmest love be given to that one of us who seeks to preserve it (your love) best
24 branchless pruned (of honor)   25 The meantime in the meantime   26–7 I'll . . .
brother I'll raise an army that will deprive your brother of his luster   28 So . . .
yours thus you have obtained your desire (to go); (or, *so* may mean "as long as")
31 cleave split   32 Should would be needed to   33 where this begins who started
this quarrel   34 our Caesar's and mine   34–6 our faults . . . them you will have to
judge between our faults and choose   36 Provide make arrangements for

ACT 3
SCENE 5

Location: Athens

Enter Enobarbus and Eros, [meeting]

ENOBARBUS How now, friend Eros?

EROS There's strange news come, sir.

ENOBARBUS What, man?

EROS Caesar and Lepidus have made wars upon Pompey.

ENOBARBUS This is old. What is the success?° 5

EROS Caesar, having made use of him° in the wars 'gainst
Pompey, presently° denied him rivality,° would not let him
partake in the glory of the action; and, not resting here,° accuses him of letters he had formerly wrote to Pompey; upon
his own appeal° seizes him. So the poor third is up,° till 10
death enlarge his confine.°

ENOBARBUS Then, world, thou hast a pair of chops, no more;°
And throw between them all the food thou hast,
They'll grind the one the other.° Where's Antony?

EROS He's walking in the garden—thus,° and spurns° 15
The rush° that lies before him; cries, "Fool Lepidus!"
And threats the throat of that his officer°
That murdered Pompey.°

ENOBARBUS   Our great navy's rigged.

EROS For Italy and Caesar. More,° Domitius:
My lord desires you presently.° My news 20
I might have told hereafter.

ENOBARBUS   'Twill be naught,
But let it be. Bring me to Antony.

EROS   Come, sir.

Exeunt

5 **success** outcome, result 6 **him** Lepidus 7 **presently** immediately | **rivality**
rights of a partner (Caesar and Lepidus have newly gone to war against Pompey and
have defeated him) 8 **resting here** stopping with this insult 10 **his own appeal**
Caesar's own accusation | **up** shut up (in prison) 11 **enlarge his confine** set him
free 12 **a pair . . . more** a single pair of jaws, with no third partner 14 **They'll . . .
other** the jaws will still grind against each other, grind each other down 15 **thus**
(Eros imitates Antony's angry walk) | **spurns** kicks 16 **rush** strewn rushes
17 **And . . . officer** and threatens the life of the officer of his 18 **Pompey** (after his
defeat by Caesar and Lepidus, Pompey was murdered—perhaps, according to
history, on Antony's orders, but here Antony blames his officer) 19 **More** I have
more to say 20 **presently** immediately

❖

ACT 3
SCENE 6

Location: Rome

Enter Agrippa, Maecenas, and Caesar

CAESAR   Contemning° Rome, he has done all this and more
In Alexandria. Here's the manner of't:
I'th' marketplace, on a tribunal° silvered,
Cleopatra and himself in chairs of gold
Were publicly enthroned. At the feet sat   5
Caesarion, whom they call my father's° son,
And all the unlawful issue that their lust
Since then hath made between them. Unto her
He gave the stablishment° of Egypt, made her
Of lower Syria, Cyprus, Lydia,   10
Absolute queen.

MAECENAS   This in the public eye?

CAESAR   I'th' common showplace, where they exercise.°
His sons he there proclaimed the kings of kings:
Great Media, Parthia, and Armenia
He gave to Alexander; to Ptolemy he assigned   15
Syria, Cilicia, and Phoenicia. She
In th' habiliments° of the goddess Isis
That day appeared, and oft before gave audience,
As 'tis reported, so.

MAECENAS   Let Rome be thus informed.   20

AGRIPPA   Who, queasy° with his insolence already,
Will their good thoughts call° from him.

CAESAR   The people knows it, and have now received
His accusations.

AGRIPPA   Who does he accuse?

---

1 Contemning disdaining **3 tribunal** seat of state, dais **6 my father's** Julius
Caesar's (Julius Caesar had adopted his grandnephew Octavius as his son)
9 stablishment settled possession **12 exercise** put on entertainments and sports
17 habiliments attire **21 queasy** nauseated, "fed up" (refers to the Roman people)
22 call withdraw

CAESAR   Caesar, and that, having in Sicily   25
   Sextus Pompeius spoiled,° we had not rated him°
   His part o'th'isle.° Then does he say he lent me
   Some shipping, unrestored.° Lastly, he frets
   That Lepidus of° the triumvirate
   Should be deposed, and, being,° that we detain   30
   All his revenue.
AGRIPPA   Sir, this should be answered.
CAESAR   'Tis done already, and the messenger gone.
   I have told him Lepidus was grown too cruel,
   That he his high authority abused
   And did deserve his change. For° what I have conquered, 35
   I grant him part; but then in his Armenia,
   And other of his conquered kingdoms, I
   Demand the like.
MAECENAS   He'll never yield to that.
CAESAR   Nor must not then be yielded to in this.

                    Enter Octavia with her train

OCTAVIA   Hail, Caesar, and my lord! Hail, most dear Caesar!   40
CAESAR   That ever I should call thee castaway!
OCTAVIA   You have not called me so, nor have you cause.
CAESAR   Why have you stol'n upon us thus? You come not
   Like Caesar's sister. The wife of Antony
   Should have an army for an usher and   45
   The neighs of horse° to tell of her approach
   Long ere she did appear. The trees by° th' way
   Should have borne men, and expectation fainted,
   Longing for what it had not. Nay, the dust
   Should have ascended to the roof of heaven,   50
   Raised by your populous troops. But you are come
   A market maid to Rome, and have prevented°
   The ostentation° of our love, which, left unshown,
   Is often left unloved.° We should have met you

---

26 **spoiled** despoiled, plundered | **rated him** allotted to Antony   27 **o'th'isle** of Sicily   28 **unrestored** that I did not return to him   29 **of** from   30 **being** having been deposed   35 **For** as for   46 **horse** horses   47 **by** along   52 **prevented** forestalled (by your unannounced arrival)   53 **ostentation** ceremonial display   53–4 **which . . . unloved** which, if not made manifest through ceremonious display, often remains unappreciated or ceases to exist

By sea and land, supplying every stage°   55
With an augmented greeting.
OCTAVIA   Good my lord,
  To come thus was I not constrained, but did it
  On my free will. My lord, Mark Antony,
  Hearing that you prepared for war, acquainted
  My grievèd ear withal, whereon I begged   60
  His pardon° for return.
CAESAR   Which soon he granted,
  Being an obstruct 'tween his lust and him.°
OCTAVIA   Do not say so, my lord.
CAESAR   I have eyes upon him,
  And his affairs come to me on the wind.
  Where is he now?   65
OCTAVIA   My lord, in Athens.
CAESAR   No, my most wrongèd sister. Cleopatra
  Hath nodded him to her. He hath given his empire
  Up to a whore; who° now are levying
  The kings o'th'earth for war. He hath assembled   70
  Bocchus, the King of Libya; Archelaus,
  Of Cappadocia; Philadelphos, King
  Of Paphlagonia; the Thracian king, Adallas;
  King Manchus of Arabia; King of Pont;
  Herod of Jewry; Mithridates, King   75
  Of Comagene; Polemon and Amyntas,
  The Kings of Mede and Lycaonia,
  With a more larger° list of scepters.
OCTAVIA   Ay me, most wretched,
  That have my heart parted betwixt two friends   80
  That does afflict each other!
CAESAR   Welcome hither.
  Your letters did withhold our breaking forth°
  Till we perceived both how you were wrong led°

---

55 **stage** stage of your journey   61 **pardon** permission   62 **Being . . . him** since your
return to Rome removed the obstacle between him and the gratification of his
desires   69 **who** and they   78 **a more larger** an even longer   82 **withhold . . . forth**
restrain my advancing to battle   83 **wrong led** wronged, abused

And we in negligent danger.° Cheer your heart.
Be you not troubled with the time,° which drives   85
O'er your content these strong necessities,°
But let determined things to destiny
Hold unbewailed their way.° Welcome to Rome,
Nothing more dear to me.° You are abused
Beyond the mark° of thought, and the high gods,   90
To do you justice, makes his ministers
Of us and those that love you.° Best of comfort,
And ever welcome to us.
AGRIPPA Welcome, lady.
MAECENAS Welcome, dear madam.   95
Each heart in Rome does love and pity you.
Only th'adulterous Antony, most large°
In his abominations, turns you off°
And gives his potent regiment° to a trull°
That noises it° against us.
OCTAVIA   Is it so, sir?   100
CAESAR Most certain. Sister, welcome. Pray you
Be ever known to patience.° My dear'st sister!

                                              Exeunt

                        ❖

                      ACT 3
                      SCENE 7

        Location: Near Actium, on the northwestern
            coast of Greece. Antony's camp.

                Enter Cleopatra and Enobarbus

CLEOPATRA I will be even with thee, doubt it not.
ENOBARBUS But why, why, why?

84 negligent danger danger through neglect of taking necessary action **85 the time** the present state of affairs **85–6 which . . . necessities** which tramples your happiness underfoot like a team of animals pulling a wagon **87–8 let . . . way** allow inevitable events to go unbewailed to their destined conclusion **89 Nothing . . . me** you who are more dear to me than anything **90 mark** reach **90–2 the high . . . you** the high gods (here treated as a singular subject of the verb "makes," and referred to as "his" in l. 91) make us and those that love you their ministers of justice in your cause **97 large** unrestrained **98 turns you off** rejects you **99 regiment** government, rule | **trull** prostitute **100 noises it** is clamorous **102 Be . . . patience** be patient

CLEOPATRA Thou hast forspoke° my being in these wars,
  And say'st it is not fit.°
ENOBARBUS   Well, is it, is it?
CLEOPATRA If not denounced against us,° why should not we   5
  Be there in person?
ENOBARBUS [*aside*]   Well, I could reply.
  If we should serve with horse° and mares together,
  The horse were merely° lost; the mares would bear
  A soldier and his horse.°
CLEOPATRA   What is't you say?
ENOBARBUS Your presence needs must puzzle° Antony,   10
  Take from his heart, take from his brain, from's time
  What should not then be spared. He is already
  Traduced° for levity, and 'tis said in Rome
  That Photinus, an eunuch,° and your maids
  Manage this war.
CLEOPATRA   Sink Rome, and their tongues rot   15
  That speak against us! A charge° we bear i'th' war,
  And as the president° of my kingdom will
  Appear there for° a man. Speak not against it.
  I will not stay behind.

                    Enter Antony and Canidius

ENOBARBUS   Nay, I have done.
  Here comes the Emperor.
ANTONY   Is it not strange, Canidius,   20
  That from Tarentum and Brundusium
  He could so quickly cut the Ionian° sea
  And take in° Toryne?—You have heard on't, sweet?
CLEOPATRA Celerity° is never more admired°
  Than by the negligent.
ANTONY   A good rebuke,   25

3 **forspoke** spoken against 4 **fit** appropriate 5 **If . . . us** even if the war were not declared against me (which it is) 7 **horse** stallions 8 **merely** utterly 8–9 **bear . . . horse** be mounted by a rider and a stallion 10 **puzzle** bewilder 13 **Traduced** criticized, censured 14 **an eunuch** (probably Mardian; in North's Plutarch, Caesar complains that "Mardian the eunuch, Photinus, and Iras . . . and Charmian . . . ruled the affairs of Antonius' empire," but Photinus [or Pothinus] was a eunuch, too) 16 **charge** responsibility, cost 17 **president** ruler 18 **for** in the capacity of 22 **Ionian** (often applied to the Aegean, but here the Adriatic; Tarentum and Brundusium or Brundisium are in the "heel" of Italy, across the Adriatic from Actium and Toryne) 23 **take in** conquer 24 **Celerity** swiftness l **admired** wondered at

Which might have well becomed° the best of men,
To taunt at slackness. Canidius, we
Will fight with him by sea.

CLEOPATRA   By sea, what else?

CANIDIUS   Why will my lord do so?

ANTONY   For that° he dares us to't.   30

ENOBARBUS   So hath my lord dared him to single fight.

CANIDIUS   Ay, and to wage this battle at Pharsalia,
Where Caesar fought with Pompey. But these offers,
Which serve not for his vantage, he shakes off,
And so should you.

ENOBARBUS   Your ships are not well manned;   35
Your mariners are muleteers,° reapers, people
Engrossed° by swift impress.° In Caesar's fleet
Are those that often have 'gainst Pompey fought;
Their ships are yare,° yours heavy. No disgrace
Shall fall° you for refusing him at sea,   40
Being prepared for land.

ANTONY   By sea, by sea.

ENOBARBUS   Most worthy sir, you therein throw away
The absolute soldiership you have by land,
Distract° your army, which doth most° consist
Of war-marked footmen,° leave unexecuted°   45
Your own renownèd knowledge, quite forgo
The way which promises assurance, and
Give up yourself merely° to chance and hazard
From firm security.

ANTONY   I'll fight at sea.

CLEOPATRA   I have sixty sails, Caesar none better.   50

ANTONY   Our overplus of shipping will we burn,
And with the rest full-manned, from th' head° of Actium
Beat th'approaching Caesar. But if we fail,
We then can do't at land.

Enter a Messenger

Thy business?

26 **becomed** become, suited   30 **For that** because   36 **muleteers** mule-drivers,
peasants   37 **Engrossed** collected wholesale | **impress** impressment, conscription
39 **yare** quick, maneuverable   40 **fall** befall   44 **Distract** divide, divert | **most** for
the most part   45 **footmen** foot soldiers | **unexecuted** unused   48 **merely** entirely
52 **head** promontory

MESSENGER   The news is true, my lord; he is descried.°   55
　　Caesar has taken Toryne.
ANTONY   Can he be there in person? 'Tis impossible;
　　Strange that his power° should be. Canidius,
　　Our nineteen legions thou shalt hold by land,
　　And our twelve thousand horse. We'll to our ship.   60
　　Away, my Thetis!°

　　　　　　　　　　　　　　　　　　　　Enter a Soldier

　　　　　　　　　　How now, worthy soldier?
SOLDIER   O noble Emperor, do not fight by sea;
　　Trust not to rotten planks. Do you misdoubt
　　This sword and these my wounds? Let th'Egyptians
　　And the Phoenicians go a-ducking;° we   65
　　Have used° to conquer standing on the earth°
　　And fighting foot to foot.
ANTONY   Well, well, away!
　　　　　　　Exeunt Antony, Cleopatra, and Enobarbus
SOLDIER   By Hercules, I think I am i'th' right.
CANIDIUS   Soldier, thou art; but his whole action grows
　　Not in the power on't.° So our leader's led,   70
　　And we are women's men.°
SOLDIER   You keep by land
　　The legions and the horse° whole,° do you not?
CANIDIUS   Marcus Octavius, Marcus Justeius,
　　Publicola, and Caelius are for sea;
　　But we keep whole by land. This speed of Caesar's   75
　　Carries° beyond belief.
SOLDIER   While he was yet in Rome
　　His power went out in such distractions° as
　　Beguiled all spies.
CANIDIUS   Who's his lieutenant, hear you?

---

55 he is descried he has been sighted   **58 his power** his army, let alone himself
61 Thetis sea goddess, the mother of Achilles   **65 go a-ducking** (1) get drenched
(2) cringe   **66 Have used** are accustomed ǀ **standing on the earth** (1) fighting on
land (2) standing upright, not *ducking*, or "cringing"   **69–70 his . . . on't** his
whole strategy has been developed without regard to where his power really lies
71 men servingmen   **72 horse** cavalry ǀ **whole** undivided, held in reserve
76 Carries surpasses (like an arrow in archery)   **78 distractions** detachments,
divisions

SOLDIER   They say, one Taurus.

CANIDIUS   Well I know the man.   80

Enter a Messenger

MESSENGER   The Emperor calls Canidius.

CANIDIUS   With news the time's with labor, and throws forth
Each minute some.°

Exeunt

❖

ACT 3
SCENE 8

Location: A field near Actium, as before

Enter Caesar [and Taurus] with his army, marching

CAESAR   Taurus!

TAURUS   My lord?

CAESAR   Strike not by land; keep whole. Provoke not battle
Till we have done at sea. Do not exceed
The prescript° of this scroll. [*He gives a scroll*] Our fortune lies   5
Upon this jump.°

Exeunt

❖

ACT 3
SCENE 9

Location: A field near Actium, as before

Enter Antony and Enobarbus

ANTONY   Set we our squadrons on yond side o'th' hill,
In eye° of Caesar's battle,° from which place
We may the number of the ships behold
And so proceed accordingly.

Exeunt

82–3 With . . . some more news is born each minute (*throws forth* means "gives birth")

5 prescript orders   **6 jump** chance, hazard

2 eye sight | **battle** battle line

❖

ACT 3
SCENE 10

Location: A field near Actium, as before

Canidius marcheth with his land army one way over the stage, and Taurus, the lieutenant of Caesar, the other way. After their going in is heard the noise of a sea fight

Alarum. Enter Enobarbus

ENOBARBUS Naught,° naught, all naught! I can behold no longer.
Th'*Antoniad*, the Egyptian admiral,°
With all their sixty, fly and turn the rudder.
To see't mine eyes are blasted.

Enter Scarus

SCARUS   Gods and goddesses,
All the whole synod° of them!
ENOBARBUS   What's thy passion?   5
SCARUS   The greater cantle° of the world is lost
With very ignorance;° we have kissed away
Kingdoms and provinces.
ENOBARBUS   How appears the fight?
SCARUS   On our side like the tokened pestilence,°
Where death is sure. Yon ribaudred° nag of Egypt—   10
Whom leprosy o'ertake!—i'th' midst o'th' fight,
When vantage like a pair of twins appeared
Both as the same,° or rather ours the elder,°
The breeze° upon her, like a cow in June,
Hoists sails and flies.
ENOBARBUS   That I beheld.   15
Mine eyes did sicken at the sight, and could not

1 **Naught** all has come to naught   2 **admiral** flagship   5 **synod** assembly   6 **cantle** corner; hence, piece or part   7 **With very ignorance** through utter stupidity   9 **tokened pestilence** (certain red spots appeared on the bodies of the plague-smitten, called tokens)   10 **ribaudred** foul, obscene   12–13 **When . . . same** when the advantage was equal on either side   13 **elder** more advanced, more likely to inherit   14 **breeze** (1) gadfly (2) light wind

Endure a further view.

SCARUS   She once being loofed,°
The noble ruin of° her magic, Antony,
Claps on his sea wing° and, like a doting mallard,°
Leaving the fight in° height, flies after her.   20
I never saw an action of such shame.
Experience, manhood, honor, ne'er before
Did violate so itself.

ENOBARBUS   Alack, alack!

Enter Canidius

CANIDIUS   Our fortune on the sea is out of breath,
And sinks most lamentably. Had our general   25
Been what he knew himself, it had gone well.
Oh, he has given example for our flight
Most grossly by his own!

ENOBARBUS
Ay, are you thereabouts?° Why then, good night indeed.°

CANIDIUS   Toward Peloponnesus° are they fled.   30

SCARUS   'Tis easy to't,° and there I will attend°
What further comes.

CANIDIUS   To Caesar will I render°
My legions and my horse.° Six kings already
Show me the way of yielding.

ENOBARBUS   I'll yet follow
The wounded chance° of Antony, though my reason   35
Sits in the wind against me.°

                                        [*Exeunt separately*]

♣

---

18 loofed luffed, with ship's head brought close to the wind (with a pun on *aloofed*, "becoming distant")   **18 ruin of** object ruined by   **19 Claps. . . sea wing** hoists sail, preparing for flight like a water bird | **mallard** drake   **20 in** at its   **29 thereabouts** of that mind, thinking of desertion | **good night indeed** it's all over   **30 Peloponnesus** southern Greece (from which Antony then crosses the Mediterranean to Egypt)   **31 to't** to get to it | **attend** await   **32 render** surrender   **33 horse** cavalry   **35 wounded chance** broken fortunes   **36 Sits . . . me** is on my downwind side, tracking me and hunting me down

ACT 3
SCENE 11

Location: Historically, events such as dispatching the School-master to Caesar took place in Egypt; however, the dramatic impression of this scene is that it occurs soon after the battle

Enter Antony with attendants

ANTONY Hark! The land bids me tread no more upon't;
It is ashamed to bear me. Friends, come hither.
I am so lated° in the world that I
Have lost my way forever. I have a ship
Laden with gold. Take that, divide it; fly,°   5
And make your peace with Caesar.

ALL   Fly? Not we.

ANTONY I have fled myself, and have instructed cowards
To run and show their shoulders.° Friends, begone.
I have myself resolved upon a course
Which has no need of you. Begone.   10
My treasure's in the harbor. Take it. Oh,
I followed that° I blush to look upon!
My very hairs do mutiny,° for the white
Reprove the brown for rashness, and they them°
For fear and doting. Friends, begone. You shall   15
Have letters from me to some friends that will
Sweep your way° for you. Pray you, look not sad,
Nor make replies of loathness.° Take the hint°
Which my despair proclaims. Let that° be left
Which leaves° itself. To the seaside straightway!   20
I will possess you of that ship and treasure.
Leave me, I pray, a little. Pray you now,
Nay, do so, for indeed I have lost command.°
Therefore I pray° you. I'll see you by and by.

[Exeunt attendants. Antony] sits down

---

3 **lated** belated, like a traveler still journeying when night falls 5 **fly** flee 8 **shoulders** backs 12 **that** that which 13 **mutiny** contend among themselves 14 **they them** the brown hairs reprove the white 17 **Sweep your way** clear your way (to Caesar) 18 **loathness** unwillingness | **hint** opportunity 19 **that** Antony and his cause 20 **leaves** is untrue to, deserts 23 **lost command** of myself and of my authority 24 **pray** entreat (as opposed to "command")

Enter Cleopatra led by Charmian, [Iras,] and Eros

EROS Nay, gentle madam, to him, comfort him.   25
IRAS Do, most dear Queen.
CHARMIAN Do; why, what else?
CLEOPATRA Let me sit down. O Juno!
ANTONY No, no, no, no, no.
EROS See you here, sir?   30
ANTONY Oh, fie, fie, fie!
CHARMIAN Madam!
IRAS Madam, O good Empress!
EROS Sir, sir!
ANTONY Yes, my lord, yes.° He° at Philippi kept°   35
    His sword e'en like a dancer,° while I struck
    The lean and wrinkled Cassius, and 'twas I
    That the mad Brutus ended.° He alone°
    Dealt on lieutenantry,° and no practice had
    In the brave squares° of war; yet now—no matter.   40
CLEOPATRA Ah, stand by.°
EROS   The Queen, my lord, the Queen.
IRAS Go to him, madam, speak to him.
    He's unqualitied° with very shame.
CLEOPATRA Well then, sustain me. Oh!
EROS Most noble sir, arise. The Queen approaches.   45
    Her head's declined, and death will seize her but°
    Your comfort makes the rescue.
ANTONY I have offended reputation,
    A most unnoble swerving.°
EROS   Sir, the Queen.
ANTONY Oh, whither hast thou led me, Egypt? See   50
    How I convey my shame out of thine eyes
    By looking back what I have left behind
    'Stroyed in dishonor.°

---

35 Yes . . . yes (Antony is absorbed in his own bitter thoughts, as also in ll. 29 and 31)
| **He** Octavius | **kept** kept in its sheath   **36 e'en . . . dancer** as though for ornament
only, in a dance   **38 ended** defeated (not *killed*; Brutus and Cassius committed suicide)
| **He alone** Caesar merely   **39 Dealt on lieutenantry** let his subordinates do the fighting
40 brave squares splendid squadrons, bodies of troops drawn up in square forma-
tion   **41 stand by** (Cleopatra indicates she is about to faint and needs assistance)
43 unqualitied dispossessed of his own nature, not himself   **46 but** unless   **49 swerving**
lapse, transgression   **50–3 See . . . dishonor** see how ashamed I am to have you see me
like this, looking back on what I have left behind dishonorably destroyed

CLEOPATRA   Oh, my lord, my lord,
    Forgive my fearful° sails! I little thought
    You would have followed.
ANTONY   Egypt, thou knew'st too well   55
    My heart was to thy rudder tied by th' strings,°
    And thou shouldst tow me after. O'er my spirit
    Thy full supremacy thou knew'st, and that
    Thy beck might from the bidding of the gods
    Command me.°
CLEOPATRA   Oh, my pardon!
ANTONY   Now I must   60
    To the young man send humble treaties,° dodge°
    And palter° in the shifts of lowness,° who
    With half the bulk o'th' world played as I pleased,
    Making and marring fortunes. You did know
    How much you were my conqueror, and that   65
    My sword, made weak by my affection,° would
    Obey it on all cause.°
CLEOPATRA   Pardon, pardon!
ANTONY   Fall° not a tear, I say; one of them rates°
    All that is won and lost. Give me a kiss.   [*They kiss*]
    Even this° repays me.—We sent our schoolmaster;°   70
    Is 'a come back?—Love, I am full of lead.—
    Some wine, within there, and our viands!° Fortune knows
    We scorn her most when most she offers blows.

                                              Exeunt

                            ❧

54 **fearful** timorous   56 **th' strings** (1) the heartstrings (2) towing cable   **59–60 Thy . . . Command me** your mere beckoning would command me away from doing the bidding of the gods themselves   61 **treaties** entreaties, propositions for settlement | **dodge** shuffle, cringe   62 **palter** use trickery, prevaricate, equivocate | **shifts of lowness** pitiful evasions used by those lacking power   66 **affection** passion   67 **on all cause** whatever the reason   68 **fall** let fall | **rates** equals   70 **Even this** this by itself | **schoolmaster** (identified in Plutarch as Euphronius, tutor to Antony's children by Cleopatra)   72 **viands** food

ACT 3
SCENE 12

Location: Egypt. Caesar's camp.

Enter Caesar, Agrippa, [Thidias,] and Dolabella, with others

CAESAR   Let him appear that's come from Antony.
　Know you him?
DOLABELLA 　　　　　Caesar, 'tis his schoolmaster—
　An argument° that he is plucked, when hither
　He sends so poor a pinion° of his wing,
　Which° had superfluous kings for messengers　　　　5
　Not many moons gone by.

Enter Ambassador from Antony

CAESAR 　　　　　　　Approach and speak.
AMBASSADOR   Such as I am, I come from Antony.
　I was of late as petty to° his ends
　As is the morn-dew on the myrtle leaf
　To his grand sea.°
CAESAR 　　　　　Be't so. Declare thine office.°　　　10
AMBASSADOR   Lord of his fortunes he salutes thee, and
　Requires° to live in Egypt; which not granted,°
　He lessens his requests, and to thee sues°
　To let him breathe° between the heavens and earth
　A private man in Athens. This for him.　　　　15
　Next, Cleopatra does confess thy greatness,
　Submits her to thy might, and of thee craves
　The circle° of the Ptolemies for her heirs,
　Now hazarded to thy grace.°
CAESAR 　　　　　　　For° Antony,
　I have no ears to his request. The Queen　　　20
　Of audience° nor desire shall fail, so° she
　From Egypt drive her all-disgracèd friend

---

3 An argument an indication   4 pinion pinion-feather, outer feather   5 Which who
8 petty to insignificant in terms of   10 To . . . sea compared to its, the dewdrop's,
great source, the sea | thine office your official business   12 Requires asks |
which not granted and if that request is not granted   13 sues petitions   14 breathe
live   18 circle crown   19 hazarded . . . grace dependent on your favor | For as for
21 Of audience neither of hearing | so provided that

Or take his life there. This if she perform
She shall not sue unheard. So to them both.
AMBASSADOR   Fortune pursue thee!
CAESAR   Bring° him through the bands.°   25
                              [*Exit Ambassador, attended*]
[*To Thidias*] To try thy eloquence now 'tis time. Dispatch.
From Antony win Cleopatra. Promise,
And in our name, what she requires;° add more,
From thine invention, offers.° Women are not
In their best fortunes strong, but want will perjure   30
The ne'er-touched vestal.° Try thy cunning,° Thidias.
Make thine own edict° for thy pains, which we
Will answer as a law.°
THIDIAS   Caesar, I go.
CAESAR   Observe how Antony becomes his flaw,°
And what thou think'st his very action speaks   35
In every power that moves.°
THIDIAS   Caesar, I shall.

                                              Exeunt

❖

ACT 3
SCENE 13

Location: Alexandria. Cleopatra's palace.

Enter Cleopatra, Enobarbus, Charmian, and Iras

CLEOPATRA   What shall we do, Enobarbus?
ENOBARBUS   Think, and die.°

---

25 Bring escort | **bands** troops on guard, military lines   **28 requires** asks
28–9 add . . . offers add ideas of your own   **29–31 Women . . . vestal** women are
not strong even at the height of their good fortune, but need will cause even an
untouched vestal virgin to break her vows   **31 cunning** skill   **32 Make . . . edict**
decree your own reward   **33 answer as a law** confirm as if it were a law
34 becomes his flaw bears his misfortune and disgrace   **35–6 And . . . moves** and
what you think his gestures signify in every move he makes

1 Think, and die think despondently, and die of melancholy or by suicide

CLEOPATRA   Is Antony or we° in fault for this?
ENOBARBUS   Antony only, that would make his will°
Lord of his reason. What though you fled
From that great face of war, whose several ranges°   5
Frighted each other? Why should he follow?
The itch of his affection° should not then
Have nicked° his captainship, at such a point,°
When half to half the world opposed, he being
The merèd question.° 'Twas a shame no less   10
Than was his loss, to course° your flying flags
And leave his navy gazing.
CLEOPATRA   Prithee, peace.

Enter the Ambassador with Antony

ANTONY   Is that his answer?
AMBASSADOR   Ay, my lord.
ANTONY   The Queen shall then have courtesy, so° she   15
Will yield us up.
AMBASSADOR   He says so.
ANTONY   Let her know't.—
To the boy Caesar send this grizzled head,
And he will fill thy wishes to the brim
With principalities.
CLEOPATRA   That head, my lord?
ANTONY [*to the Ambassador*]
To him again. Tell him he wears the rose   20
Of youth upon him, from which the world should note
Something particular.° His coin, ships, legions,
May be° a coward's, whose ministers° would prevail
Under the service of a child as soon
As i'th' command of Caesar. I dare him therefore   25
To lay his gay caparisons° apart

---

2 **we** I   3 **will** desire (especially sexual)   5 **ranges** ranks, lines (of ships)
7 **affection** sexual passion   8 **nicked** cut short or maimed, or got the better of |
point crisis   9–10 **When . . . question** when the two halves of the world found
themselves in conflict, Antony being the sole ground of the quarrel   11 **course**
pursue (as in hunting)   15 **so** provided that   22 **Something particular** some
exceptional exploit   23 **May be** could as well be | **ministers** agents, subordinates
26 **gay caparisons** resplendent trappings

And answer me declined,° sword against sword,
Ourselves alone. I'll write it. Follow me.

[*Exeunt Antony and Ambassador*]

ENOBARBUS [*aside*]   Yes, like° enough, high-battled° Caesar will
Unstate his happiness and be staged to th' show   30
Against a sworder!° I see men's judgments are
A parcel of their fortunes, and things outward
Do draw the inward quality after them
To suffer all alike.° That he should dream,
Knowing all measures,° the full° Caesar will   35
Answer° his emptiness! Caesar, thou hast subdued
His judgment too.

Enter a Servant

SERVANT   A messenger from Caesar.

CLEOPATRA   What, no more ceremony? See, my women,
Against the blown° rose may they stop their nose
That kneeled unto the buds.—Admit him, sir.   40

[*Exit Servant*]

ENOBARBUS [*aside*]   Mine honesty° and I begin to square.°
The loyalty well held to fools does make
Our faith mere folly;° yet he that can endure
To follow with allegiance a fall'n lord
Does conquer him that did his master conquer°   45
And earns a place i'th' story.

Enter Thidias

CLEOPATRA   Caesar's will?

27 **answer me declined** meet me as I am, lowered in fortune and advanced in years
29 **like** likely | **high-battled** provided with a mighty army   30–1 **Unstate . . .
sworder** set aside his advantageous fortune and be exhibited publicly in a sword-
fight contest with a mere gladiator   31–4 **I see . . . alike** I see that men's judgments
are inextricably linked to their fortunes, whereby outward circumstances draw after
them inward qualities of character in such a way that both suffer at the same time
35 **Knowing all measures** having experienced every degree of fortune | **full** at full
fortune   36 **Answer** (1) meet man to man with (2) correspond with   39 **blown**
overblown, starting to decay   41 **honesty** (with meaning also of "honor") |
square quarrel   42–3 **The . . . folly** a stubborn loyalty bestowed on fools is folly
itself   45 **Does . . . conquer** achieves a moral victory over the very fortune or the
person that subdued one's own master

THIDIAS Hear it apart.°

CLEOPATRA   None but friends. Say boldly.

THIDIAS So haply° are they friends to Antony.

ENOBARBUS He needs as many, sir, as Caesar has,
   Or needs not us.° If Caesar please, our master   50
   Will leap to be his friend. For° us, you know
   Whose he is we are, and that is Caesar's.°

THIDIAS   So.
   Thus then, thou most renowned: Caesar entreats
   Not to consider in what case thou stand'st
   Further than he is Caesar.°

CLEOPATRA   Go on: right royal.°   55

THIDIAS He knows that you embrace not Antony
   As you did love, but as you feared him.

CLEOPATRA   Oh!

THIDIAS The scars upon your honor therefore he
   Does pity as constrainèd blemishes,
   Not as deserved.

CLEOPATRA   He is a god and knows   60
   What is most right.° Mine honor was not yielded,
   But conquered merely.°

ENOBARBUS [*aside*]   To be sure of that,
   I will ask Antony. Sir, sir, thou art so leaky
   That we must leave thee to thy sinking, for
   Thy dearest quit thee.   *Exit Enobarbus*

THIDIAS   Shall I say to Caesar   65
   What you require° of him? For he partly° begs
   To be desired to give. It much would please him
   That of his fortunes you should make a staff
   To lean upon; but it would warm his spirits
   To hear from me you had left Antony   70
   And put yourself under his shroud,°

---

47 apart in private   **48 haply** perhaps   **50 Or . . . us** or else he doesn't need even us, his case being hopeless   **51 For** as for   **52 Whose . . . Caesar's** we are Antony's friends, and he is Caesar's, so that we, too, are Caesar's   **54–5 Not . . . Caesar** not to worry about your situation other than to consider that you are dealing with Caesar, the embodiment of magnanimity   **55 right royal** that is very magnanimous   **61 right** true   **62 merely** utterly   **66 require** ask | **partly** as commensurate with his dignity   **71 shroud** shelter (with suggestion too of a burial cloth)

The universal landlord.

CLEOPATRA   What's your name?

THIDIAS   My name is Thidias.

CLEOPATRA   Most kind messenger,
Say to great Caesar this in deputation:°
I kiss his conquering hand. Tell him I am prompt°   75
To lay my crown at 's feet, and there to kneel
Till from his all-obeying° breath I hear
The doom of Egypt.°

THIDIAS   'Tis your noblest course.
Wisdom and fortune combating together,
If that the former dare but what it can,   80
No chance may shake it.° Give me grace to lay
My duty on your hand.   [He kisses her hand]

CLEOPATRA   Your Caesar's father° oft,
When he hath mused of taking kingdoms in,°
Bestowed his lips on that unworthy place,   85
As° it rained kisses.

Enter Antony and Enobarbus

ANTONY   Favors? By Jove that thunders!
What art thou, fellow?

THIDIAS   One that but performs
The bidding of the fullest° man, and worthiest
To have command obeyed.

ENOBARBUS [*aside*]   You will be whipped.

ANTONY [*calling for Servants*]
Approach, there!—Ah, you kite!°—Now, gods and devils!   90
Authority melts from me of late. When I cried "Ho!",
Like boys unto a muss° kings would start forth

---

74 **in deputation** by you as deputy   75 **prompt** ready   77 **all-obeying** obeyed by all
78 **The doom of Egypt** my fate   79–81 **Wisdom . . . shake it** when wisdom and
fortune are at odds, if the wise person will have the resolution to desire only what
fortune will allow, then fortune cannot shake that wisdom   83 **Your Caesar's
father** Julius Caesar, actually Octavius's great-uncle (see note at 3.6.6)   84 **mused . .
. in** thought about conquering kingdoms   86 **As** as if   88 **fullest** most fortunate,
best   90 **kite** a rapacious bird of prey that feeds on ignoble objects, and a slang
word for "whore" (said of Cleopatra)   92 **muss** game in which small objects are
thrown down to be scrambled for

And cry, "Your will?"—Have you no ears? I am
Antony yet.

Enter a Servant [followed by others]

    Take hence this jack° and whip him.

ENOBARBUS *[aside]*
 'Tis better playing with a lion's whelp°   95
 Than with an old one dying.

ANTONY   Moon and stars!
 Whip him. Were't twenty of the greatest tributaries°
 That do acknowledge Caesar, should I find them
 So saucy with the hand of she here—what's her name
 Since she was Cleopatra? Whip him, fellows,   100
 Till like a boy you see him cringe° his face
 And whine aloud for mercy. Take him hence.

THIDIAS Mark Antony—

ANTONY   Tug him away! Being whipped,
 Bring him again. This jack of Caesar's shall
 Bear us an errand to him.   105

       Exeunt [Servants] with Thidias

 [To Cleopatra] You were half blasted° ere I knew you. Ha?
 Have I my pillow left unpressed in Rome,
 Forborne the getting° of a lawful° race,
 And by a gem of women, to be abused°
 By one that looks on feeders?°   110

CLEOPATRA Good my lord—

ANTONY You have been a boggler° ever.
 But when we in our viciousness grow hard—
 Oh, misery on't!—the wise gods seel° our eyes,
 In our own filth drop our clear judgments, make us 115
 Adore our errors, laugh at 's while we strut
 To our confusion.°

CLEOPATRA   Oh, is't come to this?

---

94 jack fellow (contemptuous) **95 whelp** cub **97 tributaries** rulers paying tribute
101 cringe contract in pain **106 blasted** withered, blighted **108 getting** begetting |
lawful legitimate **109 abused** deceived, betrayed **110 feeders** servants
112 boggler waverer, shifty person (often used of shying horses) **114 seel** blind (a
term in falconry for sewing shut the eyes of wild hawks in order to tame them)
117 confusion destruction

ANTONY   I found you as a morsel cold upon
    Dead Caesar's trencher;° nay, you were a fragment°
    Of Gnaeus Pompey's,° besides what hotter hours,   120
    Unregistered in vulgar fame,° you have
    Luxuriously° picked out. For I am sure,
    Though you can guess what temperance should be,
    You know not what it is.
CLEOPATRA   Wherefore is this?°
ANTONY   To let a fellow that will take rewards   125
    And say "God quit° you!" be familiar with
    My playfellow, your hand, this kingly seal
    And plighter° of high hearts! Oh, that I were
    Upon the hill of Basan, to outroar
    The hornèd herd!° For I have savage cause,   130
    And to proclaim it civilly were like
    A haltered neck which does the hangman thank
    For being yare° about him.

Enter a Servant with Thidias

              Is he whipped?
SERVANT   Soundly, my lord.
ANTONY   Cried he? And begged 'a pardon?   135
SERVANT   He did ask favor.
ANTONY [*to Thidias*]
    If that thy father live, let him repent
    Thou wast not made his daughter; and be thou sorry
    To follow Caesar in his triumph, since
    Thou hast been whipped for following him. Henceforth   140
    The white hand of a lady fever thee;°
    Shake thou to look on't. Get thee back to Caesar.
    Tell him thy entertainment.° Look° thou say

---

119 trencher wooden plate | **fragment** leftover   **120 Gnaeus Pompey's** (see 1.5.32 and note)   **121 vulgar fame** common gossip   **122 Luxuriously** lustfully **124 Wherefore is this?** what brought this on?   **126 quit** reward (*God quit you* is said obsequiously to acknowledge a tip)   **128 plighter** pledger   **129–30 hill of Basan . . . The hornèd herd** (allusion to the strong bulls of Bashan, Psalms 22.12 and 68.15. Antony imagines himself as the greatest horned beast, cuckold, of that herd) **133 yare** deft, quick   **141 fever thee** make you shiver   **143 entertainment** reception | **Look** be sure that

He makes me angry with him; for he seems
Proud and disdainful, harping on what I am,   145
Not what he knew I was. He makes me angry,
And at this time most easy 'tis to do't,
When my good stars, that were my former guides,
Have empty left their orbs° and shot their fires
Into th'abysm° of hell. If he mislike   150
My speech and what is done, tell him he has
Hipparchus,° my enfranchèd° bondman, whom
He may at pleasure whip, or hang, or torture,
As he shall like, to quit° me. Urge it thou.
Hence with thy stripes, begone!
                          Exit [Servant with] Thidias
CLEOPATRA   Have you done yet?   155
ANTONY   Alack, our terrene moon is now eclipsed,°
And it portends alone the fall of Antony.
CLEOPATRA   I must stay his time.°
ANTONY   To flatter Caesar, would you mingle eyes
With one that ties his points?°
CLEOPATRA   Not know me yet?   160
ANTONY   Coldhearted toward me?
CLEOPATRA   Ah, dear, if I be so,
From my cold heart let heaven engender hail,
And poison it in the source, and the first stone
Drop in my neck;° as it determines,° so
Dissolve my life! The next Caesarion smite,   165
Till by degrees the memory of my womb,°
Together with my brave° Egyptians all,
By the discandying° of this pelleted° storm
Lie graveless till the flies and gnats of Nile

---

149 orbs spheres   **150 th'abysm** the abyss   **152 Hipparchus** (according to
Plutarch, the man was a deserter to Caesar's side) | **enfranchèd** enfranchised, freed
154 quit requite, pay back   **156 our . . . eclipsed** (1) the moon in eclipse portends
disaster (2) the waning of the love of Cleopatra (equated with Isis, the moon
goddess) spells the end for me   **158 stay his time** be patient until his fury has
subsided   **160 ties his points** helps Caesar as a valet with the metal-tipped laces used
to fasten articles of clothing   **164 neck** throat or head | **determines** comes to an end,
dissolves (see l. 168)   **166 memory of my womb** my offspring   **167 brave** splendid
(also in l. 180)   **168 discandying** melting | **pelleted** falling in pellets

Have buried them for prey!°

ANTONY   I am satisfied.   170
Caesar sits down in° Alexandria, where
I will oppose his fate.° Our force by land
Hath nobly held; our severed navy too
Have knit again, and fleet,° threat'ning most sealike.
Where hast thou been, my heart?° Dost thou hear, lady?   175
If from the field I shall return once more
To kiss these lips, I will appear in blood;°
I and my sword will earn our chronicle.°
There's hope in't yet.

CLEOPATRA   That's my brave lord!   180

ANTONY   I will be treble-sinewed, hearted, breathed,°
And fight maliciously.° For when mine hours
Were nice° and lucky, men did ransom lives
Of me for jests;° but now I'll set my teeth
And send to darkness° all that stop me. Come,   185
Let's have one other gaudy° night. Call to me
All my sad captains. Fill our bowls once more;
Let's mock the midnight bell.

CLEOPATRA   It is my birthday.
I had thought t'have held it poor;° but since my lord
Is Antony again, I will be Cleopatra.   190

ANTONY   We will yet do well.

CLEOPATRA [*to attendants*]
Call all his noble captains to my lord.

ANTONY   Do so. We'll speak to them, and tonight I'll force
The wine peep through their scars. Come on, my queen,
There's sap in't° yet. The next time I do fight   195
I'll make Death love me, for I will contend
Even with his pestilent scythe.°

                         Exeunt [all but Enobarbus]

170 for prey by eating them   **171 sits down in** lays siege to   **172 oppose his fate** confront his (seemingly irresistible) fortune   **174 fleet** float   **175 heart** courage **177 in blood** (1) bloody from battle (2) full-spirited   **178 chronicle** place in history **181 treble-sinewed . . . breathed** thrice myself in strength, courage, and endurance **182 maliciously** violently, fiercely   **183 nice** delicate, refined   **183–4 men . . . jests** I allowed enemies to be ransomed for trifles or as a magnanimous gesture   **185 to darkness** to death, the underworld   **186 gaudy** festive   **189 held it poor** celebrated it simply   **195 sap in't** life in our enterprise   **196–7 I will . . . scythe** I will outdo even Death himself and his scythe of *pestilence* or plague

ENOBARBUS   Now he'll outstare° the lightning. To be furious°
  Is to be frighted out of fear, and in that mood
  The dove will peck the estridge;° and I see still°   200
  A diminution in our captain's brain
  Restores his heart. When valor preys on reason,
  It eats the sword it fights with.° I will seek
  Some way to leave him.

                                                    Exit

                          ❖

                       ACT 4
                       SCENE 1

       Location: Before Alexandria. Caesar's camp.

              Enter Caesar, Agrippa, and Maecenas,
                with his army, Caesar reading a letter

CAESAR   He calls me boy, and chides as° he had power
  To beat me out of Egypt. My messenger
  He hath whipped with rods, dares me to personal combat,
  Caesar to Antony. Let the old ruffian know
  I have many other ways to die, meantime   5
  Laugh at his challenge.
MAECENAS   Caesar must think,
  When one so great begins to rage,° he's hunted
  Even to falling. Give him no breath,° but now
  Make boot° of his distraction.° Never anger   10
  Made good guard for itself.
CAESAR   Let our best heads°
  Know that tomorrow the last of many battles
  We mean to fight. Within our files° there are,
  Of those that served Mark Antony but late,°

---

198 **outstare** stare down | **furious** frenzied   200 **estridge** ostrich, or, a kind of
hawk | **still** constantly   202–3 **When . . . with** when valor turns to unreasonable
fury, it destroys the very quality of reasonableness that valor depends on in battle

1 **as** as if   8 **rage** rave   9 **breath** breathing space   10 **boot** advantage | **distraction**
frenzy   11 **best heads** commanding officers   13 **files** (as in "rank and file")
14 **late** lately

Enough to fetch him in.° See it done,   15
And feast the army; we have store° to do't,
And they have earned the waste.° Poor Antony!

Exeunt

❧

ACT 4
SCENE 2

Location: Alexandria. Cleopatra's palace.

Enter Antony, Cleopatra, Enobarbus,
Charmian, Iras, Alexas, with others

ANTONY   He will not fight with me, Domitius?
ENOBARBUS   No.
ANTONY   Why should he not?
ENOBARBUS   He thinks, being twenty times of better fortune,
He is twenty men to one.
ANTONY   Tomorrow, soldier,   5
By sea and land I'll fight. Or° I will live
Or bathe my dying honor in the blood
Shall° make it live again. Woo't° thou fight well?
ENOBARBUS   I'll strike, and cry, "Take all."°
ANTONY   Well said. Come on!
Call forth my household servants. Let's tonight   10

Enter three or four servitors°

Be bounteous at our meal.—Give me thy hand.
Thou hast been rightly honest°—so hast thou—
Thou—and thou—and thou. You have served me well,
And kings have been your fellows.°
CLEOPATRA *[aside to Enobarbus]*   What means this?

---

15 **fetch him in** surround, capture him   16 **store** provisions   17 **waste** lavish
expenditure

6 **or** either   8 **Shall** that will | **Woo't** wilt   9 **strike . . . Take all** (1) fight to the
finish, crying, "winner take all" (2) strike sail and surrender   10.1 *servitors*
attendants   12 **honest** true, loyal   14 **fellows** fellow servants of me

ENOBARBUS [*aside to Cleopatra*]
'Tis one of those odd tricks which sorrow shoots   15
Out of the mind.

ANTONY   And thou art honest too.
I wish I could be made so many men,°
And all of you clapped up° together in
An Antony, that I might do you service
So good as you have done.

ALL   The gods forbid!   20

ANTONY
Well, my good fellows, wait on me tonight:
Scant not my cups,° and make as much of me
As when mine empire was your fellow° too,
And suffered° my command.

CLEOPATRA [*aside to Enobarbus*]   What does he mean?

ENOBARBUS [*aside to Cleopatra*]
To make his followers weep.

ANTONY   Tend me tonight;   25
May be it is the period° of your duty.
Haply° you shall not see me more, or if,°
A mangled shadow.° Perchance tomorrow
You'll serve another master. I look on you
As one that takes his leave. Mine honest friends,   30
I turn you not away, but, like a master
Married to your good service, stay till death.
Tend me tonight two hours, I ask no more,
And the gods yield° you for't!

ENOBARBUS   What mean you, sir,
To give them this discomfort? Look, they weep,   35
And I, an ass, am onion-eyed. For shame,
Transform us not to women.

ANTONY   Ho, ho, ho!
Now the witch take me° if I meant it thus!
Grace grow° where those drops fall! My hearty° friends,

---

17 **made . . . men** divided into as many men as you are   18 **clapped up** combined
22 **Scant not my cups** provide generously   23 **fellow** fellow servant   24 **suffered**
acknowledged, submitted to   26 **period** end   27 **Haply** perhaps | **if** if you do
28 **shadow** ghost   34 **yield** reward   38 **the witch take me** may I be bewitched
39 **Grace grow** (1) may rue or herb of grace grow (2) may gracious fortune flourish |
hearty loving

You take me in too dolorous a sense,   40
For I spake to you for your comfort, did desire you
To burn this night with torches.° Know, my hearts,
I hope well of tomorrow, and will lead you
Where rather I'll expect victorious life
Than death and honor. Let's to supper, come,   45
And drown consideration.°

                                                        Exeunt

                            ❖

                           ACT 4
                          SCENE 3

              Location: Alexandria. Before the palace.

                        Enter a company of Soldiers

FIRST SOLDIER   Brother, good night. Tomorrow is the day.
SECOND SOLDIER   It will determine one way.° Fare you well.
    Heard you of nothing strange about° the streets?
FIRST SOLDIER   Nothing. What news?
SECOND SOLDIER   Belike° 'tis but a rumor. Good night to you.   5
FIRST SOLDIER   Well, sir, good night.

                            They meet other Soldiers

SECOND SOLDIER   Soldiers, have careful watch.
THIRD SOLDIER   And you. Good night, good night.
            They place themselves in every corner of the stage
SECOND SOLDIER   Here we.° And if tomorrow
    Our navy thrive, I have an absolute hope   10
    Our landmen will stand up.
FIRST SOLDIER   'Tis a brave° army, and full of purpose.
                    Music of the hautboys° is under the stage
SECOND SOLDIER   Peace! What noise?
FIRST SOLDIER   List,° list!

---

42 burn . . . torches revel through the night   **46 drown consideration** drown
brooding thought in our winecups

2 determine one way be decided, come to an end one way or the other   **3 about** in
5 Belike probably   **9 Here we** here's our station   **12 brave** splendid, gallant
12.1 *hautboys* oboelike instruments   **14 List** listen

SECOND SOLDIER   Hark!   15
FIRST SOLDIER   Music i'th'air.
THIRD SOLDIER   Under the earth.
FOURTH SOLDIER   It signs well,° does it not?
THIRD SOLDIER   No.
FIRST SOLDIER   Peace, I say! What should this mean?   20
SECOND SOLDIER
    'Tis the god Hercules, whom Antony loved,
    Now leaves him.
FIRST SOLDIER   Walk; let's see if other watchmen
    Do hear what we do.
                [*They advance toward their fellow watchmen*]
SECOND SOLDIER   How now, masters?°
ALL [*speak together*]   How now? How now? Do you hear this?   25
FIRST SOLDIER   Ay. Is't not strange?
THIRD SOLDIER   Do you hear, masters? Do you hear?
FIRST SOLDIER   Follow the noise so far as we have quarter;°
    Let's see how it will give off.°
ALL   Content. 'Tis strange.   30
                                        Exeunt

❖

ACT 4
SCENE 4

Location: Alexandria. The palace.

> *Enter Antony and Cleopatra, with*
> [*Charmian and*] *others* [*attending*]

ANTONY   Eros! Mine armor, Eros!
CLEOPATRA   Sleep a little.
ANTONY   No, my chuck.°—Eros, come, mine armor, Eros!

> *Enter Eros* [*with armor*]

    Come, good fellow, put thine iron° on.

---

18 signs well is a good sign   **24 masters** good sirs (also in l. 27)   **28 as we have quarter** as our watch post extends   **29 give off** cease

2 chuck (a term of endearment)   **3 thine iron** my armor that you have there (or perhaps he is telling Eros to arm)

If fortune be not ours today, it is
Because we brave° her. Come.
CLEOPATRA   Nay, I'll help too.   5
   What's this for?   [*She helps to arm him*]
ANTONY   Ah, let be, let be! Thou art
   The armorer of my heart. False,° false; this, this.
CLEOPATRA   Sooth,° la, I'll help. Thus it must be.
ANTONY   Well, well,
   We shall thrive now. See'st thou, my good fellow?
   Go, put on thy defenses.°
EROS   Briefly,° sir.   10
CLEOPATRA   Is not this buckled well?
ANTONY   Rarely,° rarely.
   He that unbuckles this, till we do please
   To doff't for our repose, shall hear a storm.°
   Thou fumblest, Eros, and my queen's a squire°
   More tight° at this than thou. Dispatch.° O love,   15
   That thou couldst see my wars today, and knew'st
   The royal occupation!° Thou shouldst see
   A workman° in't.

Enter an armed Soldier

           Good morrow to thee. Welcome.
   Thou look'st like him that knows a warlike charge.°
   To business that we love we rise betimes°   20
   And go to't with delight.
SOLDIER   A thousand, sir,
   Early though 't be, have on their riveted trim°
   And at the port° expect you.   *Shout. Trumpets flourish*

Enter Captains and soldiers

---

5 **brave** defy   7 **False** you're putting it on wrong   8 **Sooth** in truth   10 **defenses**
armor | **Briefly** in a moment   11 **Rarely** excellently   12–13 **He . . . storm** anyone
who attempts to burst my armor in the fight, before I choose myself to unarm and
rest, will be greeted by a storm of blows   14 **squire** armor-bearer of a knight
15 **tight** deft, skillful | **Dispatch** finish up   16–17 **knew'st . . . occupation** (would
that) you could appreciate how excellently I carry out the royal art of warfare
18 **workman** craftsman, professional   19 **charge** duty, responsibility   20 **betimes**
early   22 **riveted trim** armor riveted into place   23 **port** gate

CAPTAIN   The morn is fair. Good morrow, General.

ALL   Good morrow, General.

ANTONY   'Tis well blown,° lads.   25
   This morning, like the spirit of a youth
   That means to be of note, begins betimes.
   So, so. Come, give me that. This way. Well said.°
   Fare thee well, dame. Whate'er becomes of me,
   This is a soldier's kiss. [*He kisses her*] Rebukable,   30
   And worthy shameful check° it were, to stand
   On more mechanic compliment.° I'll leave thee
   Now like a man of steel.—You that will fight,
   Follow me close. I'll bring you to't. Adieu.
             Exeunt [Antony, Eros, Captains, and soldiers]

CHARMIAN   Please you, retire to your chamber?

CLEOPATRA   Lead me.   35
   He goes forth gallantly. That he and Caesar might
   Determine this great war in single fight!
   Then Antony—but now—Well, on.
                           Exeunt

❧

ACT 4
SCENE 5

Location: Before Alexandria. Antony's camp.

*Trumpets sound. Enter Antony and
Eros; [a Soldier meeting them]*

SOLDIER   The gods make this a happy° day to Antony!

ANTONY   Would thou and those thy scars had once° prevailed
   To make me fight at land!

SOLDIER   Hadst thou done so,
   The kings that have revolted,° and the soldier
   That has this morning left thee, would have still   5

---

25 **'tis well blown** the morning begins well (or, refers to trumpets in line 23 s.d.)
28 **well said** well done   31 **check** reproof   31–2 **stand . . . compliment** insist on
vulgar and routine ceremonies of leavetaking

1 **happy** fortunate   2 **once** formerly   4 **revolted** deserted

Followed thy heels.

ANTONY   Who's gone this morning?

SOLDIER   Who?

One ever near thee. Call for Enobarbus,
He shall not hear thee, or from Caesar's camp
Say, "I am none of thine."

ANTONY   What sayest thou?

SOLDIER   Sir,

He is with Caesar.

EROS   Sir, his chests and treasure   10

He has not with him.

ANTONY   Is he gone?

SOLDIER   Most certain.

ANTONY   Go, Eros, send his treasure after. Do it.
Detain no jot, I charge thee. Write to him—
I will subscribe°—gentle adieus and greetings.
Say that I wish he never find more cause   15
To change a master. Oh, my fortunes have
Corrupted honest men! Dispatch.°—Enobarbus!

                                     Exeunt

❖

ACT 4
SCENE 6

Location: Before Alexandria. Caesar's camp.

                Flourish. Enter Agrippa, Caesar,
                   with Enobarbus, and Dolabella

CAESAR   Go forth, Agrippa, and begin the fight.
Our will is Antony be took alive;
Make it so known.

AGRIPPA   Caesar, I shall.   [*Exit*]

CAESAR   The time of universal peace is near.°   5

---

14 subscribe sign   **17 Dispatch** make haste, get on with it

5 The . . . near (the Renaissance identified Octavius Caesar, or the Emperor Augustus as he was subsequently titled, with this *Pax Romana,* peace under the Roman Empire)

Prove this° a prosp'rous day, the three-nooked° world
Shall bear° the olive° freely.

Enter a Messenger

MESSENGER   Antony
  Is come into the field.
CAESAR   Go charge Agrippa°
  Plant those that have revolted in the van,°
  That Antony may seem to spend his fury   10
  Upon himself.   *Exeunt [all but Enobarbus]*
ENOBARBUS   Alexas did revolt and went to Jewry° on
  Affairs of Antony, there did dissuade°
  Great Herod to incline himself to Caesar
  And leave his master Antony. For this pains,   15
  Caesar hath hanged him. Canidius and the rest
  That fell away have entertainment° but
  No honorable trust. I have done ill,
  Of which I do accuse myself so sorely°
  That I will joy no more.

Enter a Soldier of Caesar's

SOLDIER   Enobarbus, Antony   20
  Hath after thee sent all thy treasure, with
  His bounty overplus.° The messenger
  Came on my guard,° and at thy tent is now
  Unloading of his mules.
ENOBARBUS   I give it you.   25
SOLDIER   Mock not, Enobarbus,
  I tell you true. Best you safed° the bringer
  Out of the host.° I must attend mine office,°
  Or would have done't myself. Your emperor
  Continues still a Jove.   *Exit*   30

---

6 **Prove this** if this prove to be | **three-nooked** three-cornered (refers to Asia, Europe, and Africa)   7 **bear** (1) bring forth (2) wear as a triumphal garland | **olive** symbol of peace   8 **charge Agrippa** order Agrippa to   9 **van** vanguard, front lines   12 **Jewry** Judaea   13 **dissuade** from following Antony   17 **entertainment** employment, maintenance   19 **sorely** heavily   22 **overplus** in addition   23 **on my guard** while I was standing guard   27 **Best you safed** you would do well to provide safe conduct for   28 **host** army | **attend mine office** see to my duties

ENOBARBUS   I am alone the° villain of the earth,
   And feel I am so most.° O Antony,
   Thou mine° of bounty, how wouldst thou have paid
   My better service, when my turpitude
   Thou dost so crown with gold! This blows° my heart.   35
   If swift thought break it not, a swifter mean°
   Shall outstrike thought; but thought° will do't,° I feel.
   I fight against thee? No, I will go seek
   Some ditch wherein to die. The foul'st best fits
   My latter part of life.   40

Exit

❖

ACT 4
SCENE 7

Location: Field of battle between the camps

Alarum. Drums and trumpets. Enter Agrippa [and others]

AGRIPPA   Retire! We have engaged ourselves too far.
   Caesar himself has work,° and our oppression°
   Exceeds what we expected.   *Exeunt°*

Alarums. Enter Antony, and Scarus wounded

SCARUS   O my brave Emperor, this is fought indeed!
   Had we done so at first, we had droven° them home   5
   With clouts° about their heads.
ANTONY   Thou bleed'st apace.
SCARUS   I had a wound here that was like a T,
   But now 'tis made an H.°   *[Sound retreat] far off*
ANTONY   They do retire.

---

31 **alone the** the only, the greatest   32 **And . . . most** and am the one who feels it
most   33 **mine** abundant store   35 **blows** causes to swell to the bursting point
36 **mean** suicide   37 **thought** melancholy | **do't** break my heart

2 **has work** is hard pressed | **our oppression** the heavy attacks against us   3 s.d.
Exeunt (the cleared stage technically marks a new scene, although the alarums
provide a sense of continuous action)   5 **droven** driven   6 **clouts** (1) bandages
(2) blows and knocks   8 **H** the bottom of the T has been cut across to make an H
lying on its side (there is a pun on *ache*, pronounced *aitch*)

SCARUS   We'll beat 'em into bench holes.° I have yet
    Room for six scotches° more.   10

                                        Enter Eros

EROS   They are beaten, sir, and our advantage serves
    For a fair victory.°
SCARUS   Let us score° their backs
    And snatch 'em up, as we take hares, behind!
    'Tis sport to maul a runner.°
ANTONY   I will reward thee
    Once for thy spritely comfort and tenfold   15
    For thy good valor. Come thee on.
SCARUS   I'll halt° after.

                                        Exeunt

                            ♣

                        ACT 4
                        SCENE 8

            Location: Before Alexandria.
        The action is virtually continuous.

    Alarum. Enter Antony again in a march; Scarus, with others

ANTONY   We have beat° him to his camp. Run one° before
    And let the Queen know of our gests.°   [*Exit a Soldier*]
                                        Tomorrow,
    Before the sun shall see 's, we'll spill the blood
    That has today escaped. I thank you all,
    For doughty-handed° are you, and have fought   5
    Not as you served the cause, but as't had been
    Each man's like mine;° you have shown° all Hectors.
    Enter the city, clip° your wives, your friends,

---

9 bench holes the holes of privies, any desperate place to hide   **10 scotches** cuts
11–12 our . . . victory we are in such a favorable position that a complete victory
seems in prospect   **12 score** mark by cuts from a whip   **14 a runner** one in retreat
17 halt limp

1 beat driven | **Run one** let someone run   **2 gests** deeds   **5 doughty-handed**
valiant   **6–7 Not . . . mine** not as if you were merely serving the general cause, but
as if it were your cause personally   **7 shown** shown yourselves   **8 clip** embrace

Tell them your feats, whilst they with joyful tears
Wash the congealment from your wounds and kiss   10
The honored gashes whole.

         Enter Cleopatra [attended]

              [*To Scarus*] Give me thy hand;
To this great fairy° I'll commend thy acts,
Make her thanks bless thee. [*To Cleopatra*] O thou day°
  o'th' world,
Chain mine armed neck;° leap thou, attire and all,
Through proof of harness° to my heart, and there   15
Ride on the pants° triumphing!   [*They embrace*]
CLEOPATRA   Lord of lords,
O infinite virtue,° com'st thou smiling from
The world's great snare uncaught?
ANTONY   My nightingale,
We have beat them to their beds. What, girl, though gray
Do something° mingle with our younger brown, yet ha' we   20
A brain that nourishes our nerves° and can
Get goal for goal of° youth. Behold this man;°
Commend° unto his lips thy favoring hand.—
Kiss it, my warrior. [*Scarus kisses Cleopatra's hand*] He hath
  fought today
As if a god, in hate of mankind, had   25
Destroyed in such a shape.
CLEOPATRA   I'll give thee, friend,
An armor all of gold; it was a king's.
ANTONY   He has deserved it, were it carbuncled°
Like holy Phoebus' car.° Give me thy hand.
Through Alexandria make a jolly march;   30
Bear our hacked targets like the men that owe them.°
Had our great palace the capacity

---

12 fairy enchantress, dispenser of good fortune **13 day** light **14 Chain . . . neck**
hang around my neck in an embrace like a medal on a chain **15 proof of harness**
proof-armor, tested armor **16 pants** heartbeats **17 virtue** valor **20 something**
somewhat **21 nerves** sinews, tendons **22 Get . . . of** stay competitively equal with
this man Scarus **23 Commend** entrust, commit **28 carbuncled** set with jewels
29 Phoebus' car the chariot of the sun **31 Bear . . . them** bear our hacked shields,
well suited to the warriors who, like their shields, have sustained blows (*owe* means
"own")

To camp this host,° we all would sup together
And drink carouses° to the next day's fate,
Which promises royal peril.° Trumpeters,   35
With brazen din blast you the city's ear;
Make mingle with our rattling taborins,°
That heaven and earth may strike their sounds together,°
Applauding our approach.   [*Trumpets sound*]
                                                    Exeunt

❧

ACT 4
SCENE 9

Location: Caesar's camp

Enter a Sentry and his company. Enobarbus follows

SENTRY If we be not relieved within this hour,
    We must return to th' court of guard.° The night
    Is shiny,° and they say we shall embattle°
    By the second hour i'th' morn.
FIRST WATCH This last day was a shrewd° one to 's.   5
ENOBARBUS Oh, bear me witness, night—
SECOND WATCH What man is this?
FIRST WATCH Stand close,° and list° him.

                                    [*They stand aside*]

ENOBARBUS Be witness to me, O thou blessèd moon,
    When men revolted° shall upon record°   10
    Bear hateful memory: poor Enobarbus did
    Before thy face repent.
SENTRY Enobarbus?
SECOND WATCH Peace! Hark further.

---

33 camp this host accommodate this army   **34 carouses** toasts   **35 royal peril** war, the sport of monarchs   **37 taborins** drums   **38 That . . . together** that the heavens may echo and augment the loud noise of the drums

2 court of guard guardroom   **3 shiny** bright, moonlit | **embattle** assemble for the combat   **5 shrewd** unlucky   **8 close** concealed | **list** listen to   **10 revolted** who have broken their allegiance | **upon record** in the record of history

ENOBARBUS   O sovereign mistress of true melancholy,°   15
   The poisonous damp of night disponge° upon me,
   That life, a very rebel to my will,
   May hang no longer on me. Throw my heart
   Against the flint and hardness of my fault,
   Which,° being dried with grief,° will break to powder   20
   And finish all foul thoughts. O Antony,
   Nobler than my revolt is infamous,
   Forgive me in thine own particular,°
   But let the world rank me in register°
   A master-leaver° and a fugitive.°   25
   O Antony! O Antony!   [*He dies*]

FIRST WATCH   Let's speak to him.

SENTRY   Let's hear him, for the things he speaks
   May concern Caesar.

SECOND WATCH   Let's do so. But he sleeps.

SENTRY   Swoons rather, for so bad a prayer as his   30
   Was never yet for° sleep.

FIRST WATCH   Go we to him.
       [*They approach Enobarbus*]

SECOND WATCH   Awake, sir, awake. Speak to us.

FIRST WATCH   Hear you, sir?

SENTRY   The hand of death hath raught° him.
       Drums afar off
   Hark, the drums demurely° wake the sleepers.   35
   Let us bear him to th' court of guard;
   He is of note.° Our hour is fully out.

SECOND WATCH   Come on, then. He may recover yet.
       Exeunt [with the body]

❧

15 **mistress . . . melancholy** the moon, so addressed because of her supposed influence in causing lunacy   16 **disponge** pour down (as from a squeezed sponge)   20 **Which** the heart | **dried with grief** (cold and melancholy blood was thought to strangle and dry up the heart)   23 **in . . . particular** in your own person   24 **rank me in register** put me down in its records   25 **master-leaver** (1) one who deserts his master (2) nonpareil of deserters | **fugitive** deserter   31 **for** a prelude to   34 **raught** reached   35 **demurely** with solemn sound   37 **of note** of rank

ACT 4
SCENE 10

Location: The field of battle

Enter Antony and Scarus, with their army

ANTONY   Their preparation is today by sea;
We please them not by land.
SCARUS   For both, my lord.
ANTONY   I would they'd fight i'th' fire or i'th'air;°
We'd fight there too. But this it is: our foot°
Upon the hills adjoining to the city   5
Shall stay with us—order for sea° is given;
They have put forth° the haven—
Where their appointment° we may best discover°
And look on their endeavor.

Exeunt

❖

ACT 4
SCENE 11

Location: The field of battle

Enter Caesar and his army

CAESAR   But being° charged, we will be still° by land,
Which, as I take't, we shall;° for his best force
Is forth° to man his galleys. To the vales,°
And hold our best advantage.°

Exeunt

❖

---

3 **fire . . . air** (along with earth and water, where Antony is already prepared, fire and air make up the traditional four elements of all matter)   4 **foot** foot soldiers
6 **for sea** to fight at sea   7 **forth** forth from   8 **appointment** disposition of forces, equipment | **discover** descry

1 **But being** unless we are | **still** inactive   2 **we shall** we will be left undisturbed
3 **Is forth** has gone forth | **vales** valleys   4 **hold . . . advantage** take the most advantageous position

ACT 4
SCENE 12

Location: The field of battle at first, though by scene's end the action appears to be located in Alexandria.

Enter Antony and Scarus

ANTONY   Yet they are not joined. Where yond pine does stand,
I shall discover all. I'll bring thee word
Straight° how 'tis like° to go.   *Exit*

                              Alarum afar off, as at a sea fight

SCARUS   Swallows have built
In Cleopatra's sails their nests. The augurers°
Say they know not, they cannot tell, look grimly,   5
And dare not speak their knowledge. Antony
Is valiant, and dejected, and by starts
His fretted° fortunes give him hope and fear
Of what he has and has not.

                                   Enter Antony

ANTONY   All is lost!
This foul Egyptian hath betrayèd me.   10
My fleet hath yielded to the foe, and yonder
They cast their caps up and carouse together
Like friends long lost. Triple-turned° whore! 'Tis thou
Hast sold me to this novice, and my heart
Makes only wars on thee. Bid them all fly;   15
For when I am revenged upon my charm,°
I have done all. Bid them all fly. Begone!

                                   [*Exit Scarus*]

O sun, thy uprise shall I see no more.
Fortune and Antony part here; even here
Do we shake hands.° All come to this? The hearts°   20
That spanieled° me at heels, to whom I gave
Their wishes,° do discandy,° melt their sweets

---

3 **Straight** immediately | **like** likely   4 **augurers** augurs, soothsayers   8 **fretted** worn away, vexed, checkered   13 **Triple-turned** three times faithless (to Julius Caesar, Gnaeus Pompey, and now Antony)   16 **charm** practicer of charms or spells   20 **shake hands** in parting | **hearts** good fellows   21 **spanieled** fawned upon like a spaniel   22 **Their wishes** whatever they wished | **discandy** melt, dissolve

On blossoming Caesar; and this pine° is barked°
That overtopped them all. Betrayed I am.
Oh, this false soul of Egypt! This grave° charm,   25
Whose eye becked° forth my wars and called them home,
Whose bosom was my crownet, my chief end,°
Like a right° gypsy hath at fast and loose°
Beguiled me to the very heart of loss.°
[*Calling*] What, Eros, Eros!

                                        Enter Cleopatra

                              Ah, thou spell!° Avaunt!°   30
CLEOPATRA   Why is my lord enraged against his love?
ANTONY   Vanish, or I shall give thee thy deserving
And blemish Caesar's triumph.° Let him take thee
And hoist thee up to the shouting plebeians!
Follow his chariot, like the greatest spot°   35
Of all thy sex; most monsterlike be shown°
For poor'st diminutives,° for dolts, and let
Patient Octavia plow thy visage up
With her preparèd nails!   *Exit Cleopatra*
                        'Tis well thou'rt gone,
If it be well to live; but better 'twere   40
Thou fell'st into° my fury, for one death
Might have prevented many.°—Eros, ho!—
The shirt of Nessus is upon me. Teach me,
Alcides, thou mine ancestor, thy rage.
Let me lodge Lichas° on the horns o'th' moon,   45

---

23 **this pine** Antony | **barked** stripped of its bark and thus killed   25 **This grave charm** this sorceress who casts fatal spells   26 **becked** beckoned   27 **Whose . . . end** whose embraces were the crown of my achievement and my goal   28 **right** veritable | **fast and loose** a cheating game in which the victim bets that he can make fast a knot in an ingeniously coiled rope, whereupon the knot is pulled loose   29 **loss** ruin   30 **spell** enchantment | **Avaunt!** begone!   33 **blemish Caesar's triumph** mutilate you and thereby frustrate Caesar's plan to display you in his triumphal procession into Rome   35 **spot** blemish, disgrace   36 **shown** exhibited   37 **diminutives** underlings, the populace   41 **Thou fell'st into** you had fallen a victim to   42 **many** many other deaths resulting from my rage   43–5 **Nessus . . . Lichas** (when Hercules or *Alcides* had fatally wounded the centaur *Nessus* for trying to rape Hercules's wife Deianira, Nessus vengefully gave his blood-soaked shirt to Deianira as a supposed love charm for her husband; the poison gave Hercules such agony that he cast his page *Lichas* into the air)

And with those hands, that grasped the heaviest club,
Subdue my worthiest self. The witch shall die.
To the young Roman boy she hath sold me, and I fall
Under this plot. She dies for't.—Eros, ho!

Exit

❖

ACT 4
SCENE 13

*Location: Alexandria. This scene appears to follow
scene 12 closely. The sense of location is very fluid, and it
is not clear where the end of scene 12 takes place.*

Enter Cleopatra, Charmian, Iras, [and] Mardian

CLEOPATRA Help me, my women! Oh, he's more mad
Than Telamon° for his shield; the boar of Thessaly°
Was never so embossed.°
CHARMIAN   To th' monument!°
There lock yourself and send him word you are dead.
The soul and body rive° not more in parting   5
Than greatness going off.°
CLEOPATRA   To th' monument!
Mardian, go tell him I have slain myself.
Say that the last I spoke was "Antony,"
And word it, prithee, piteously. Hence, Mardian,
And bring me how he takes my death. To th' monument!   10

Exeunt

❖

2 **Telamon** Ajax Telamon, who after the capture of Troy went mad and slew himself
when he was not awarded the shield and armor of Achilles | **the boar of Thessaly**
the boar sent by Diana or Artemis to ravage the fields of Calydon, slain by Meleager
3 **embossed** foaming at the mouth from rage and exhaustion | **monument** tomb
presumably built to house Cleopatra's royal remains after her death, like the
pyramids   5 **rive** split, sever   6 **going off** bidding farewell to its glory

ACT 4
SCENE 14

Location: Alexandria. (See location of scene 13;
again, the sense of time is immediate and the place is fluid.)

Enter Antony and Eros

ANTONY   Eros, thou yet behold'st me?
EROS   Ay, noble lord.
ANTONY   Sometime we see a cloud that's dragonish,°
   A vapor sometime like a bear or lion,
   A towered citadel, a pendant° rock,
   A forkèd mountain, or blue promontory   5
   With trees upon't that nod unto the world
   And mock our eyes with air. Thou hast seen these signs;
   They are black vesper's pageants.°
EROS   Ay, my lord.
ANTONY   That which is now a horse, even with a thought
   The rack dislimns° and makes it indistinct   10
   As water is in water.
EROS   It does, my lord.
ANTONY   My good knave° Eros, now thy captain is
   Even such a body. Here I am Antony,
   Yet cannot hold this visible shape, my knave.
   I made these wars for Egypt, and the Queen,   15
   Whose heart I thought I had, for she had mine—
   Which whilst it was mine had annexed unto't
   A million more, now lost—she, Eros, has
   Packed cards° with Caesar and false-played° my glory
   Unto an enemy's triumph.°   20
   Nay, weep not, gentle Eros. There is left us
   Ourselves to end ourselves.

Enter Mardian

Oh, thy vile lady!

---

2 dragonish shaped like a dragon   **4 pendant** overhanging   **8 black . . . pageants**
the evanescent splendor of a sunset heralding the approach of night   **10 The rack
dislimns** the mass of cloud changes its shape   **12 knave** lad   **19 Packed cards**
stacked the deck | **false-played** falsely played away   **20 triumph** (1) victory
(2) trump card

She has robbed me of my sword.°
MARDIAN   No, Antony,
  My mistress loved thee, and her fortunes mingled
  With thine entirely.
ANTONY   Hence, saucy eunuch, peace!   25
  She hath betrayed me and shall die the death.°
MARDIAN   Death of° one person can be paid but once,
  And that she has discharged.° What thou wouldst do
  Is done unto thy hand.° The last she spake
  Was, "Antony, most noble Antony!"   30
  Then in the midst a tearing groan did break
  The name of Antony; it was divided
  Between her heart and lips.° She rendered life
  Thy name so buried in her.°
ANTONY   Dead, then?
MARDIAN   Dead.
ANTONY   Unarm, Eros. The long day's task is done,   35
  And we must sleep. [*To Mardian*] That thou depart'st hence
      safe
  Does pay thy labor richly; go.   *Exit Mardian*
                          Off, pluck off!
                          [*Eros unarms him*]
  The sevenfold° shield of Ajax cannot keep
  The battery° from my heart. Oh, cleave, my sides!
  Heart, once be stronger than thy continent;°   40
  Crack thy frail case! Apace,° Eros, apace.
  No more a soldier. Bruisèd pieces, go;
  You have been nobly borne.—From° me awhile.
                                    Exit Eros
  I will o'ertake thee, Cleopatra, and
  Weep for my pardon. So it must be, for now   45
  All length° is torture; since the torch° is out,

23 **sword** prowess as a soldier, masculinity 26 **die the death** be put to death 27 **of** by 28 **discharged** paid 29 **unto thy hand** for you, without your having to lift a finger 32–3 **it . . . lips** she groaned out half of Antony's name and then died with the unspoken part in her heart only 33–4 **She . . . in her** she gave back to nature that part of your name thus buried in her heart 38 **sevenfold** with seven thicknesses (the shield of Ajax was of brass reinforced with seven thicknesses of oxhide) 39 **battery** battering 40 **thy continent** that which contains you 41 **Apace** quickly 43 **From** go from 46 **length** prolongation of life | **the torch** the life of Cleopatra

Lie down, and stray no farther. Now all labor
Mars what it does; yea, very force° entangles
Itself with strength.° Seal° then, and all is done.
Eros!°—I come, my queen.—Eros!—Stay for me.   50
Where souls do couch° on flowers, we'll hand in hand,
And with our sprightly° port° make the ghosts gaze.
Dido and her Aeneas shall want troops,°
And all the haunt be ours.°—Come, Eros, Eros!

                                                   Enter Eros

EROS   What would my lord?
ANTONY   Since Cleopatra died   55
  I have lived in such dishonor that the gods
  Detest my baseness. I, that with my sword
  Quartered the world, and o'er green Neptune's back
  With ships made cities,° condemn myself to lack°
  The courage of a woman—less noble mind   60
  Than she which by her death our Caesar tells
  "I am conqueror of myself." Thou art sworn, Eros,
  That when the exigent° should come which now
  Is come indeed, when I should see behind me
  Th'inevitable prosecution° of   65
  Disgrace and horror, that on my command
  Thou then wouldst kill me. Do't. The time is come.
  Thou strik'st not me, 'tis Caesar thou defeat'st.
  Put color in thy cheek.
EROS   The gods withhold me!°
  Shall I do that which all the Parthian darts,   70

---

48 very force any resolute action **49 with strength** with its own strength | **Seal** finish the business (as in sealing a letter) **50 Eros** (the meaning of Eros's name, erotic love, is especially apt here) **51 couch** lie (here, in the Elysian fields) **52 sprightly** (1) high-spirited (2) spiritlike, ghostly | **port** bearing **53 Dido . . . troops** we will be the most distinguished lovers in the Elysian fields, outshining even the Queen of Carthage and her famous lover (in the *Aeneid,* Aeneas deserts Dido in order to found Rome, putting public good ahead of private passion as Antony does not; Dido scorns Aeneas when they meet in the underworld; Antony here imagines himself and Cleopatra in the Elysian fields) | **want troops** lack followers **54 all . . . ours** we shall be the objects of everyone's attention **58–9 Quartered . . . cities** divided and conquered the world, and at sea assembled flotillas as dense and populous as cities **59 to lack** for lacking **63 exigent** exigency, time of compelling need **65 prosecution** consequence **69 The gods withhold me!** God forbid!

Though enemy, lost aim and could not?

ANTONY   Eros,
Wouldst thou be windowed° in great Rome and see
Thy master thus with pleached° arms, bending down
His corrigible° neck, his face subdued
To penetrative° shame, whilst the wheeled seat°   75
Of fortunate Caesar, drawn before him, branded
His baseness that ensued?°

EROS   I would not see't.

ANTONY   Come, then, for with a wound I must be cured.
Draw that thy honest° sword, which thou hast worn
Most useful for thy country.

EROS   Oh, sir, pardon me!°   80

ANTONY   When I did make thee free, swor'st thou not then
To do this when I bade thee? Do it at once,
Or thy precedent° services are all
But accidents unpurposed.° Draw, and come.

EROS   Turn from me then that noble countenance   85
Wherein the worship° of the whole world lies.

ANTONY   Lo thee!   [*He turns away*]

EROS [*drawing his sword*]
My sword is drawn.

ANTONY   Then let it do at once
That thing why thou hast drawn it.

EROS   My dear master,
My captain, and my emperor, let me say,   90
Before I strike this bloody stroke, farewell.

ANTONY   'Tis said, man, and farewell.

EROS   Farewell, great chief. Shall I strike now?

ANTONY   Now, Eros.

EROS (*kills himself*)
Why, there then! Thus I do escape the sorrow
Of Antony's death.   [*He dies*]

ANTONY   Thrice nobler than myself!   95

---

72 windowed placed as in a window   **73 pleached** folded or bound   **74 corrigible**
submissive to correction   **75 penetrative** penetrating | **wheeled seat** chariot
76–7 branded . . . ensued stigmatized, as by a brand, the shame of him that followed
79 honest honorable   **80 pardon me!** excuse me from doing this!   **83 precedent** former
84 accidents unpurposed events leading to no purpose   **86 worship** honor, worth

Thou teachest me, O valiant Eros, what
I should, and thou couldst not.° My queen and Eros
Have by their brave instruction got upon me
A nobleness in record.° But I will be
A bridegroom in my death, and run into't   100
As to a lover's bed. Come, then, and Eros,
Thy master dies thy scholar. To do thus
I learned of thee.   [*He falls on his sword*]
                    How, not dead? Not dead?
The guard, ho! Oh, dispatch° me!

                    Enter [Dercetus and others of] a Guard

FIRST GUARD   What's the noise?   105
ANTONY   I have done my work ill, friends.
    Oh, make an end of what I have begun!
SECOND GUARD   The star is fallen.
FIRST GUARD   And time is at his period.°
ALL   Alas, and woe!   110
ANTONY   Let him that loves me strike me dead.
FIRST GUARD   Not I.
SECOND GUARD   Nor I.
THIRD GUARD   Nor anyone.   *Exeunt [Guard]*
DERCETUS   Thy death and fortunes bid thy followers fly.   115
    This sword but shown to Caesar, with this tidings,
    Shall enter me with him.°   [*He takes up Antony's sword*]

                    Enter Diomedes

DIOMEDES   Where's Antony?
DERCETUS   There, Diomed, there.
DIOMEDES   Lives he? Wilt thou not answer, man?   120
                    [*Exit Dercetus*]
ANTONY   Art thou there, Diomed? Draw thy sword and give me
    Sufficing strokes for death.
DIOMEDES   Most absolute lord,

---

97 I should . . . not I should have done for myself and you couldn't do for me
98–9 got . . . record won a noble place in history before I have   104 dispatch finish
109 his period its end   117 enter . . . him admit me to his service, put me in his
good graces

My mistress Cleopatra sent me to thee.

ANTONY   When did she send thee?

DIOMEDES   Now, my lord.

ANTONY   Where is she?

DIOMEDES   Locked in her monument. She had a prophesying fear   125
Of what hath come to pass. For when she saw—
Which never shall be found°—you did suspect
She had disposed with° Caesar, and that your rage
Would not be purged, she sent you word she was dead;
But, fearing since how it might work, hath sent   130
Me to proclaim the truth, and I am come,
I dread, too late.

ANTONY   Too late, good Diomed. Call my guard, I prithee.

DIOMEDES [calling]
What ho, the Emperor's guard! The guard, what ho!
Come, your lord calls.   135

Enter four or five of the Guard of Antony

ANTONY   Bear me, good friends, where Cleopatra bides.°
'Tis the last service that I shall command you.

FIRST GUARD   Woe, woe are we, sir, you may not live to wear
All your true followers out.°

ALL   Most heavy day!

ANTONY   Nay, good my fellows, do not please sharp fate   140
To grace° it with your sorrows. Bid that welcome
Which comes to punish us, and we punish it,
Seeming to bear it lightly. Take me up.
I have led you oft; carry me now, good friends,
And have my thanks for all.   145

Exeunt, bearing Antony [and Eros]

❖

127 found found true   128 disposed with come to terms with   136 bides abides,
dwells   138–9 live . . . out outlive those that serve you   141 To grace by gracing
or honoring

ACT 4
SCENE 15

Location: Alexandria. Cleopatra's monument.

Enter Cleopatra and her maids aloft,° with Charmian and Iras

CLEOPATRA   Oh, Charmian, I will never go from hence.
CHARMIAN   Be comforted, dear madam.
CLEOPATRA   No, I will not.
All strange and terrible events are welcome,
But comforts we despise. Our size of sorrow,
Proportioned to our cause, must be as great   5
As that which makes it.

Enter [below] Diomedes

                        How now? Is he dead?
DIOMEDES   His death's upon him, but not dead.
Look out o'th'other side your monument;
His guard have brought him thither.

Enter [below] Antony, and the Guard [bearing him]

CLEOPATRA   O sun,   10
Burn the great sphere° thou mov'st in; darkling° stand
The varying shore o'th' world! O Antony,
Antony, Antony! Help, Charmian, help, Iras, help!
Help, friends below! Let's draw him hither.
ANTONY   Peace!
Not Caesar's valor hath o'erthrown Antony,   15
But Antony's hath triumphed on itself.
CLEOPATRA   So it should be, that none but Antony
Should conquer Antony; but woe 'tis so!
ANTONY   I am dying, Egypt, dying. Only
I here importune° death awhile, until   20
Of many thousand kisses the poor last
I lay upon thy lips.
CLEOPATRA   I dare not,° dear—

0.1 *aloft* in the gallery above the main stage   11 **sphere** concentric sphere in which, according to Ptolemaic astronomy, the sun moved about the earth as did the planets and stars | **darkling** in darkness   20 **importune** beg a delay of   22 **I dare not** I dare not come down

Dear my lord, pardon—I dare not,
Lest I be taken. Not th'imperious show°
Of the full-fortuned Caesar ever shall   25
Be brooched° with me. If knife, drugs, serpents, have
Edge, sting, or operation,° I am safe.
Your wife Octavia, with her modest eyes
And still conclusion,° shall acquire no honor
Demuring° upon me. But come, come, Antony—   30
Help me, my women—we must draw thee up.
Assist, good friends.

ANTONY   Oh, quick, or I am gone.

                              [*They begin lifting*]

CLEOPATRA Here's sport indeed! How heavy weighs my lord!
Our strength is all gone into heaviness,°
That makes the weight. Had I great Juno's power,   35
The strong-winged Mercury should fetch thee up
And set thee by Jove's side. Yet come a little;
Wishers were ever fools.° Oh, come, come, come!

                They heave Antony aloft to Cleopatra

And welcome, welcome! Die when thou hast lived;°
Quicken° with kissing. Had my lips that power,   40
Thus would I wear them out.   [*She kisses him*]

ALL   A heavy° sight!

ANTONY   I am dying, Egypt, dying.
Give me some wine, and let me speak a little.

CLEOPATRA   No, let me speak, and let me rail so high   45
That the false huswife° Fortune break her wheel,
Provoked by my offense.°

ANTONY   One word, sweet Queen:
Of° Caesar seek your honor, with your safety. Oh!

CLEOPATRA   They do not go together.

ANTONY   Gentle, hear me.
None about Caesar trust but Proculeius.   50

---

24 th'imperious show the imperial triumphal procession   **26 brooched** adorned (as
with a brooch)   **27 operation** power, efficacy   **29 still conclusion** silent judgment
30 Demuring looking demurely   **34 heaviness** (1) sadness (2) weight   **38 Wishers . . .
fools** those who wish for things are always fools   **39 Die . . . lived** die after living
intensely (with a pun on *die* suggesting sexual consummation; hence *Quicken* in
l. 40)   **40 Quicken** revive   **42 heavy** doleful   **46 false huswife** treacherous hussy
47 offense offensive speech   **48 Of** from

CLEOPATRA   My resolution and my hands I'll trust,
  None about Caesar.
ANTONY   The miserable change now at my end
  Lament° nor sorrow at, but please your thoughts
  In feeding them with those my former fortunes,   55
  Wherein I lived the greatest prince o'th' world,
  The noblest; and do now not basely die,
  Not cowardly put off my helmet to
  My countryman—a Roman by a Roman
  Valiantly vanquished. Now my spirit is going;   60
  I can no more.
CLEOPATRA   Noblest of men, woo't° die?
  Hast thou no care of me? Shall I abide
  In this dull world, which in thy absence is
  No better than a sty? [*Antony dies*] Oh, see, my women,
  The crown o'th'earth doth melt. My lord!   65
  Oh, withered is the garland of the war;
  The soldier's pole° is fall'n! Young boys and girls
  Are level now with men. The odds is gone,°
  And there is nothing left remarkable
  Beneath the visiting moon.   [*She faints*] 70
CHARMIAN   Oh, quietness, lady!
IRAS   She's dead too, our sovereign.
CHARMIAN   Lady!
IRAS   Madam!
CHARMIAN   Oh, madam, madam, madam!   75
IRAS   Royal Egypt, Empress!   [*Cleopatra stirs*]
CHARMIAN   Peace, peace, Iras.
CLEOPATRA
  No more but e'en a woman, and commanded
  By such poor passion as the maid that milks
  And does the meanest chares.° It were° for me   80
  To throw my scepter at the injurious gods,
  To tell them that this world did equal theirs

---

54 **Lament** neither lament   61 **woo't** wilt thou   67 **pole** polestar or battle standard (probably with a suggestion of a sexual potency now withered and fallen through death)   68 **The odds is gone** the distinction between great and small has disappeared   80 **chares** chores, drudgery | **were** would be fitting

Till they had stol'n our jewel. All's but naught;
Patience is sottish, and impatience does
Become a dog that's mad.° Then is it sin   85
To rush into the secret house of death
Ere death dare come to us? How do you, women?
What, what, good cheer! Why, how now, Charmian?
My noble girls! Ah, women, women! Look,
Our lamp is spent, it's out. Good sirs,° take heart.   90
We'll bury him; and then, what's brave,° what's noble,
Let's do't after the high Roman fashion
And make death proud to take us. Come, away.
This case of that huge spirit now is cold.
Ah, women, women! Come. We have no friend   95
But resolution, and the briefest° end.
                    Exeunt, [those above] bearing off Antony's body

❖

ACT 5
SCENE 1

Location: Alexandria. Caesar's camp.

Enter Caesar, Agrippa, Dolabella, Maecenas,
[Gallus, Proculeius,] with his council of war

CAESAR   Go to him, Dolabella, bid him yield;
   Being so frustrate,° tell him, he mocks
   The pauses that he makes.°
DOLABELLA   Caesar, I shall.   [*Exit*]

        Enter Dercetus, with the sword of Antony

CAESAR   Wherefore is that? And what art thou that dar'st
   Appear thus to us?
DERCETUS   I am called Dercetus.   5

84–5 Patience . . . mad patience is for fools, and impatience is for the mad; both are useless here   90 Good sirs (addressed to the women)   91 brave fine   96 briefest swiftest

2 frustrate helpless, baffled   2–3 mocks . . . makes makes himself ridiculous by his delays (in yielding)

Mark Antony I served, who best was worthy
Best to be served. Whilst he stood up and spoke
He was my master, and I wore my life
To spend° upon his haters. If thou please
To take me to thee, as I was to him   10
I'll be to Caesar; if thou pleasest not,
I yield thee up my life.
CAESAR   What is't thou say'st?
DERCETUS   I say, O Caesar, Antony is dead.
CAESAR   The breaking° of so great a thing should make
A greater crack.° The round world   15
Should have shook lions into civil° streets
And citizens to their° dens. The death of Antony
Is not a single doom;° in the name lay
A moiety° of the world.
DERCETUS   He is dead, Caesar,
Not by a public minister of justice,   20
Nor by a hirèd knife; but that self° hand
Which writ his honor in the acts it did
Hath, with the courage which the heart did lend it,
Splitted the heart. This is his sword.
                         [*He offers the sword*]
I robbed his wound of it. Behold it stained   25
With his most noble blood.
CAESAR   Look you sad, friends?
The gods rebuke me, but it is° tidings
To wash the eyes of kings.
AGRIPPA   And strange it is
That nature must compel us to lament
Our most persisted° deeds.
MAECENAS   His taints and honors   30
Waged equal with° him.
AGRIPPA   A rarer spirit never

9 **spend** expend   14 **breaking** (1) destruction (2) disclosure   15 **crack** (1) cracking apart (2) loud report   16 **civil** city   17 **their** the lions', or else, the citizens scurry to safety indoors, in their own "dens" (in either case, nature is inverted in a kind of disorder that earlier accompanied the death of Julius Caesar)   18 **Is . . . doom** signifies the death and destruction of much more than a single man   19 **moiety** half   21 **self** same   27 **but it is** if it is not   30 **persisted** persistently desired or pursued   31 **Waged equal with** battled equally in

Did steer humanity;° but you gods will give° us
Some faults to make us men. Caesar is touched.

MAECENAS   When such a spacious mirror's set before him,
He needs must see himself.

CAESAR   O Antony,   35
I have followed° thee to this; but we do launch
Diseases in our bodies.° I must perforce°
Have shown to thee° such a declining day,
Or look on thine; we could not stall° together
In the whole world. But yet let me lament   40
With tears as sovereign as the blood of hearts°
That thou, my brother, my competitor°
In top of all design,° my mate in empire,
Friend and companion in the front° of war,
The arm of mine own body, and the heart   45
Where mine his thoughts did kindle°—that our stars,
Unreconciliable, should divide
Our equalness to this.° Hear me, good friends—

Enter an Egyptian

But I will tell you at some meeter season.°
The business of this man looks out of him;°   50
We'll hear him what he says.—Whence are you?°
EGYPTIAN   A poor Egyptian yet,° the Queen my mistress,
Confined in all she has, her monument,
Of thy intents desires instruction,
That she preparedly may frame herself°   55
To th' way she's forced to.

CAESAR   Bid her have good heart.

32 **steer humanity** govern any individual | **will give** insist on giving   36 **followed** pursued   36–7 **but . . . bodies** I have hurt you to cure myself, as men lance diseases in their own bodies   37 **perforce** necessarily   38 **shown to thee** suffered myself at your hands   39 **stall** dwell   41 **as sovereign . . . hearts** as precious or efficacious as heart's blood   42 **competitor** associate, partner (and rival)   43 **In . . . design** at the head of every grand enterprise   44 **front** forehead, face   45–6 **the heart . . . kindle** the brave heart where my heart kindled its (*his*) thoughts of courage   47–8 **should . . . this** should divide our equal partnership to this extreme   49 **meeter season** more suitable time   50 **looks . . . him** reveals itself in his expression   51 **Whence are you?** where do you come from?   52 **A . . . yet** Egyptian Cleopatra, still reduced in circumstance (and awaiting your will), or, I am a poor Egyptian still, though subject to Rome's authority   55 **frame herself** shape her course of action

She soon shall know of us, by some of ours,°
How honorable and how kindly we
Determine for her; for Caesar cannot live
To be ungentle.

EGYPTIAN   So the gods preserve thee!   *Exit*   60

CAESAR   Come hither, Proculeius. Go and say
We purpose° her no shame. Give her what comforts
The quality of her passion° shall require,
Lest, in her greatness,° by some mortal stroke
She do defeat us; for her life in Rome°   65
Would be eternal in our triumph.° Go,
And with your speediest° bring us what she says
And how you find of° her.

PROCULEIUS   Caesar, I shall.

                                                    Exit Proculeius

CAESAR   Gallus, go you along.   [*Exit Gallus*]
                                        Where's Dolabella,
To second Proculeius?

ALL   Dolabella!   70

CAESAR   Let him alone,° for I remember now
How he's employed. He shall in time be ready.
Go with me to my tent, where you shall see
How hardly° I was drawn into this war,
How calm and gentle I proceeded still°   75
In all my writings.° Go with me and see
What I can show in this.

                                                    Exeunt

❧

ACT 5
SCENE 2

Location: Alexandria. Cleopatra's monument.

Enter Cleopatra, Charmian, Iras, and Mardian

CLEOPATRA   My desolation does begin to make
A better° life. 'Tis paltry to be Caesar;
Not being Fortune, he's but Fortune's knave,°
A minister of her will. And it is great
To do that thing that ends all other deeds,   5
Which shackles accidents and bolts up change,
Which sleeps and never palates more the dung,
The beggar's nurse and Caesar's.°

              Enter [to the gates of the monument] Proculeius

PROCULEIUS   Caesar sends greeting to the Queen of Egypt,
And bids thee study on° what fair demands   10
Thou mean'st to have him grant thee.

CLEOPATRA   What's thy name?

PROCULEIUS   My name is Proculeius.

CLEOPATRA   Antony
Did tell me of you, bade me trust you; but
I do not greatly care to be° deceived,
That° have no use for trusting. If your master   15
Would have a queen his beggar, you must tell him
That majesty, to keep decorum, must
No less beg than a kingdom. If he please
To give me conquered Egypt for my son,
He gives me so much of mine own as° I   20
Will kneel to him with thanks.

PROCULEIUS   Be of good cheer;
You're fall'n into a princely hand. Fear nothing.
Make your full reference° freely to my lord,
Who is so full of grace that it flows over
On all that need. Let me report to him   25

---

2 **better** rising above the vicissitudes of fortune   3 **knave** servant   5–8 **To do . . . Caesar's** to commit suicide, a sleep that arrests accident and change, and in which the sleeper relishes no more the dungy earth that sustains both Caesar and the beggar   10 **study on** consider carefully   14 **do . . . to be** am wary of being   15 **That** since I   20 **as** that   23 **Make . . . reference** refer your case

Your sweet dependency,° and you shall find
A conqueror that will pray in aid for kindness°
Where he for grace is kneeled to.

CLEOPATRA   Pray you, tell him
  I am his fortune's vassal, and I send him
  The greatness he has got.° I hourly learn   30
  A doctrine of obedience, and would gladly
  Look him i'th' face.

PROCULEIUS   This I'll report, dear lady.
  Have comfort, for I know your plight is pitied
  Of° him that caused it.

                      [*Roman soldiers° enter from behind*
                       Cleopatra and take her prisoner]
  You see how easily she may be surprised.   35
  [*To the soldiers*] Guard her till Caesar come.

IRAS   Royal Queen!

CHARMIAN   Oh, Cleopatra! Thou art taken, Queen.

CLEOPATRA [*drawing a dagger*]
  Quick, quick, good hands.

PROCULEIUS   Hold, worthy lady, hold!
                            [*He disarms her*]
  Do not yourself such wrong, who are in this
  Relieved,° but not betrayed.

CLEOPATRA   What, of death too,°   40
  That rids our dogs of languish?°

PROCULEIUS   Cleopatra,
  Do not abuse my master's bounty by
  Th'undoing of yourself. Let the world see
  His nobleness well acted,° which your death
  Will never let come forth.°

CLEOPATRA   Where art thou, Death?   45
  Come hither, come! Come, come, and take a queen

---

26 **dependency** submissiveness   27 **pray . . . kindness** beg your assistance to ensure
that he may omit no kindness   29–30 **I send . . . got** I acknowledge his superiority
over all he has won, including myself   34 **Of** by   34.1 *Roman soldiers* (perhaps led
by Gallus; see 5.1.69; possibly some speech for him has been omitted)   40 **Relieved**
rescued | **of death too** (1) am I *relieved* or deprived even of death (2) am I *betrayed*
even of the right to die   41 **our dogs of languish** even our dogs of lingering disease
44 **acted** accomplished   45 **let come forth** allow to be displayed

Worth many babes and beggars!°
PROCULEIUS   Oh, temperance, lady!
CLEOPATRA   Sir, I will eat no meat, I'll not drink, sir;
　　If idle talk will once be necessary,°
　　I'll not sleep, neither. This mortal house I'll ruin,   50
　　Do Caesar what he can. Know, sir, that I
　　Will not wait pinioned° at your master's court,
　　Nor once be chastised with the sober eye
　　Of dull Octavia. Shall they hoist me up
　　And show me to the shouting varletry°   55
　　Of censuring Rome? Rather a ditch in Egypt
　　Be gentle grave unto me! Rather on Nilus' mud
　　Lay me stark nak'd and let the waterflies
　　Blow me into abhorring!° Rather make
　　My country's high pyramides my gibbet°   60
　　And hang me up in chains!
PROCULEIUS   You do extend
　　These thoughts of horror further than you shall
　　Find cause in Caesar.

                                   Enter Dolabella

DOLABELLA   Proculeius,
　　What thou hast done thy master Caesar knows,
　　And he hath sent for thee. For° the Queen,   65
　　I'll take her to my guard.
PROCULEIUS   So, Dolabella,
　　It shall content me best. Be gentle to her.
　　[*To Cleopatra*] To Caesar I will speak what° you shall please,
　　If you'll employ me to him.
CLEOPATRA   Say I would die.
                                   Exit Proculeius [*with soldiers*]
DOLABELLA   Most noble Empress, you have heard of me?   70
CLEOPATRA   I cannot tell.
DOLABELLA   Assuredly you know me.

---

47 **babes and beggars** those whom death takes easily and often   49 **If . . . necessary**
even if on occasion I must resort to idle talk (to keep myself awake)   52 **wait
pinioned** wait in attendance, like a bird with clipped wings, unable to fly
55 **varletry** rabble   59 **Blow . . . abhorring** cause me to swell abhorrently with
maggots, or, deposit their eggs on me until I become abhorrent   60 **gibbet** gallows
65 **For** as for   68 **what** whatever

CLEOPATRA   No matter, sir, what I have heard or known.
You laugh when boys or women tell their dreams;
Is't not your trick?°
DOLABELLA   I understand not, madam.
CLEOPATRA   I dreamt there was an emperor Antony.   75
Oh, such another sleep, that I might see
But such another man!
DOLABELLA   If it might please ye—
CLEOPATRA   His face was as the heavens, and therein stuck°
A sun and moon, which kept their course and lighted
The little O, the earth.
DOLABELLA   Most sovereign creature—   80
CLEOPATRA   His legs bestrid° the ocean; his reared arm
Crested° the world; his voice was propertied
As all the tunèd spheres, and that to friends;°
But when he meant to quail° and shake the orb,°
He was as rattling thunder. For° his bounty,   85
There was no winter in't; an autumn 'twas
That grew the more by reaping. His delights
Were dolphinlike; they showed his back above
The element they lived in.° In his livery
Walked crowns and crownets;° realms and islands were   90
As plates° dropped from his pocket.
DOLABELLA   Cleopatra—
CLEOPATRA   Think you there was or might be such a man
As this I dreamt of?
DOLABELLA   Gentle madam, no.
CLEOPATRA   You lie, up to the hearing of the gods.
But if there be nor ever were° one such,   95

---

74 **trick** manner, way   78 **stuck** were set   81 **bestrid** straddled (like the Colossus
of Rhodes)   82 **Crested** surmounted   82–3 **propertied . . . friends** endowed with
qualities which, when he spoke to friends, recalled the harmony of the heavenly
bodies in their spheres   84 **quail** make quail, overawe | **orb** world   85 **For** as for
87–9 **His . . . in** like the dolphin sportfully rising up out of the sea, his pleasures
arose out of the element in which he lived, both glorying in and transcending that
element   89–90 **In . . . crownets** among his retainers (those who would wear his
livery) were kings and princes   91 **plates** coins   95 **nor ever were** or if there never
existed

It's past the size of dreaming.° Nature wants stuff
To vie strange forms with fancy; yet t'imagine
An Antony were nature's piece 'gainst fancy,
Condemning shadows quite.°

DOLABELLA   Hear me, good madam:
Your loss is as yourself, great; and you bear it   100
As answering to the weight.° Would I might never
O'ertake pursued success but I do feel,°
By the rebound of yours, a grief that smites
My very heart at root.

CLEOPATRA   I thank you, sir.
Know you what Caesar means to do with me?   105

DOLABELLA I am loath to tell you what I would you knew.

CLEOPATRA Nay, pray you, sir.

DOLABELLA   Though he be honorable—

CLEOPATRA He'll lead me, then, in triumph.

DOLABELLA Madam, he will, I know't.   *Flourish*

> *Enter Proculeius, Caesar, Gallus,*
> *Maecenas, and others of his train*

ALL   Make way there! Caesar!   110

CAESAR Which is the Queen of Egypt?

DOLABELLA It is the Emperor, madam.

                    Cleopatra kneels

CAESAR Arise, you shall not kneel. I pray you, rise.
Rise, Egypt.

CLEOPATRA [*rising*] Sir, the gods will have it thus;
My master and my lord I must obey.   115

CAESAR Take to you no hard thoughts.°
The record of what injuries you did us,
Though written in our flesh, we shall remember
As things but done by chance.

CLEOPATRA   Sole sir° o'th' world,

---

96 It's . . . dreaming no dream can come up to it, my image of him   96–9 Nature . . .
quite nature lacks material to equal the remarkable forms produced by fancy or
imagination; yet an Antony such as I have pictured forth would himself be a work
of nature, in fact would be Nature's masterpiece in competition with the
imagination   101 As . . . weight commensurate with the weightiness of the loss
101–2 Would . . . feel may I never succeed at what I desire if I do not feel   116 Take
. . . thoughts don't torment yourself with reproaches   119 sir master

I cannot project° mine own cause so well   120
To make it clear,° but do confess I have
Been laden with like frailties which before
Have often shamed our sex.
CAESAR   Cleopatra, know
    We will extenuate rather than enforce.°
    If you apply yourself to our intents,°   125
    Which towards you are most gentle, you shall find
    A benefit in this change; but if you seek
    To lay on me a cruelty° by taking
    Antony's course, you shall bereave° yourself
    Of my good purposes and put your children   130
    To that destruction which I'll guard them from
    If thereon you rely. I'll take my leave.
CLEOPATRA
    And may,° through all the world! 'Tis yours, and we,
    Your scutcheons° and your signs of conquest, shall
    Hang° in what place you please. Here, my good lord.   135
                              [*She gives him a scroll*]
CAESAR   You shall advise me in all for Cleopatra.°
CLEOPATRA   This is the brief° of money, plate, and jewels
    I am possessed of. 'Tis exactly valued,
    Not petty things admitted.° Where's Seleucus?

                              [*Enter Seleucus*]

SELEUCUS   Here, madam.   140
CLEOPATRA   This is my treasurer. Let him speak, my lord,
    Upon his peril, that I have reserved
    To myself nothing.—Speak the truth, Seleucus.
SELEUCUS   Madam, I had rather seal my lips
    Than to my peril speak that which is not.   145
CLEOPATRA   What have I kept back?

---

120 project set forth   **121 clear** free of blame   **124 enforce** press home   **125 If . . . intents** if you comply with my plans   **128 lay . . . cruelty** force me to be cruel   **129 bereave** rob   **133 And may** (1) you may leave when you choose (2) you may have your will in anything   **134 scutcheons** shields showing armorial bearings; hence, shields hung up as monuments of victory   **135 Hang** be hung up in display as your trophies (but with a hidden suggestion of "be hanged as your captives")   **136 in all for Cleopatra** in all matters pertaining to yourself   **137 brief** list   **139 Not . . . admitted** petty things omitted

SELEUCUS   Enough to purchase what you have made known.

CAESAR   Nay, blush not, Cleopatra. I approve
    Your wisdom in the deed.

CLEOPATRA   See, Caesar! Oh, behold
    How pomp is followed!° Mine° will now be yours,   150
    And, should we shift estates,° yours would be mine.
    The ingratitude of this Seleucus does
    Even make me wild.—Oh, slave, of no more trust
    Than love that's hired!°   [Seleucus retreats from her]
                    What, goest thou back? Thou shalt
    Go back, I warrant thee! But I'll catch thine eyes,   155
    Though they had wings. Slave, soulless villain, dog!
    Oh, rarely° base!

CAESAR   Good Queen, let us entreat you.

CLEOPATRA   Oh, Caesar, what a wounding shame is this,
    That thou vouchsafing° here to visit me,
    Doing the honor of thy lordliness   160
    To one so meek, that mine own servant should
    Parcel° the sum of my disgraces by
    Addition of his envy!° Say, good Caesar,
    That I some lady° trifles have reserved,
    Immoment toys,° things of such dignity   165
    As we greet modern° friends withal,° and say
    Some nobler token I have kept apart
    For Livia° and Octavia, to induce
    Their mediation; must I be unfolded
    With one that I have bred?° The gods! It smites me   170
    Beneath the fall I have. [To Seleucus] Prithee, go hence,
    Or I shall show the cinders° of my spirits
    Through th'ashes of my chance.° Wert thou a man,
    Thou wouldst have mercy on me.

CAESAR   Forbear,° Seleucus.   [Exit Seleucus]   175

---

150 How . . . followed! how greatness is served! | Mine all the pomp and following
that attends me   151 shift estates reverse fortunes, exchange places   154 hired
paid for   157 rarely exceptionally   159 vouchsafing deigning to come   162 Parcel
particularize   163 envy malice   164 lady ladylike, feminine   165 Immoment toys
trifles of no moment or importance   166 modern common | withal with   168 Livia
Octavius Caesar's wife   169–70 unfolded . . . bred exposed by one of my household
172 cinders smoldering hot coals   173 chance (fallen) fortune   175 Forbear
withdraw

CLEOPATRA   Be it known that we, the greatest, are misthought°
　　For things that others do; and when we fall
　　We answer others' merits in our name,°
　　Are therefore to be pitied.
CAESAR　　　　　　　　　Cleopatra,
　　Not what you have reserved nor what acknowledged　　　　180
　　Put we i'th' roll of conquest. Still be't yours;
　　Bestow° it at your pleasure, and believe
　　Caesar's no merchant, to make prize° with you
　　Of things that merchants sold. Therefore be cheered.
　　Make not your thoughts your prisons.° No, dear Queen,　　185
　　For we intend so to dispose° you as
　　Yourself shall give us counsel. Feed and sleep.
　　Our care and pity is so much upon you
　　That we remain your friend; and so adieu.
CLEOPATRA   My master, and my lord!
CAESAR　　　　　　　　　Not so. Adieu.　　　190
　　　　　　　　Flourish. Exeunt Caesar and his train
CLEOPATRA   He words me, girls, he words me, that I should not
　　Be noble to myself.° But hark thee, Charmian.
　　　　　　　　　　[*She whispers to Charmian*]
IRAS   Finish, good lady. The bright day is done,
　　And we are for the dark.
CLEOPATRA [*to Charmian*]   Hie thee again.°
　　I have spoke° already, and it is provided;　　　　　195
　　Go put it to the haste.
CHARMIAN　　　　　Madam, I will.

　　　　　　　　　　　Enter Dolabella

DOLABELLA   Where's the Queen?
CHARMIAN　　　　　　Behold, sir.　　　　[*Exit*]
CLEOPATRA　　　　　　　　Dolabella!
DOLABELLA   Madam, as thereto sworn by your command,
　　Which my love makes religion to obey,

176 **misthought** misjudged　178 **We ... name** we are accountable for the deeds of
others done in our name　182 **Bestow** use　183 **make prize** haggle　185 **Make ...
prisons** don't imprison yourself in your thoughts by misconceiving of your situation
186 **dispose** dispose of　191–2 **He words ... myself** he tries to deceive me with mere
words to keep me from suicide　194 **Hie thee again** return quickly　195 **spoke**
given orders (for the means of suicide)

I tell you this: Caesar through Syria   200
Intends his journey, and within three days
You with your children will he send before.
Make your best use of this. I have performed
Your pleasure and my promise.
CLEOPATRA   Dolabella,
I shall remain your debtor.
DOLABELLA   I your servant.   205
Adieu, good Queen. I must attend on Caesar.
CLEOPATRA   Farewell, and thanks.   *Exit [Dolabella]*
                    Now, Iras, what think'st thou?
Thou an Egyptian puppet shall be shown
In Rome as well as I. Mechanic slaves°
With greasy aprons, rules,° and hammers shall   210
Uplift us to the view. In their thick breaths,
Rank of gross diet,° shall we be enclouded
And forced to drink° their vapor.
IRAS   The gods forbid!
CLEOPATRA   Nay, 'tis most certain, Iras. Saucy lictors°
Will catch at us like strumpets, and scald° rhymers   215
Ballad us° out o' tune. The quick° comedians
Extemporally° will stage us and present
Our Alexandrian revels; Antony
Shall be brought drunken forth, and I shall see
Some squeaking Cleopatra boy° my greatness   220
I'th' posture of a whore.
IRAS   O the good gods!
CLEOPATRA   Nay, that's certain.
IRAS   I'll never see't! For I am sure my nails
Are stronger than mine eyes.
CLEOPATRA   Why, that's the way
To fool their preparation and to conquer   225

---

209 Mechanic slaves common laborers   **210 rules** straight-edged measuring sticks
212 Rank . . . diet reeking of coarse food   **213 drink** drink in, breathe deeply
214 lictors minor officials in attendance on Roman magistrates   **215 scald** scurvy
216 Ballad us sing ballads about us | **quick** quick-witted   **217 Extemporally** in
improvised performance   **220 boy** (allusion to the practice of having women's parts
acted by boys on the Elizabethan stage)

Their most absurd intents.

Enter Charmian

Now, Charmian!
Show° me, my women, like a queen. Go fetch
My best attires. I am again for Cydnus,
To meet Mark Antony. Sirrah° Iras, go—
Now, noble Charmian, we'll dispatch° indeed— 230
And when thou hast done this chare° I'll give thee leave
To play till doomsday. Bring our crown and all.
                    [*Exit Iras.°*] *A noise within*
Wherefore's this noise?

Enter a Guardsman

GUARDSMAN   Here is a rural fellow
That will not be denied Your Highness' presence.
He brings you figs.   235
CLEOPATRA   Let him come in.   *Exit Guardsman*
                    What° poor an instrument
May do a noble deed! He brings me liberty.
My resolution's placed,° and I have nothing
Of woman in me. Now from head to foot
I am marble-constant; now the fleeting° moon 240
No planet is of mine.

Enter Guardsman, and Clown° [bringing in a basket]

GUARDSMAN   This is the man.
CLEOPATRA   Avoid,° and leave him.   *Exit Guardsman*
    Hast thou the pretty worm° of Nilus there,
    That kills and pains not?
CLOWN   Truly, I have him, but I would not be the party that 245
    should desire you to touch him, for his biting is immortal.°
    Those that do die of it do seldom or never recover.
CLEOPATRA   Remember'st thou any that have died on't?

227 **Show** display   229 **Sirrah** (compare *sirs*, addressed to the women, in 4.15.90)
230 **dispatch** (1) finish (2) hasten   231 **chare** task, chore   232.1 **Exit Iras** (it is
possible that Charmian leaves, too)   236 **What** how   238 **placed** fixed   240 **fleeting**
inconstant, changing   241.1 *Clown* rustic   242 **Avoid** withdraw   243 **worm**
snake, serpent (but elsewhere in this scene with the added connotation of "the male
sexual organ" and "earthworm")   246 **immortal** (blunder for "mortal")

CLOWN Very many, men and women too. I heard of° one of
them no longer than yesterday—a very honest woman, but 250
something given to lie,° as a woman should not do but in the
way of honesty—how she died of the biting of it, what pain
she felt. Truly, she makes a very good report o'th' worm. But
he that will believe all that they say shall never be saved by
half° that they do. But this is most falliable,° the worm's an 255
odd worm.

CLEOPATRA Get thee hence, farewell.

CLOWN I wish you all joy of the worm.

[*He sets down his basket*]

CLEOPATRA Farewell.

CLOWN You must think this, look you, that the worm will do 260
his kind.°

CLEOPATRA Ay, ay; farewell.

CLOWN Look you, the worm is not to be trusted but in the
keeping of wise people, for indeed there is no goodness in
the worm. 265

CLEOPATRA Take thou no care;° it shall be heeded.

CLOWN Very good. Give it nothing, I pray you, for it is not
worth the feeding.

CLEOPATRA Will it eat me?

CLOWN You must not think I am so simple but I know the 270
devil himself will not eat a woman. I know that a woman is
a dish for the gods, if the devil dress° her not. But truly, these
same whoreson° devils do the gods great harm in their
women, for in every ten that they make, the devils mar five.

CLEOPATRA Well, get thee gone. Farewell. 275

CLOWN Yes, forsooth. I wish you joy o'th' worm.

Exit

[*Enter Iras with royal attire*]

CLEOPATRA Give me my robe. Put on my crown. I have
Immortal longings° in me. Now no more

249 heard of heard from **251 to lie** (with sexual second meaning hinted at also in
honest, "chaste," *die,* "reach orgasm," and *worm*) **254–5 all . . . half** (the Clown
comically reverses the sensible order of these two words) **255 falliable** (blunder for
"infallible") **261 his kind** its natural function **266 Take thou no care** don't worry
272 dress prepare, as in cooking (with a suggestion also of dressing in alluring
clothes) **273 whoreson** rascally, abominable (a slang expression) **278 Immortal
longings** longings for immortality

The juice of Egypt's grape shall moist this lip.

[*The women dress her*]

Yare,° yare, good Iras; quick. Methinks I hear   280
Antony call; I see him rouse himself
To praise my noble act. I hear him mock
The luck of Caesar, which the gods give men
To excuse their after wrath.° Husband, I come!
Now to that name my courage prove my title!°   285
I am fire and air; my other elements°
I give to baser life. So, have you done?
Come then, and take the last warmth of my lips.
Farewell, kind Charmian. Iras, long farewell.

[*She kisses them. Iras falls and dies*]

Have I the aspic° in my lips? Dost fall?   290
If thou and nature can so gently part,
The stroke of death is as a lover's pinch,
Which hurts, and is desired. Dost thou lie still?
If thus thou vanishest, thou tell'st the world
It is not worth leave-taking.°   295

CHARMIAN   Dissolve, thick cloud, and rain, that I may say
The gods themselves do weep!

CLEOPATRA   This proves me base.
If she first meet the curlèd° Antony,
He'll make demand° of her, and spend that kiss°
Which is my heaven to have. [*To an asp*] Come, thou mortal°
    wretch,°   300
With thy sharp teeth this knot intrinsicate°
Of life at once untie. Poor venomous fool,
Be angry, and dispatch. Oh, couldst thou speak,
That I might hear thee call great Caesar ass
Unpolicied!°

CHARMIAN   O eastern star!°

CLEOPATRA   Peace, peace!   305

280 **Yare** quickly   283–4 **which . . . wrath** the luck that the gods give men when they
intend to mock and punish them subsequently for their hubris   285 **to . . . title!** may
my courage prove my right to call myself Antony's wife!   286 **other elements** earth
and water, the heavier elements   290 **aspic** asp   295 **is . . . leave-taking** does not
deserve a ceremonious farewell   298 **curlèd** with curled hair   299 **make demand**
(1) ask questions (2) ask pleasure | **spend that kiss** expend his desire on her   300 **mortal**
deadly | **wretch** (an affectionate term of abuse, like *fool* in l. 302)   301 **intrinsicate**
intricate   305 **Unpolicied** outwitted | **eastern star** Venus, the morning star

Dost thou not see my baby at my breast,
That sucks the nurse asleep?
CHARMIAN   Oh, break! Oh, break!
CLEOPATRA   As sweet as balm, as soft as air, as gentle—
O Antony!—Nay, I will take thee too.
                                    [*Applying another asp to her arm*]
What° should I stay—   *Dies*   310
CHARMIAN   In this wild° world? So, fare thee well.
Now boast thee, Death, in thy possession lies
A lass unparalleled. Downy° windows, close;
And golden Phoebus never be beheld
Of° eyes again so royal! Your crown's awry;   315
I'll mend° it, and then play—

                              Enter the Guard, rustling in

FIRST GUARD   Where's the Queen?
CHARMIAN   Speak softly. Wake her not.
FIRST GUARD   Caesar hath sent—
CHARMIAN   Too slow a messenger.
                              [*She applies an asp to herself*]
Oh, come apace, dispatch! I partly feel thee.
FIRST GUARD   Approach, ho! All's not well. Caesar's beguiled.°   320
SECOND GUARD   There's Dolabella sent from Caesar. Call him.
                                    [*Exit a guard*]
FIRST GUARD   What work is here, Charmian? Is this well done?
CHARMIAN   It is well done, and fitting for a princess
Descended of so many royal kings.
Ah, soldier!   *Charmian dies*   325

                              Enter Dolabella

DOLABELLA   How goes it here?
SECOND GUARD   All dead.
DOLABELLA   Caesar, thy thoughts
Touch their effects° in this. Thyself art coming
To see performed the dreaded act which thou
So sought'st to hinder.

---

310 **What** why   311 **wild** savage (sometimes emended to *vild*, "vile")   313 **Downy**
windows soft eyelids   315 **Of** by   316 **mend** fix, straighten   320 **beguiled** cheated,
tricked   327 **Touch their effects** meet with realization

Enter Caesar and all his train, marching

ALL   A way° there, a way for Caesar!   330
DOLABELLA   Oh, sir, you are too sure an augurer;
   That° you did fear is done.
CAESAR   Bravest at the last,
   She leveled at° our purposes and, being royal,
   Took her own way. The manner of their deaths?
   I do not see them bleed.
DOLABELLA   Who was last with them?   335
FIRST GUARD   A simple° countryman, that brought her figs.
   This was his basket.
CAESAR   Poisoned, then.
FIRST GUARD   Oh, Caesar,
   This Charmian lived but now; she stood and spake.
   I found her trimming up the diadem
   On her dead mistress; tremblingly she stood,   340
   And on the sudden dropped.
CAESAR   Oh, noble weakness!
   If they had swallowed poison, 'twould appear
   By external swelling; but she looks like sleep,°
   As° she would catch another Antony
   In her strong toil° of grace.
DOLABELLA   Here on her breast   345
   There is a vent° of blood and something blown;°
   The like is on her arm.
FIRST GUARD   This is an aspic's trail, and these fig leaves
   Have slime upon them, such as th'aspic leaves
   Upon the caves of Nile.
CAESAR   Most probable   350
   That so she died; for her physician tells me
   She hath pursued conclusions° infinite
   Of easy ways to die. Take up her bed,
   And bear her women from the monument.
   She shall be buried by her Antony.   355
   No grave upon the earth shall clip° in it

---

330 **A way** make a path   332 **That** that which   333 **leveled at** aimed at, guessed
336 **simple** humbly born   343 **like sleep** as if asleep   344 **As** as if   345 **toil** net
346 **vent** discharge | **blown** deposited, or, swollen   352 **conclusions** experiments
356 **clip** embrace, clasp

A pair so famous. High events as these
Strike those that make them;° and their story is
No less in pity than his glory which
Brought them to be lamented.° Our army shall   360
In solemn show attend this funeral,
And then to Rome. Come, Dolabella, see
High order in this great solemnity.

Exeunt omnes,° [*bearing the dead bodies*]

358 **Strike . . . them** touch with sorrow those who brought about these deeds
358–60 **their story . . . lamented** the story of these famous lovers is no less pitiable
than the fame of him who brought them low is glorious   363.1 *omnes* all

CONTEXTS

The Historical Background

The events depicted in *Antony and Cleopatra* span ten years, from the death of Antony's first wife, Fulvia, in 40 BCE to the Alexandrian War and the deaths of Antony and Cleopatra in 30 BCE. The play's allusions take us back at least two decades earlier, and its audience would know the sequel as well: The power struggle between Octavius Caesar and Antony culminated the civil wars that destroyed Rome's republic and replaced it with the one-man rule of Octavius (soon awarded the title of Augustus), the head of a long line of Roman emperors. These Roman events were intertwined with the ambitions of Cleopatra VII (70–30 BCE), heir to the throne of the Ptolemies, the Greek dynasty that had ruled Egypt since the conquests of Alexander the Great in the late fourth century BCE.

Modern readers may welcome a historical synopsis, based partly on Shakespeare's primary source, Plutarch's *Life of Marcus Antonius* (see pp. 149–90).

Rome's conquests in the eastern Mediterranean in the second century BCE enormously enriched her ruling senatorial class and so put her republican form of government at risk. Flouting and reshaping at will the constitution they claimed to uphold, Roman generals fought one another over the booty of empire. Pompey the Great, Julius Caesar, and Marcus Licinius Crassus formed the First Triumvirate in 60 BCE in order to share power and divide up the commands over Rome's armies. Crassus led a disastrous expedition against the only other great power neighboring on Roman dominions, the Parthian empire centered in present-day northern Iraq and

Octavius Caesar, later Augustus (63 BCE–14 CE).
By permission of Alinari/Art Resource, NY.

Iran. His army was destroyed at Carrhae, and he was subsequently killed, in 53 BCE. Antony's general Ventidius avenged this defeat fifteen years later in his campaigns against the Parthians in 39–38 BCE. [Shakespeare records this event in **3.1.**]

With the triumvirate reduced to Pompey and Julius Caesar, a showdown between the two was inevitable. In 49 BCE, Caesar led his army, which had conquered Gaul, across the Rubicon river into Italy. Most of the senate, the upholders of what was left of Rome's constitutional government, fled the city to take the side of Pompey, and civil war ensued. At the battle of Pharsalia in 48 BCE, Caesar's army defeated Pompey, who escaped to Egypt, hoping to raise a new army there. Instead, he was treacherously murdered by agents of King Ptolemy XIII, who presented his head to Caesar, when the latter arrived, with a small force of soldiers, at the Egyptian capital in the great city of Alexandria.

Ptolemy, now thirteen years old, had previously ruled Egypt with his elder half-sister Cleopatra, and they may have been married in the manner of Ptolemaic monarchs. The regents of the boy-king had deposed and driven away Cleopatra, twenty-two and capable of ruling on her own. She managed to have herself smuggled into Caesar's lodgings; the story goes that she was concealed in a rolled-up rug or bed mattress [2.6.70–72]. She and Caesar found political and personal use for each other. Egypt—with its enormous production of grain ensured by the fertile mud of the Nile, with the great trade and luxury manufactures of Alexandria, and with the fabled treasury of the Ptolemies—was the richest prize in the Mediterranean not yet under the direct rule of Rome. Cleopatra needed the Roman general to put her back on her throne and to guarantee the independence of her kingdom, even if under Rome's protection. Caesar needed her as an ally in extorting money from Ptolemy to pay his army. The two began a sexual liaison, and Cleopatra gave birth to their son, Caesarion, the following year. [Shakespeare's Cleopatra looks back on her relationship with Julius Caesar at 1.5.69–78, 2.5.109–11, and 3.13.83–86; his jealous Antony reminds her of it at 3.13.118–22. Following a suggestion of Plutarch, Shakespeare also has Antony accuse her of having had an affair with Gnaeus Pompey, the son of Pompey the Great, who had visited Egypt a year earlier in 49 BCE; but this charge seems unlikely.]

Ptolemy and another older sister, Arsinoe IV, rose up with their Egyptian troops and the city of Alexandria against Caesar and Cleopatra. Ptolemy was killed; Arsinoe would later be led as a captive in Caesar's triumphal procession in Rome. Caesar reinstated Cleopatra as queen of Egypt, which now also housed three of Cae-

sar's Roman legions as a foreign garrison to protect Rome's interests. With the defeat of the remaining adherents of Pompey, Caesar
now became Dictator and supreme power in the Roman state.
Cleopatra joined him in the city of Rome itself and was staying
there as his guest and mistress when he was assassinated on the Ides
of March in 44 BCE. She quickly returned to Egypt to ensure her
position there.

Caesar's death cast Rome into another cycle of civil war. At
Caesar's funeral, Mark Antony, one of his leading lieutenants,
enflamed the Roman mob against the conspirators who had
killed him; Brutus and Cassius fled into Asia minor to raise
troops. The now dominant Antony was soon challenged by
Octavius, Julius Caesar's nineteen-year-old grand-nephew and
designated heir. Octavius initially put himself on the side of the
senate against Antony; he was siding with many of the constitu-
tionalist opponents of Julius Caesar and even with some of the
very murderers of Caesar upon whom he had sworn revenge. His
troops, along with those of the consuls Hirtius and Pansa,
besieged and drove Antony and his army out of Mutina (Modena)
in 43 BCE. [Shakespeare's (Octavius) Caesar recalls this campaign
against his once and future adversary at **1.4.57ff.**]

Octavius allowed Antony to escape with his legions to southern
France, where they joined up with the troops of another Caesarian
general, Marcus Lepidus. Octavius meanwhile imitated his grand-
uncle and marched on Rome, where he seized the public treasury to
pay off his troops. He forced the senate to confirm him as the adoptive son of Julius Caesar (receiving the name of Octavian, by which
he is known historically) and to declare war on the conspirators
against Caesar. For this war, he allied himself with Antony and Lepidus to form the Second Triumvirate. Their first act was the bloody
proscriptions: Lists of names were drawn of citizens who were to be
killed and whose property was to be confiscated. Among them was
the great orator and philosopher, Cicero, who had helped Octavius
come to power and who had attacked Antony in a series of orations, the *Philippics*; now, with Octavius's acquiescence, Antony
had his revenge. But Cicero was just one of over three hundred senators who lost their lives in a terrifying bloodbath whose motives
were overridingly and cynically mercenary: The targets were rich
men, whose property went to the generals and their soldiers.

While Lepidus stayed in Italy, Antony and Octavius tracked down Brutus and Cassius in northern Greece and defeated them at Philippi in November 42 BCE, thus putting an end to the last defenders of the republic. [Shakespeare's (Sextus) Pompey evokes the republican resistance at Philippi as justification for his own piracy and making war at **2.6.10–19.**]

It was in the following spring of 41 BCE that Antony fatefully summoned Cleopatra to meet with him at Tarsus on the banks of the Cydnus river (in present-day southeastern Turkey). He was preparing for a military campaign against the Parthians and wanted both Egypt's financial support and her aid in maintaining Roman rule in the Near East in his army's absence. Cleopatra's arrival in a pageant in which she impersonated the love-goddess Aphrodite, the Roman Venus, is the stuff of legend, recorded by Plutarch [and famously recalled by Enobarbus in the play at **2.2.195ff**]. On the one hand, she was following Egyptian custom, which deified its living rulers as incarnations of gods, in this case the goddess Isis [see **3.6.17**], with whom the Greek Aphrodite was identified. On the other hand, she was flattering Antony's own identification with Dionysus, the mythical conqueror of the East, associated in Egypt with Osiris, the brother and consort of Isis. [In Plutarch, it is Dionysus who deserts Antony in Alexandria, rather than Hercules as told in Shakespeare's version, **4.3.**] This scenario was propaganda for the Roman–Egyptian alliance the general and queen were forging, but they soon seemed to be living it out when Antony wintered in Alexandria during 41–40 BCE, and the two became lovers. Cleopatra bore Antony twin children, Alexander Helios and Cleopatra Selene, in 40 BCE.

The action of Shakespeare's play properly begins here, during Antony's first sojourn in Alexandria [**1.1–1.3**]. Antony received the news there that his wife Fulvia, a formidable matron-politician, and his brother Lucius had raised a rebellion among Italian landowners whose fields had been expropriated to reward Octavius's veterans. Antony had not sanctioned this war against his fellow triumvir, which ended in Fulvia's defeat and flight from Italy. Fulvia was already ill when Antony reached her in Athens; he refused to support her insurrection, and she died soon thereafter. [Shakespeare telescopes events so that Fulvia dies while Antony is still in Egypt with Cleopatra, **1.2.116ff.**] Antony would not see Cleopatra again for four years.

Octavius's own aggression began civil war with Antony, but the two warlords were soon reconciled at Brindisi in 40 BCE. They formally divided the empire: Antony would rule the rich, Greek-speaking East, Octavius the rest of Western Europe. While Antony retained the right to recruit in Italy, where the best soldiers were to be found, his trouble in exercising this right would contribute to his final military failure. Lepidus, the third triumvir, was granted only Roman Africa, west of Libya. When Antony abandoned his previous support for Sextus Pompey, the son of Pompey the Great, Octavius was free to make war on him. In a further gesture of accord, Antony married Octavia, Octavius's beautiful, accomplished, and recently widowed sister [2.2–2.5].

But Octavius's war against Sextus Pompey fared so badly that there were violent public demonstrations in Rome in favor of peace and of Pompey himself. In 39 BCE the three triumvirs met with Pompey at Misenum on the coast of Campania and agreed to grant him grain-rich Sicily and Sardinia in return for his promise to rid the sea of pirates [2.6–2.7, 3.2]. Within a year, however, Octavius and Pompey were at war again. Pompey won two naval victories, but in 36 BCE his forces were finally crushed by Octavius's general, Marcus Agrippa. Pompey fled into Asia Minor, where he was betrayed to the troops of Antony, who had him put to death. Secure at last from Pompey, Octavius stripped Lepidus of his triumviral power and sent him into retirement as a private citizen. [On both of these developments, see 3.5, where Antony is said to regret the killing of Pompey.] Once again, a triumvirate had been reduced to two dueling rivals.

Meanwhile, Antony returned to the conquest of Parthia, an episode that Shakespeare elides. Had Antony succeeded, he would have achieved a feat of arms comparable to that of Alexander the Great, enriched himself and his army, and made his position in the Roman state unassailable. By the terms of the treaty of Tarentum in 37 BCE, Octavius was supposed to send Antony four legions for the Parthian campaign in exchange for the ships Antony sent him for the conflict against Pompey. These legions were not forthcoming, and Octavius's default helped to bring Antony once more into alliance and personal association with Cleopatra. In 37 BCE, he sent Octavia back to Italy and joined Cleopatra in Antioch in Syria. Antony lost the Parthian

Octavia Minor (70–11 BCE), sister of Octavius Caesar. Gold coin of 40 BCE commemorating the marriage in that year of Octavia to Mark Antony (who is depicted on its reverse side) and the reconciliation of Antony and Octavius. By permission of Bildarchiv Preussischer Kulturbesitz/Art Resource, NY.

war in 36 BCE, a disaster mitigated only by his skillful military retreat and compensated only by a minor victory against the treacherous king of Armenia two year later.

Antony and Octavius headed toward confrontation, and the propaganda war was already in play. In 35 BCE, Antony again ordered Octavia, who had set out to join him in the East, to return to Rome. In the following year, he held a public spectacle at Alexandria in which he invested Caesarion with the crown of Egypt as co-ruler with his mother: Here, he proclaimed, in a direct affront to Octavius, was Julius Caesar's true son and heir. He granted to his own sons by Cleopatra, Alexander Helios and Ptolemy, kingships and overlordships over Armenia and Syria. [Shakespeare conflates these events in 3.4 and 3.6.] As he was setting up a personal dynasty, Antony also restored a limited amount of self-government to Rome's Greek-speaking subject peoples, under the ultimate sway of Roman arms based in Cleopatra's

Alexandria. These "Donations" provoked outrage at Rome and allowed Octavius's supporters to portray the impending struggle against Antony as a conflict between West and East. The senate proclaimed war not against Antony but on Cleopatra in 32 BCE; earlier that year, Antony had formally divorced Octavia.

Cleopatra's participation in the ensuing military campaign in fact precluded Antony from attacking Italy while he still enjoyed a superiority in troops and resources over Octavius: It would have smacked of invasion by a foreign power and rallied even Antony's Roman friends to his rival's side. Cleopatra had raised a navy in Egypt and insisted on accompanying it to protect her interests. The forces of Octavius and Antony eventually collided at the naval battle of Actium on September 2, 31 BCE, at the mouth of the Gulf of Ambracia in northwestern Greece. Antony and Cleopatra sought to break out of the gulf where Agrippa had bottled up their fleet. Octavius's propaganda cloaks subsequent accounts of this decisive encounter that depict Antony relinquishing the fight and potential victory in order to follow the sails of a Cleopatra who fled the battle out of fear or potential treachery [3.7–3.11]. More crippling to Antony than the battle itself was the desertion to Octavius of his allies and legions on land [3.10.32–34], a relatively bloodless and inglorious victory.

Antony and Cleopatra returned to Alexandria to wait for Octavius's attack a year later. Antony fell upon and drove back the advance forces of Octavius's army and enjoyed a brief moment of triumph [4.4–4.8]. But on August 1, 30 BCE (the future name of the month would commemorate this day), Antony's army and navy went over to Octavius, who entered Alexandria. Antony committed suicide [4.10–4.15]; Cleopatra barricaded herself in the tomb of the Ptolemies, where she had amassed and now threatened to burn the Egyptian royal treasure that Octavius desperately needed to pay his troops. She was captured [5.1–5.2] and the treasure recovered.

Two weeks later, having observed the funeral rites of Antony as his wife, Cleopatra committed suicide [5.2], almost certainly with the collusion and sufferance of Octavius: He would have encouraged her to take her life by threatening to lead her in triumph in Rome. The story goes that she poisoned herself with an asp. If so, this was the royal cobra of Egypt that was also identified with Isis: Its bite was believed to confer immortal life. Octavius buried

Cleopatra beside Antony. He had Caesarion put to death, as well as Antyllus, Antony's son by Fulvia; he spared Antony's other children by Cleopatra. After two and a half millennia, the line of Pharaohs ended. Egypt henceforth became a Roman province. The Alexandrians raised statues of Cleopatra's attendants, her hairdresser Iras and her lady-in-waiting Charmion, as monuments to servants so faithful that they chose to die with their royal mistress.

Classical Writers on Mark Antony and Cleopatra

Although famously charged by his contemporary and rival playwright Ben Jonson with possessing "small Latine and lesse Greeke," Shakespeare could have known a variety of classical texts that treated the figures of Octavius Caesar, Antony, and Cleopatra. In addition to the writings presented here, printed editions and translations circulated in the sixteenth century of the Greek historian Appian (fl. 130–47 CE) and the Latin historians Suetonius (c. 70–after 122 CE) and Velleius Paterculus (19 BCE–30 CE). Cicero's *Letters* and his series of speeches against Antony, the *Philippics*, shed light on the happenings and protagonists up until Cicero's proscription and murder in 43 BCE, three years before the events of *Antony and Cleopatra* begin. The writings selected here—from the Greek language historians Plutarch and Dio Cassius and from the Roman poets Virgil, Horace, and Propertius—have been chosen both because of the likelihood of Shakespeare's use of and familiarity with them and for their own intrinsic interest and beauty.

The Historians:
Plutarch and Dio Cassius

Plutarch (46–120 ce)

Shakespeare's principal source for Antony and Cleopatra *is the* Life of
Marcus Antonius, *written in Greek by the first-century historian
Plutarch in his* Parallel Lives. *The version that Shakespeare read was
translated by Thomas North (1579) from the French translation of the
Greek by Jacques Amyot (1559). Plutarch parallels the life of Antony
with that of the fourth-century* bce *Macedonian king, Demetrius; both
were womanizers who lost their kingdoms. Plutarch's severest judgment
on Antony emerges in his comparison of the two men in an epilogue to
the* Life. *As a triumvir with Octavius Caesar and Marcus Lepidus,
Antony countenanced the killing of his own uncle as a trade-off for the
murder of his enemy, Cicero, the great orator, statesman, and philosopher. Worse, Antony had destroyed the last vestiges of the Roman republic. His desire was "altogether wicked and tyrannical: who sought to
keep the people of Rome in bondage and subjection, but lately before rid
of [Julius] Caesar's reign and government. For the greatest and most
famous exploit Antonius ever did in wars (to wit, the war in which he
overthrew Cassius and Brutus) was begun to no other end but to deprive
his countrymen of their liberty and freedom." This last charge applied
equally well to Octavius, to whom Plutarch is no more sympathetic and
whom he accuses of using his sister, Octavia, as a political pawn. Shakespeare picks up on this republican argument in the speech of Sextus
Pompey at 2.6.8–19, although Pompey's motives may be no purer, as
Menas's offer in the next scene to make him "lord of all the world"
(2.7.61) suggests. Plutarch criticizes Antony for his love of wine, women,
and song, even as he acknowledges that this behavior, as well as Antony's
courage and soldierly prowess, won him the admiration and loyalty of
his troops. He makes clear that this love of pleasure—and Shakespeare
may have liked Antony's fondness for players and theater—was already
part of his character before he met Cleopatra, but she encouraged it to
his destruction. Yet the Greek Plutarch can admire Cleopatra herself: He
generally prefers his Greek historical figures over his Roman ones.
Cleopatra was the heir of the Ptolemies, a Macedonian Greek dynasty.
She might have made the Greek-speaking Eastern Mediterranean and
her capital Alexandria the master over the Roman world.*

Silver denarius showing Antony and Cleopatra on reverse sides, celebrating Antony's so-called conquest of Armenia, 32 BCE. Cleopatra is called "Queen of Kings and Sons of Kings" on the inscription, two years after the "Donations of Alexandria." By permission of Yale University Art Gallery.

Shakespeare picks and chooses from Plutarch: He closely imitates Plutarch's version of Antony's dying speech (p. 184), but he does not use Cleopatra's moving speech (pp. 188–89) at the tomb of Antony (other Renaissance dramatists did). The following excerpts from the Life of Marcus Antonius *are those most relevant to* Antony and Cleopatra. *The long account of Antony's unsuccessful war against the Parthians is omitted. Corresponding scenes in the play are indicated in brackets.*

from *Life of Marcus Antonius*,[1] trans. Sir Thomas North (1579)

[Antony's Character]

But besides all this, he had a noble presence, and showed a countenance of one of a noble house; he had a goodly thick beard, a broad forehead, crook-nosed, and there appeared such a manly look in his countenance as is commonly seen in Hercules' pictures, stamped or graven in metal. Now it had been a speech of old time that the family of the Antonii were descended from one Anton the son of Hercules, whereof the family took name. This opinion did Antonius seek to confirm in all his doings, not only resembling him in the likeness of his body, as we have said before, but also in the wearing of his garments. For when he would openly show himself abroad before many people, he would always wear his cassock girt down low upon his hips, with a great sword hanging by his side, and upon that some ill-favored cloak. Furthermore, things that seem intolerable in other men, as to boast commonly, to jest with one or other, to drink like a good fellow with everybody, to sit with the soldiers when they dine, and to eat and drink with them soldierlike—it is incredible what wonderful love it won him amongst them. And furthermore, being given to love, that made him the more desired and by that means he brought many to love him. For he would further every man's love, and also would not be angry that men should merrily tell him of those he loved. [1.3.84; 4.3.21–22; 4.12.43–47]

But besides all this, that which most procured his rising and advancement was his liberality, who gave all to the soldiers and kept nothing for himself; and when he was grown to great credit then was

---

[1]*The Lives of the Noble Grecians and Romans Compared Together by That Grave, Learned Philosopher and Historiographer Plutarch of Chaeronea*, trans. out of Greek into French by James Amyot and out of French into English by Thomas North, ed. Roland Baughman, Vol. 7 (New York: The Limited Editions Club, 1941).

his authority and power also very great, the which notwithstanding himself did overthrow by a thousand other faults he had. [**5.2.85ff.**] In this place I will show you one example only of his wonderful liberality. He commanded one day his cofferer that kept his money to give a friend of his twenty-five myriads, which the Romans call in their tongue *Decies*. His cofferer marveling at it and being angry withal in his mind, brought him all this money in a heap together, to show him what a marvelous mass of money it was. Antonius, seeing it as he went by, asked what it was; his cofferer answered him it was the money he willed him to give unto his friend. Then Antonius perceiving the spite of his man, "I thought," said he, "that *Decies* had been a greater sum of money than it is, for this is but a trifle"; and therefore he gave his friend as much more another time, but that was afterwards.

[*Antony as Lieutenant of Julius Cæsar*]

But by this means he got the ill will of the common people, and on the other side, the noblemen (as Cicero saith) did not only mislike him, but also hate him for his naughty life; for they did abhor his banquets and drunken feasts he made at unseasonable times, and his extreme wasteful expenses upon vain light huswives; and then in the daytime he would sleep or walk out his drunkenness, thinking to wear away the fume of the abundance of wine which he had taken overnight. In his house they did nothing but feast, dance, and mask; and himself passed away the time in hearing of foolish plays, or in marrying these players, tumblers, jesters, and such sort of people. As for proof hereof, it is reported that at Hippias' marriage, one of his jesters, he drank wine so lustily all night, that the next morning when he came to plead before the people assembled in council, who had sent for him, he being queasy-stomached with his surfeit he had taken was compelled to lay all before them, and one of his friends held him his gown instead of a basin.

He had another pleasant player called Sergius, that was one of the chiefest men about him, and a woman also called Cytheride, of the same profession, whom he loved dearly; he carried her up and down in a litter unto all the towns he went, and had as many men waiting upon her litter, she being but a player, as were attending upon his own mother. It grieved honest men also very much to see that when he went into the country he carried with him a great number of cupboards full of silver and gold plate, openly in the face of the world, as it had been the pomp or show of some triumph; and that eftsoons in the middest of his journey he would set up his halls and tents hard by some green grove or pleasant river, and there his cooks should prepare him a sumptuous dinner. And furthermore, lions were harnessed in traces to draw his carts; and besides also, in honest men's houses in the cities where he came, he would have common harlots, courtesans, and these tumbling gillots lodged. Now it grieved men much to see that Cæsar should be out of Italy following of his enemies, to end this great war with such great peril and danger; and that others in the meantime, abusing his name and authority, should commit such insolent and out-rageous parts unto their citizens.

This methinks was the cause that made the conspiracy against Cæsar increase more and more, and laid the reins of the bridle upon the soldiers' necks, whereby they durst boldlier commit many extor-tions, cruelties, and robberies. And therefore Cæsar after his return pardoned Dolabella, and being created consul the third time, he took not Antonius, but chose Lepidus his colleague and fellow con-sul. Afterwards when Pompey's house was put to open sale, Anto-nius bought it [2.6.27–29], but when they asked him money for it, he made it very strange and was offended with them, and writeth himself that he would not go with Cæsar into the wars of Africa, because he was not well recompensed for the service he had done him before. Yet Cæsar did somewhat bridle his madness and inso-lency, not suffering him to pass his fault so lightly away, making as though he saw them not. And therefore he left his dissolute manner of life, and married Fulvia, that was Clodius' widow, a woman not so basely minded to spend her time in spinning and housewifery, and was not contented to master her husband at home, but would also rule him in his office abroad, and command him that commanded legions and great armies; so that Cleopatra was to give Fulvia thanks for that she had taught Antonius this obedience to women, that learned so well to be at their commandment.

[After Julius Cæsar's murder; Battle of Philippi]

Now things remaining in this state at Rome, Octavius Cæsar the younger came to Rome, who was the son of Julius Cæsar's niece, as you have heard before, and was left his lawful heir by will, remain-ing, at the time of the death of his great-uncle that was slain, in the city of Apollonia. This young man at his first arrival went to salute

Antonius, as one of his late dead father Cæsar's friends, who by his last will and testament had made him his heir; and withal, he was presently in hand with him for money and other things which were left of trust in his hands, because Cæsar had by will bequeathed unto the people of Rome three score and fifteen silver drachmas to be given to every man, the which he as heir stood charged withal.

Antonius at the first made no reckoning of him, because he was very young; and said he lacked wit and good friends to advise him, if he looked to take such a charge in hand as to undertake to be Cæsar's heir. But when Antonius saw that he could not shake him off with those words, and that he was still in hand with him for his father's goods, but specially for the ready money, then he spoke and did what he could against him. And first of all, it was he that did keep him from being tribune of the people; and also when Octavius Cæsar began to meddle with the dedicating of the chair of gold, which was prepared by the senate to honor Cæsar with, he threatened to send him to prison; and moreover desisted not to put the people in an uproar. This young Cæsar, seeing his doings, went unto Cicero and others, which were Antonius' enemies, and by them crept into favor with the senate; and he himself sought the people's good will every manner of way, gathering together the old soldiers of the late deceased Cæsar, which were dispersed in divers cities and colonies. Antonius, being afraid of it, talked with Octavius in the capitol and became his friend.

But the very same night Antonius had a strange dream, who thought that lightning fell upon him and burnt his right hand. Shortly after word was brought him that Cæsar lay in wait to kill him. Cæsar cleared himself unto him, and told him there was no such matter; but he could not make Antonius believe the contrary. Whereupon they became further enemies than ever they were; insomuch that both of them made friends of either side to gather together all the old soldiers through Italy, that were dispersed in divers towns, and made them large promises, and sought also to win the legions of their side, which were already in arms.

Cicero, on the other side, being at that time the chiefest man of authority and estimation in the city, he stirred up all men against Antonius; so that in the end he made the senate pronounce him an enemy to his country, and appointed young Cæsar sergeants to carry axes before him, and such other signs as were incident to the dignity of a consul or prætor; and moreover sent Hirtius and Pansa, then consuls, to drive Antonius out of Italy. These two consuls together with Cæsar, who also had an army, went against Antonius that beseiged the city of Modena, and there overthrew him in battle, but both the consuls were slain there.

Antonius, flying upon this overthrow, fell into great misery all at once, but the chiefest want of all other, and that pinched him most, was famine. Howbeit, he was of such a strong nature that by patience he would overcome any adversity, and the heavier fortune lay upon him, the more constant showed he himself. Every man that feeleth want or adversity knoweth by virtue and discretion what he should do, but when indeed they are overlaid with extremity and be sore oppressed, few have the hearts to follow that which they praise and commend, and much less to avoid that they reprove and mislike. But rather to the contrary, they yield to their accustomed easy life, and through faint heart and lack of courage, do change their first mind and purpose. And therefore it was a wonderful example to the soldiers, to see Antonius, that was brought up in all fineness and superfluity, so easily to drink puddle water, and to eat wild fruits and roots; and moreover it is reported that even as they passed the Alps, they did eat the bark of trees, and such beasts as man never tasted of their flesh before. [1.4.57–72] . . .

So Octavius Cæsar would not lean to Cicero, when he saw that his whole travail and endeavor was only to restore the commonwealth to her former liberty. Therefore he sent certain of his friends to Antonius, to make them friends again, and thereupon all three met together (to wit, Cæsar, Antonius, and Lepidus) in an island environed round about with a little river, and there remained three days together. Now as touching all other matters, they were easily agreed, and did divide all the empire of Rome between them, as if it had been their own inheritance. But yet they could hardly agree whom they would put to death, for everyone of them would kill their enemies and save their kinsmen and friends. Yet at length, giving place to their greedy desire to be revenged of their enemies, they spurned all reverence of blood and holiness of friendship at their feet. For Cæsar left Cicero to Antonius' will. Antonius also forsook Lucius Cæsar, who was his uncle by his mother, and both of them together suffered Lepidus to kill his own brother Paulus. Yet some writers affirm that Cæsar and Antonius requested Paulus might be slain, and that Lepidus was contented with it. In my opinion there was never a more horrible, unnatural, and crueler change than this was. For thus changing murder for murder, they did as well kill those whom they did forsake and leave unto others, as those also which others left unto them to kill; but so much more was their wickedness and cruelty great unto their friends, for that they put them to death, being innocents, and having no cause to hate them.

After this plot was agreed upon between them; the soldiers that were thereabouts, would have this friendship and league betwixt them confirmed by marriage, and that Cæsar should marry Claudia, the daughter of Fulvia, Antonius' wife. This marriage also being agreed upon, they condemned three hundred of the chiefest citizens of Rome to be put to death by proscription. And Antonius also commanded them to whom he had given commission to kill Cicero, that they should strike off his head and right hand, with the which he had written the invective orations (called *Philippides*) against Antonius. So when the murderers brought him Cicero's head and hand cut off, he beheld them a long time with great joy and laughed heartily, and that oftentimes, for the great joy he felt. Then when he had taken his pleasure of the sight of them, he caused them to be set up in an open place, over the pulpit for orations (where, when he was alive, he had often spoken to the people), as if he had done the dead man hurt, and not blemished his own fortune—showing himself (to his great shame and infamy) a cruel man and unworthy the office and authority he bare. . . .

Now the government of these triumviri grew odious and hateful to the Romans, for divers respects; but they most blamed Antonius, because he, being elder than Cæsar, and of more power and force than Lepidus, gave himself again to his former riot and excess, when he left to deal in the affairs of the commonwealth. But setting aside the ill name he had for his insolency, he was yet much more hated in respect of the house he dwelt in, the which was the house of Pompey the Great—a man as famous for his temperance, modesty, and civil life as for his three triumphs. For it grieved them to see the gates commonly shut against the captains, magistrates of the city, and also ambassadors of strange nations, which were sometimes thrust from the gate with violence, and that the house within was full of tumblers, antic dancers, jugglers, players, jesters and drunkards, quaffing and guzzling; and that on them he spent and bestowed the most part of his money he got by all kind of possible extortions, bribery and policy. For they did not only sell by the crier the goods of those whom they had outlawed and appointed to murder, slanderously deceived the poor widows and young orphans, and also raised all kinds of imposts, subsidies and taxes; but understanding also that the holy Vestal nuns had certain goods and money put in their custody to keep, both of men's in the city, and those also that were abroad, they went thither and took them away by force. Octavius Cæsar perceiving that no money would serve Antonius' turn, he prayed that they might divide the money between them, and so did they also divide the army, for them both to go into Macedon to make war against Brutus and Cassius; and in the meantime they left the government of the city of Rome unto Lepidus.

When they had passed over the seas and that they began to make war, they being both camped by their enemies—to wit, Antonius against Cassius, and Cæsar against Brutus—Cæsar did no great matter, but Antonius had always the upper hand, and did all. For at the first battle Cæsar was overthrown by Brutus and lost his camp, and very hardly saved himself by flying from them that followed him. [3.11.35–40] Howbeit he writeth himself in his *Commentaries*, that he fled before the charge was given, because of a dream one of his friends had. Antonius on the other side overthrew Cassius in battle, though some write that he was not there himself at the battle, but that he came after the overthrow, whilst his men had the enemies in chase. So Cassius at his earnest request was slain by a faithful servant of his own called Pindarus whom he had enfranchised, because he knew not in time that Brutus had overcome Cæsar. Shortly after they fought another battle again, in the which Brutus was overthrown, who afterwards also slew himself.

Thus Antonius had the chiefest glory of all this victory, specially because Cæsar was sick at that time.

[Antony and Cleopatra]

Antonius being thus inclined, the last and extremest mischief of all other (to wit, the love of Cleopatra) lighted on him, who did waken and stir up many vices yet hidden in him, and were never seen to any; and if any spark of goodness or hope of rising were left him, Cleopatra quenched it straight and made it worse than before. The manner how he fell in love with her was this.

Antonius, going to make war with the Parthians, sent to command Cleopatra to appear personally before him when he came into Cilicia, to answer unto such accusations as were laid against her, being this: that she had aided Cassius and Brutus in their war against him. The messenger sent unto Cleopatra to make this summons unto her was called Dellius, who when he had thoroughly considered her beauty, the excellent grace and sweetness of her tongue, he nothing mistrusted that Antonius would do any hurt to so noble a lady, but rather assured himself that within few days she should be in great favor with him. Thereupon he did her great honor and persuaded her to come into Cilicia as honorably furnished as she could possible, and bade her not to be afraid at all of Antonius, for he was a more courteous lord than any that she had ever seen. Cleopatra, on th'other side, believing Dellius' words, and guessing by the former access and credit she had with Julius Cæsar and Gnaeus Pompey (the son of Pompey the Great) [1.5.69–78; 2.5.109; 3.13.118–20] only for her beauty, she began to have good hope that she might more easily win Antonius. For Cæsar and Pompey knew her when she was but a young thing, and knew not then what the world meant; but now she went to Antonius at the age when a woman's beauty is at the prime, and she also of best judgment. So she furnished herself with a world of gifts, store of gold and silver, and of riches and other sumptuous ornaments, as is credible enough she might bring from so great a house and from so wealthy and rich a realm as Egypt was. But yet she carried nothing with her wherein she trusted more than in herself, and in the charms and enchantment of her passing beauty and grace.

Therefore, when she was sent unto by divers letters, both from Antonius himself and also from his friends, she made so light of it and mocked Antonius so much, that she disdained to set forward otherwise but to take her barge in the river of Cydnus, the poop whereof was of gold, the sails of purple, and the oars of silver; which kept stroke in rowing after the sound of the music of flutes, hautboys, citterns, viols, and such other instruments as they played upon in the barge. And now for the person of herself: she was laid under a pavilion of cloth of gold of tissue, apparelled and attired like the goddess Venus commonly drawn in picture; and hard by her, on either hand of her, pretty fair boys, apparelled as painters do set forth god Cupid, with little fans in their hands, with the which they fanned wind upon her. Her ladies and gentlewomen also, the fairest of them were apparelled like the nymphs Nereides (which are the mermaids of the waters) and like the Graces, some steering the helm, others tending the tackle and robes of the barge, out of the which there came a wonderful passing sweet savor of perfumes, that perfumed the wharf's side, pestered with innumerable multitudes of people. Some of them followed the barge all alongst the river's side; others also ran out of the city to see her coming in. So that in th'end there ran such multitudes of people one after another to see her, that Antonius was left post alone in the market place, in his imperial seat to give audience; and there went a rumor in the people's mouths that the goddess Venus was come to play with the god Bacchus for the general good of all Asia. [2.2.195–235]

When Cleopatra landed, Antonius sent to invite her to supper to him. But she sent him word again he should do better rather to come and sup with her. Antonius therefore to show himself courteous unto her at her arrival, was contented to obey her, and went to supper to her; where he found such passing sumptuous fare that no tongue can express it. But amongst all other things, he most wondered at the infinite number of lights and torches hanged on the top of the house, giving light in every place, so artificially set and ordered by devices—some round, some square—that it was the rarest thing to behold that eye could discern or that ever books could mention. The next night, Antonius feasting her, contended to pass her in magnificence and fineness, but she overcame him in both. So that he himself began to scorn the gross service of his house, in respect of Cleopatra's sumptuousness and fineness. And when Cleopatra found Antonius' jests and slents to be but gross and soldierlike in plain manner, she gave it him finely and without fear taunted him thoroughly.

Now her beauty (as it is reported) was not so passing, as unmatchable of other women, nor yet such as upon present view did enamor men with her; but so sweet was her company and conversation that a man could not possibly but be taken. And besides her beauty, the good grace she had to talk and discourse, her courteous nature that tempered her words and deeds, was a spur that pricked to the quick. Furthermore, besides all these, her voice and words were marvelous pleasant; for her tongue was an instrument of music to divers sports and pastimes, the which she easily turned to any language that pleased her. She spoke unto few barbarous people by interpreter, but made them answer herself, or at the least the most part of them; as the Ethiopians, the Arabians, the Troglodytes, the Hebrews, the Syrians, the Medes, and the Parthians, and to many others also, whose languages she had learned. Whereas divers of her progenitors, the kings of Egypt, could scarce learn the Egyptian tongue only, and many of them forgot to speak the Macedonian.

Now Antonius was so ravished with the love of Cleopatra that, though his wife Fulvia had great wars and much ado with Cæsar for his affairs, and that the army of the Parthians (the which the king's lieutenants had given to the only leading of Labienus) was now assembled in Mesopotamia ready to invade Syria, yet, as though all this had nothing touched him, he yielded himself to go with Cleopatra into Alexandria, where he spent and lost in childish sports (as a man might say) and idle pastimes, the most precious thing a man can spend, as Antiphon saith; and that is, time. For they made an order between them, which they called *Amimetobion* (as much to say, no life comparable and matchable with it) one feasting each other by turns, and in cost exceeding all measure and reason.

And for proof hereof I have heard my grandfather Lampryas report that one Philotas, a physician born in the city of Amphissa, told him that he was at that present time in Alexandria, and studied physic; and that, having acquaintance with one of Antonius' cooks, he took him with him to Antonius' house (being a young man desirous to see things) to show him the wonderful sumptuous charge and preparation of one only supper. When he was in the kitchen, and saw a world of diversities of meats—and amongst others, eight wild boars roasted whole—he began to wonder at it, and said, "Sure you have a great number of guests to supper." The cook fell a-laughing and answered him: "No," quoth he, "not many guests, nor above twelve in all; but yet all that is boiled or roasted must be served in whole, or else it would be marred straight. For Antonius peradventure will sup presently, or it may be a pretty while hence, or likely enough he will defer it longer, for that he hath drunk well today, or else hath had some other great matters in hand; and therefore we do not dress one supper only, but many suppers, because we are uncertain of the hour he will sup in." [2.2.188–89] . . .

But now again to Cleopatra. Plato writeth that there are four kinds of flattery, but Cleopatra divided it into many kinds. For she, were it in sport, or in matter of earnest, still devised sundry new delights to have Antonius at commandment, never leaving him night nor day, nor once letting him go out of her sight. For she would play at dice with him, drink with him, and hunt commonly with him, and also be with him when he went to any exercise or activity of body. And sometime also, when he would go up and down the city disguised like a slave in the night, and would peer into poor men's windows and their shops, and scold and brawl with them within the house, Cleopatra would also be in a chambermaid's array, and amble up and down the streets with him, so that oftentimes Antonius bore away both mocks and blows. [1.4.18–21] Now, though most men misliked this manner, yet the Alexandrians were commonly glad of this jollity and liked it well, saying very gallantly and wisely that Antonius showed them a comical face, to wit, a merry countenance, and the Romans a tragical face, to say, a grim look.

But to reckon up all the foolish sports they made, reveling in this sort, it were too fond a part of me, and therefore I will only tell you one among the rest. On a time he went to angle for fish, and when he could take none, he was as angry as he could be, because Cleopatra stood by. Wherefore he secretly commanded the fishermen that, when he cast in his line, they should straight dive under the water and put a fish on his hook which they had taken before; and so snatched up his angling rod and brought up fish twice or thrice. Cleopatra found it straight, yet she seemed not to see it but wondered at his excellent fishing; but when she was alone by herself among her own people, she told them how it was, and bade them the next morning to be on the water to see the fishing. A number of people came to the haven and got into the fisher boats to see this fishing. Antonius then threw in his line and Cleopatra straight commanded one of her men to dive under water before Antonius' men, and to put some old salt fish upon his bait, like unto those that are brought out of the country of Pontus. When he had hung the fish on his hook, Antonius thinking he had taken a fish indeed, snatched up his line presently. Then they all fell a-laughing. Cleopatra laughing also, said unto him, "Leave us (my lord) Egyptians (which dwell in the country of Pharus and Canobus) your angling rod: this is not thy profession; thou must hunt after conquering of realms and countries." [2.5.15–18]

Now Antonius delighting in these fond and childish pastimes, very ill news was brought him from two places. The first from Rome, that his brother Lucius and Fulvia his wife fell out first between themselves, and afterwards fell to open war with Cæsar, and had brought all to nought, that they were both driven to fly out of Italy. [1.2.85–91] The second news, as bad as the first, that Labienus conquered all Asia with the army of the Parthians, from the river of Euphrates and from Syria, unto the countries of Lydia and Ionia. [1.2.97–101] Then began Antonius, with much ado, a little to rouse himself as if he had been wakened out of a deep sleep, and as a man may say, coming out of a great drunkenness.

So, first of all, he bent himself against the Parthians, and went as far as the country of Phœnicia, but there he received lamentable letters from his wife Fulvia. Whereupon he straight returned towards Italy with two hundred sail, and as he went took up his friends by the way that fled out of Italy to come to him. By them he was informed that his wife Fulvia was the only cause of this war, who being of a peevish, crooked, and troublesome nature, had purposely raised this uproar in Italy in hope, thereby to withdraw him from Cleopatra. But by good fortune his wife Fulvia, going to meet with Antonius, sickened by the way and died in the city of Sicyon, and therefore Octavius Cæsar and he were the easilier made friends together. [1.2.116–26] For when Antonius landed in Italy, and that men saw Cæsar asked nothing of him, and that Antonius on the other side laid all the fault and burden on his wife Fulvia, the friends of both parties would not suffer them to unrip any old matters, and to prove or defend who had the wrong or right, and who was the first procurer of this war, fearing to make matters worse between them [2.2.50–104]; but they made them friends together and divided the empire of Rome between them, making the sea Ionium the bounds of their division. For they gave all the provinces eastward unto Antonius, and the countries westward unto Cæsar, and left Africa unto Lepidus; and made a law that they three one after another should make their friends consuls, when they would not be themselves.

This seemed to be a sound counsel, but yet it was to be confirmed with a straiter bond, which fortune offered thus. There was Octavia, the eldest sister of Cæsar—not by one mother, for she came of Ancharia, and Cæsar himself afterwards of Accia. It is reported that he dearly loved his sister Octavia, for indeed she was a noble lady, and left the widow of her first husband Caius Marcellus who died not long before; and it seemed also that Antonius had been widower ever since the death of his wife Fulvia. For he denied not that he kept Cleopatra, but so did he not confess that he had her as his wife, and so with reason he did defend the love he bare unto this Egyptian Cleopatra. Thereupon every man did set forward this marriage, hoping thereby that this lady Octavia, having an excellent grace, wisdom and honesty, joined unto so rare a beauty, that when she were with Antonius (he loving her as so worthy a lady deserveth) she should be a mean to keep good love and amity betwixt her brother and him. So when Cæsar and he made the match between them, they both went to Rome about this marriage, although it was against the law that a widow should be married within ten months after her husband's death. Howbeit the senate dispensed with the law, and so the marriage proceeded accordingly. [2.2.125–61]

Sextus Pompeius at that time kept in Sicily, and so made many an inroad into Italy with a great number of pinnaces and other pirates' ships, of the which were captains two notable pirates, Menas and Menecrates; who so scoured all the sea thereabouts that none durst peep out with a sail. [2.1] Furthermore, Sextus Pompeius had dealt very friendly with Antonius, for he had courteously received his mother when she fled out of Italy with Fulvia, and therefore they thought good to make peace with him. [2.2.162–66] So they met all three together by the mount of Misena upon a hill that runneth far into the sea; Pompey having his ships riding hard by at anchor, and Antonius and Cæsar their armies on the shore side, directly over against him. [2.6.1–56] Now, after they had agreed that Sextus Pompeius should have Sardinia and Sicily, with this condition, that he should rid the sea of all thieves and pirates and make it safe for passengers, and withal that he should send a certain of wheat to Rome, one of them did feast another and drew cuts who should begin. [2.6.60–83]

It was Pompeius' chance to invite them first. [2.7] Whereupon Antonius asked him, "And where shall we sup?" "There," said Pompey, and showed him his admiral galley, which had six banks of oars: "That," said he, "is my father's house they have left me." He spake it to taunt Antonius, because he had his father's house, that was Pompey the Great. [2.7.128] So he cast anchors enough into the sea to make his galley fast, and then built a bridge of wood to convey them to his galley from the head of Mount Misena; and there he welcomed them and made them great cheer. Now in the middest of the feast, when they fell to be merry with Antonius' love unto Cleopatra, Menas the pirate came to Pompey and, whispering in his ear, said unto him: "Shall I cut the cables of the anchors and make thee lord not only of Sicily and Sardinia, but of the whole empire of Rome besides?" Pompey having paused a while upon it, at length answered him: "Thou shouldest have done it and never told it me; but now we must content us with that we have. As for myself, I was never taught to break my faith, nor to be counted as a traitor." [2.7.55–84] The other two also did likewise feast him in their camp, and then he returned into Sicily.

Antonius, after this agreement made, sent Ventidius before into Asia to stay the Parthians, and to keep them they should come no further [2.3.41–43]; and he himself in the meantime, to gratify Cæsar, was contented to be chosen Julius Cæsar's priest and sacrificer, and so they jointly together dispatched all great matters concerning the state of the empire. But in all other manner of sports and exercises, wherein they passed the time away the one with the other, Antonius was ever inferior unto Cæsar and always lost, which grieved him much.

With Antonius there was a soothsayer or astronomer of Egypt that could cast a figure and judge of men's nativities to tell them what should happen to them. He, either to please Cleopatra, or else for that he found it so by his art, told Antonius plainly that his fortune (which of itself was excellent good, and very great) was altogether blemished and obscured by Cæsar's fortune; and therefore he counselled him utterly to leave his company and to get him as far from him as he could. "For thy demon," said he, "(that is to say, the good angel and spirit that keepeth thee) is afraid of his, and being courageous and high when he is alone, becometh fearful and timorous when he cometh near unto the other." Howsoever it was, the events ensuing proved the Egyptian's words true. For it is said that as often as they two drew cuts for pastime, who should have any thing, or whether they played at dice, Antonius alway lost. Oftentimes when they were disposed to see cockfight, or quails that were taught to fight one with another, Cæsar's cocks or quails did overcome. The which spited Antonius in his mind, although he made no outward show of it; and therefore he believed the Egyptian the better. [2.3.10–41]

In fine, he recommended the affairs of his house unto Cæsar, and went out of Italy with Octavia his wife, whom he carried into Greece, after he had had a daughter by her. So, Antonius lying all the winter at Athens, news came unto him of the victories of Ventidius, who had overcome the Parthians in battle, in the which also were slain Labienus and Pharnabates, the chiefest captain King Orodes had. For these good news he feasted all Athens, and kept open house for all the Grecians, and many games of price were played at Athens, of the which he himself would be judge. Wherefore, leaving his guard, his axes, and tokens of his empire at his house, he came into the show place (or lists) where these games were played, in a long gown and slippers after the Grecian fashion, and they carried tipstaves, as marshals' men do carry before the judges to make place; and he himself in person was a stickler to part the young men when they had fought enough.

After that, preparing to go to the wars, he made him a garland of the holy olive and carried a vessel with him of the water of the fountain Clepsydra, because of an oracle he had received that so commanded him. In the meantime, Ventidius once again overcame Pacorus (Orodes' son, king of Parthia) in a battle fought in the country of Cyrrestica, he being come again with a great army to invade Syria; at which battle was slain a great number of the Parthians, and among them Pacorus, the king's own son slain. [3.1] This noble exploit, as famous as ever any was, was a full revenge to the Romans of the shame and loss they had received before by the death of Marcus Crassus; and he made the Parthians fly, and glad to keep themselves within the confines and territories of Mesopotamia, and Media, after they had thrice together been overcome in several battles.

Howbeit Ventidius durst not undertake to follow them any further, fearing lest he should have gotten Antonius' displeasure by it. Notwithstanding, he led his army against them that had rebelled, and conquered them again; amongst whom he besieged Antiochus, king of Commagena, who offered him to give a thousand talents to be pardoned his rebellion, and promised ever to be at Antonius' commandment. But Ventidius made him answer that he should send unto Antonius, who was not far off, and would not suffer Ventidius to make any peace with Antiochus, to the end that yet this little exploit should pass in his name, and that they should not think he did anything but by his lieutenant Ventidius. The siege grew very long, because they that were in the town, seeing they could not be received upon no reasonable composition, determined valiantly to defend themselves to the last man. Thus Antonius did nothing and yet received great shame, repenting him much that he took not their first offer. And yet at last he was glad to make truce with Antiochus, and to take three hundred talents for composition. Thus after he had set order for the state and affairs of Syria, he returned again to Athens, and having given Ventidius such honors as he deserved, he sent him to Rome to triumph for the Parthians.

Ventidius was the only man that ever triumphed of the Parthians until this present day, a mean man born and of no noble house nor family; who only came to that he attained unto through Antonius' friendship, the which delivered him happy occasion to achieve to great matters. And yet to say truly, he did so well quit himself in all his enterprises, that he confirmed that which was spoken of Antonius and Cæsar: to wit, that they were alway more fortunate when they made war by their lieutenants, than by themselves. For Sossius, one of Antonius' lieutenants in Syria, did notable good service; and Canidius whom he had also left his lieutenant in the borders of Armenia, did conquer it all. So did he also overcome the kings of the Iberians and Albanians, and went on with his conquests unto Mount Caucasus. By these conquests, the fame of Antonius' power increased more and more, and grew dreadful unto all the barbarous nations.

But Antonius, notwithstanding, grew to be marvelously offended with Cæsar, upon certain reports that had been brought unto him; and so took sea to go towards Italy with three hundred sail. And because those of Brundusium would not receive his army into their haven, he went further unto Tarentum. There his wife Octavia, that came out of Greece with him, besought him to send her unto her brother, the which he did. [3.4.10–38] Octavia at that time was great with child, and moreover had a second daughter by him, and yet she put herself in journey and met with her brother Octavius Cæsar by the way, who brought his two chief friends, Mæcenas and Agrippa, with him. She took them aside and with all the instance she could possible, entreated them they would not suffer her that was the happiest woman of the world, to become now the most wretched and unfortunatest creature of all other. "For now," said she, "every man's eye doth gaze on me, that am the sister of one of the Emperors and wife of the other. And if the worse counsel take place (which the gods forbid) and that they grow to wars, for yourselves it is uncertain to which of them two the gods have assigned the victory or overthrow. But for me, on which side soever victory fall, my state can be but most miserable still. [3.4.12–20]

These words of Octavia so softened Cæsar's heart, that he went quickly unto Tarentum. But it was a noble sight for them that were present to see so great an army by land, and so many ships afloat in the road, quietly and safe, and furthermore the meeting and kindness of friends lovingly embracing one another. First, Antonius feasted Cæsar, which he granted unto for his sister's sake. Afterwards they agreed together that Cæsar should give Antoniuis two legions to go against the Parthians, and that Antonius should let Cæsar have a hundred galleys armed with brazen spurs at the prows. Besides all this, Octavia obtained of her husband twenty brigantines for her brother, and of her brother for her husband, a thousand armed men. After they had taken leave of each other, Cæsar went immediately to make war with Sextus Pompeius, to get Sicily into his hands. Antonius also, leaving his wife Octavia and little children begotten of her with Cæsar, and his other children which he had by Fulvia, he went directly into Asia.

Then began this pestilent plague and mischief of Cleopatra's love (which had slept a long time, and seemed to have been utterly forgotten, and that Antonius had given place to better counsel) again to kindle and to be in force, so soon as Antonius came near unto Syria. And in the end, the horse of the mind, as Plato termeth it, that is so hard of rein (I mean the unreined lust of concupiscence) did put out of Antonius' head all honest and commendable thoughts, for he sent Fonteius Capito to bring Cleopatra into Syria. Unto whom, to welcome her, he gave no trifling things, but unto those that she had already, he added the provinces of Phœnicia, those of the nethermost Syria, the Isle of Cyprus and a great part of Cilicia, and that country of Jewry where the true balm is, and that part of Arabia where the Nabathæians do dwell, which stretcheth out towards the ocean. These great gifts much misliked the Romans. But now, though Antonius did easily give away great seigniories, realms, and mighty nations unto some private men, and that also he took from other kings their lawful realms (as from Antigonus, king of the Jews, whom he openly beheaded, where never king before had suffered like death), yet all this did not so much offend the Romans, as the unmeasurable honors which he did unto Cleopatra.

But yet he did much more aggravate their malice and ill will towards him, because that Cleopatra having brought him two twins, a son and a daughter, he named his son Alexander, and his daughter Cleopatra, and gave them to their surnames, the sun to the one, and the moon to the other. This notwithstanding, he, that could finely cloak his shameful deeds with fine words, said that the greatness and magnificence of the empire of Rome appeared most, not where the Romans took, but where they gave much; and nobility was multiplied amongst men by the posterity of kings, when they left of their seed in divers places; and that by this means his first ancestor was begotten of Hercules, who had not left the hope and continuance of his line and posterity in the womb of one only woman, fearing Solon's laws, or regarding the ordinances of men touching the procreation of children; but that he gave it unto nature, and established the foundation of many noble races and families in divers places.

[Antony Wages War in Parthia (Omitted)]
[The Run-up to Actium]

Now whilst Antonius was busy in this preparation, Octavia his wife, whom he had left at Rome, would needs take sea to come unto him. Her brother Octavius Cæsar was willing unto it, not for his respect at all (as most authors do report) as for that he might have an honest color to make war with Antonius if he did misuse her, and not esteem of her as she ought to be. [2.6.113–28] But when she was come to Athens, she received letters from Antonius, willing her to stay there until his coming, and did advertise her of his journey and determination. The which though it grieved her much, and that she knew it was but an excuse, yet by her letters to him of answer, she asked him whether he would have those things sent unto him which she had brought him, being great store of apparel for soldiers, a great number of horse, sum of money and gifts to bestow on his friends and captains he had about him; and besides all those, she had two thousand soldiers, chosen men, all well armed, like unto the prætors' bands.

When Niger, one of Antonius' friends whom he had sent unto Athens, had brought these news from his wife Octavia, and withal did greatly praise her as she was worthy and well deserved; Cleopatra knowing that Octavia would have Antonius from her, and fearing also that if with her virtue and honest behavior (besides the great power of her brother Cæsar) she did add thereunto her modest kind love to please her husband, that she would then be too strong for her and in the end win him away, she subtly seemed to languish for the love of Antonius, pining her body for lack of meat. Furthermore, she every way so framed her countenance that, when Antonius came to see her, she cast her eyes upon him like a woman ravished for joy. Straight again when he went from her, she fell a-weeping and blubbering, looking ruefully of the matter, and still found the means that Antonius should oftentimes find her weeping; and then, when he came suddenly upon her, she made as though she dried her eyes, and turned her face away, as if she were unwilling that he should see her weep. All these tricks she used, Antonius being in readiness to go into Syria to speak with the king of Medes.

Then the flatterers that furthered Cleopatra's mind blamed Antonius, and told him that he was a hard-natured man, and that he had small love in him, that would see a poor lady in such torment for his sake, whose life depended only upon him alone.

"For, Octavia," said they, "that was married unto him as it were of necessity because her brother Cæsar's affairs so required it, hath the honor to be called Antonius' lawful spouse and wife [2.6.128–29]; and Cleopatra, being born a queen of so many thousands of men, is only named Antonius' leman, and yet that she disdained not so to be called, if it might please him she might enjoy his company and live with him; but if he once leave her, that then it is unpossible she should live." To be short, by these their flatteries and enticements, they so wrought Antonius' effeminate mind, that, fearing lest she should make herself away, he returned again unto Alexandria, and referred the king of Medes to the next year following, although he received news that the Parthians at that time were at civil wars among themselves. This notwithstanding, he went afterwards and made peace with him. For he married his daughter which was very young unto one of the sons that Cleopatra had by him, and then returned, being fully bent to make war with Cæsar.

When Octavia was returned to Rome from Athens Cæsar commanded her to go out of Antonius' house and to dwell by herself, because he had abused her. Octavia answered him again that she would not forsake her husband's house, and that, if he had no other occasion to make war with him, she prayed him then to take no thought for her. "For," said she, "it were too shameful a thing, that two so famous captains should bring in civil wars among the Romans, the one for the love of a woman, and the other for the jealousy betwixt one another." Now as she spake the word, so did she also perform the deed. For she kept still in Antonius' house, as if he had been there, and very honestly and honorably kept his children, not those only she had by him, but the other which her husband had by Fulvia. Furthermore, when Antonius sent any of his men to Rome to sue for any office in the commonwealth, she received him very courteously, and so used herself unto her brother that she obtained the thing she requested.

Howbeit, thereby, thinking no hurt, she did Antonius great hurt. For her honest love and regard to her husband made every man hate him, when they saw he did so unkindly use so noble a lady [3.6.89–100]: but yet the greatest cause of their malice unto him was for the division of lands he made amongst his children in the city of Alexandria. [3.6.1–19] And to confess a truth, it was too arrogant and insolent a part, and done (as a man would say) in derision and contempt of the Romans. For he assembled all the people in the show place where young men do exercise themselves, and there, upon a high tribunal silvered, he set two chairs of gold, the one for himself and the other for Cleopatra, and lower chairs for his children; then he openly published before the assembly that first of all he did establish Cleopatra queen of Egypt, of Cyprus, of Lydia, and of the lower Syria, and at that time also, Cæsarion king of the same realms. This Cæsarion was supposed to be the son of Julius Cæsar, who had left Cleopatra great with child.

Secondly, he called the sons he had by her the kings of kings, and gave Alexander for his portion Armenia, Media, and Parthia, when he had conquered the country; and unto Ptolemy for his portion Phœnicia, Syria, and Cilicia. And therewithal he brought out Alexander in a long gown after the fashion of the Medes, with a high copped tank hat on his head, narrow in the top, as the kings of the Medes and Armenians do use to wear them; and Ptolemy appeared in a cloak after the Macedonian manner, with slippers on his feet, and a broad hat, with a royal band or diadem. Such was the apparel and old attire of the ancient kings and successors of Alexander the Great. So, after his sons had done their humble duties and kissed their father and mother, presently a company of Armenian soldiers, set there of purpose, compassed the one about, and a like company of Macedonians the other. Now for Cleopatra, she did not only wear at that time, but at all other times else when she came abroad, the apparel of the goddess Isis, and so gave audience unto all her subjects as a new Isis.

Octavius Cæsar reporting all these things unto the senate, and oftentimes accusing him to the whole people and assembly in Rome, he thereby stirred up all the Romans against him. Antonius on th'other side sent to Rome likewise to accuse him, and the chiefest points of his accusations he charged him with, were these. First, that having spoiled Sextus Pompeius in Sicily, he did not give him his part of the isle. Secondly, that he did detain in his hands the ships he lent him to make that war. Thirdly, that having put Lepidus their companion and triumvirate out of his part of the empire, and having deprived him of all honors, he retained for himself the lands and revenues thereof, which had been assigned unto him for his part. And last of all, that he had in manner divided all Italy amongst his own soldiers, and had left no part of it for his soldiers. [3.6.23–31]

Octavius Cæsar answered him again that, for Lepidus, he had indeed deposed him and taken his part of the empire from him, because he did over-cruelly use his authority. And secondly, for the conquests he had made by force of arms, he was contented Antonius should have his part of Armenia. And thirdly, that, for his soldiers, they should seek for nothing in Italy because they possessed Media and Parthia, the which provinces they had added to the empire of Rome, valiantly fighting with their Emperor and captain. [3.6.32–39]

Antonius hearing these news, being yet in Armenia, commanded Canidius to go presently to the seaside with his sixteen legions he had, and he himself with Cleopatra went unto the city of Ephesus, and there gathered together his galleys and ships out of all parts, which came to the number of eight hundred, reckoning the great ships of burden; and of those Cleopatra furnished him with two hundred, and twenty thousand talents besides, and provision of victuals also to maintain all the whole army in this war. [3.7.1–19] So Antonius through the persuasions of Domitius, commanded Cleopatra to return again into Egypt, and there to understand the success of this war. But Cleopatra fearing lest Antonius should again be made friends with Octavius Cæsar by means of his wife Octavia, she so plied Canidius with money and filled his purse, that he became her spokesman unto Antonius, and told him there was no reason to send her from this war, who defrayed so great a charge; neither that it was for his profit, because that thereby the Egyptians would then be utterly discouraged, which were the chiefest strength of the army by sea; considering that he could see no king of all the kings their confederates that Cleopatra was inferior unto, either for wisdom or judgment, seeing that long before she had wisely governed so great a realm as Egypt, and besides that she had been so long acquainted with him, by whom she had learned to manage great affairs.

These fair persuasions won him, for it was predestined that the government of all the world should fall into Octavius Cæsar's hands. Thus, all their forces being joined together, they hoist sail towards the Isle of Samos, and there gave themselves to feasts and solace. For as all the kings, princes, and commonalties, peoples and cities from Syria unto the marshes Mæotides, and from the Armenians to the Illyrians, were sent unto to send and bring all munition and warlike preparation they could; even so all players, minstrels, tumblers, fools and jesters, were commanded to assemble in the Isle of Samos. So that, where in manner all the world in every place was full of lamentations, sighs and tears, only in this Isle of Samos there was nothing for many days' space but singing and piping, and all the theatre full of these common players, minstrels and singing men. Besides all this, every city sent an ox thither to sacrifice, and kings did strive one with another who should make the noblest feasts and give the richest gifts. So that every man said, "What can they do more for joy of victory, if they win the battle, when they make already such sumptuous feasts at the beginning of the war?"

When this was done, he gave the whole rabble of these minstrels, and such kind of people, the city of Priene to keep them withal during this war. Then he went unto the city of Athens, and there gave himself again to see plays and pastimes and to keep the theatres. Cleopatra, on the other side, being jealous of the honors which Octavia had received in this city, where indeed she was marvelously honored and beloved of the Athenians, to win the people's good will also at Athens, she gave them great gifts, and they likewise gave her many great honors and appointed certain ambassadors to carry the decree to her house; among the which Antonius was one, who as a citizen of Athens reported the matter unto her, and made an oration in the behalf of the city. Afterwards he sent to Rome to put his wife Octavia out of his house, who (as it is reported) went out of his house with all Antonius' children, saving the eldest of them he had by Fulvia, who was with her father, bewailing and lamenting her cursed hap that had brought her to this, that she was accounted one of the chiefest causes of this civil war. The Romans did pity her, but much more Antonius, and those specially that had seen Cleopatra, who neither exceeded Octavia in beauty, nor yet in young years.

Octavius Cæsar understanding the sudden and wonderful great preparation of Antonius, he was not a little astonied at it (fearing he should be driven to fight that summer) because he wanted many things, and the great and grievous exactions of money did sorely oppress the people. [2.1.13–14] For all manner of men else, were driven to pay the fourth part of their goods and revenue, but the Libertines (to wit, those whose fathers or other predecessors had sometime been bondmen), they were sessed to pay the eighth part of all their goods at one payment. Hereupon there rose a wonderful exclamation and great uproar all Italy over, so that among the greatest faults that ever Antonius committed, they blamed him most for that he delayed to give Cæsar battle. For he gave Cæsar leisure to make his preparations, and also to appease the complaints of the people. When such a great sum of money was demanded of them, they grudged at it and grew to mutiny upon it, but when they had once paid it, they remembered it no more.

[*Actium*]

Now after Cæsar had made sufficient preparation, he proclaimed open war against Cleopatra, and made the people to abolish the power and empire of Antonius, because he had before given it up unto a woman. And Cæsar said furthermore, that Antonius was not master of himself, but that Cleopatra had brought him beside himself by her charms and amorous poisons, and that they that should make war with them should be Mardian the eunuch, Photinus, and Iras, a woman of Cleopatra's bed chamber that frizzled her hair and dressed her head, and Charmion; the which were those that ruled all the affairs of Antonius' empire. . . .

Now Antonius was made so subject to a woman's will that, though he was a great deal stronger by land, yet for Cleopatra's sake, he would needs have this battle tried by sea [3.7.27–54]; though he saw before his eyes that, for lack of watermen, his captains did press by force all sorts of men out of Greece that they could take up in the field—as travelers, muleteers, reapers, harvest men, and young boys; and yet could they not sufficiently furnish his galleys, so that the most part of them were empty, and could scant row, because they lacked watermen enow. But on the contrary side, Cæsar's ships were not built for pomp, high and great, only for a sight and bravery; but they were light of yarage, armed, and furnished with watermen as many as they needed, and had them all in readiness in the havens of Tarentum, and Brundusium.

So Octavius sent unto Antonius to will him to delay no more time, but to come on with his army into Italy, and that for his own part he would give him safe harbor, and that he would withdraw his army from the sea as far as one horse could run, until he had put his army ashore and had lodged his men. Antonius on the other side bravely sent him word again, and challenged the combat of him man to man, though he were the elder; and that if he refused him so, he would then fight a battle with him in the fields of Pharsalia, as Julius Cæsar and Pompey had done before. [3.7.31–35] Now whilst Antonius rode at anchor, lying idly in harbor at the head of Actium, in the place where the city of Nicopolis standeth at this present, Cæsar had quickly passed the sea Ionium and taken a place called Toryne, before Antonius understood that he had taken ship. Then began his men to be afraid, because his army by land was left behind. But Cleopatra making light of it; "And what danger, I pray you," said she, "if Cæsar keep at Toryne?"

The next morning by break of day, his enemies coming with full force of oars in battle against him, Antonius was afraid that, if they came to join, they would take and carry away his ships that had no men of war in them. So he armed all his watermen and set them in order of battle upon the forecastle of their ships, and then lift up all his ranks of oars towards the element, as well of the one side as the other, with the prows against the enemies, at the entry and mouth of the gulf which beginneth at the point of Actium; and so kept them in order of battle, as if they had been armed and furnished with watermen and soldiers. Thus Octavius Cæsar being finely deceived by this stratagem, retired presently, and therewithal Antonius very wisely and suddenly did cut him off from fresh water. For, understanding that the places where Octavius Cæsar landed had very little store of water, and yet very bad, he shut them in with strong ditches and trenches he cast, to keep them from sailing out at their pleasure, and so to go seek water further off. Furthermore he dealt very friendly and courteously with Domitius, and against Cleopatra's mind. For he being sick of an ague, when he went and took a little boat to go to Cæsar's camp, Antonius was very sorry for it, but yet he sent after him all his carriage, train, and men; and the same Domitius, as though he gave him to understand that he repented his open treason, he died immediately after. [3.13.198–204; 4.5; 4.6.20–40; 4.9]

There were certain kings also that forsook him, and turned on Cæsar's side, as Amyntas and Deiotarus. Furthermore, his fleet and navy that was unfortunate in all things and unready for service, compelled him to change his mind, and to hazard battle by land. And Canidius also, who had charge of his army by land, when time came to follow Antonius' determination, he turned him clean contrary and counselled him to send Cleopatra back again and himself to retire into Macedon, to fight there on the mainland. And furthermore told him that Dicomes, king of the Getes, promised him to aid him with a great power; and that it should be no shame nor dishonor to let Cæsar have the sea (because himself and his men both had been well practised and exercised in battles by sea, in the war of Sicily against Sextus Pompeius), but rather that he should do against all reason—he having so great skill and experience of battles by land as he had—if he should not employ the force and valiantness of so many lusty armed footmen as he had ready, but would weaken his army by dividing them into ships.

But now, notwithstanding all these good persuasions, Cleopatra forced him to put all to the hazard of battle by sea, considering with herself how she might fly and provide for her safety, not to help him to win the victory, but to fly more easily after the battle lost. Betwixt Antonius' camp and his fleet of ships, there was a great high point of firm land that ran a good way into the sea, the which Antonius often used for a walk, without mistrust of fear or danger. One of Cæsar's men perceived it, and told his master that he would laugh and they could take up Antonius in the middest of his walk. Thereupon Cæsar sent some of his men to lie in ambush for him, and they missed not much of taking of him (for they took him that came before him), because they discovered too soon, and so Antonius scaped very hardly.

So when Antonius had determined to fight by sea, he set all the other ships afire but three score ships of Egypt, and reserved only but the best and greatest galleys, from three banks unto ten banks of oars. Into them he put two and twenty thousand fighting men, with two thousand darters and slingers. Now, as he was setting his men in order of battle, there was a captain and a valiant man, that had served Antonius in many battles and conflicts, and had all his body hacked and cut, who, as Antonius passed by, cried out unto him and said, "O noble Emperor, how cometh it to pass that you trust to these vile brittle ships? What, do you mistrust these wounds of mine, and by this sword? Let the Egyptians and Phœnicians fight by sea, and set us on the mainland, where we use to conquer or to be slain on our feet." Antonius passed by him and said never a word, but only beckoned to him with his hand and head, as though he willed him to be of good courage, although indeed he had no great courage himself. For when the masters of the galleys and pilots would have let their sails alone, he made them clap them on, saying—to color the matter withal—that not one of his enemies should scape. [3.7.61–67] . . .

When the skirmish began, and that they came to join, there was no great hurt at the first meeting, neither did the ships hit vehemently one against the other, as they do commonly in fight by sea. For on the one side, Antonius' ships for their heaviness could not have the strength and swiftness to make their blows of any force; and Cæsar's ships on th'other side took great heed not to rush and shock with the forecastles of Antonius' ships, whose prows were armed with great brazen spurs. Furthermore they durst not flank them, because their points were easily broken which way soever they came to set upon his ships—that were made of great main square pieces of timber, bound together with great iron pins—so that the battle was much like to a battle by land, or to speak more properly, to the assault of a city. For there were always three or four of Cæsar's ships about one of Antonius' ships, and the soldiers fought with their pikes, halberds, and darts, and threw pots and darts with fire. Antonius' ships on the other side bestowed among them, with their crossbows and engines of battery, great store of shot from their high towers of wood that were upon their ships.

Now Publicola seeing Agrippa put forth his left wing of Cæsar's army, to compass in Antonius' ships that fought, he was driven also to loose off to have more room, and, going a little at one side, to put those further off that were afraid, and in the middest of the battle. For they were sore distressed by Aruntius. Howbeit the battle was yet of even hand and the victory doubtful, being indifferent to both, when suddenly they saw the three score ships of Cleopatra busy about their yard masts and hoisting sails to fly. So they fled through the middest of them that were in fight, for they had been placed behind the great ships, and did marvelously disorder the other ships. For the enemies themselves wondered much to see them sail in that sort, with full sail towards Peloponnesus.

There Antonius showed plainly that he had not only lost the courage and heart of an emperor, but also of a valiant man, and that he was not his own man (proving that true which an old man spoke in mirth, that the soul of a lover lived in another body, and not in his own); he was so carried away with the vain love of this woman, as if he had been glued unto her, and that she could not have removed without moving of him also. For when he saw Cleopatra's ship under sail, he forgot, forsook, and betrayed them that fought for him, and embarked upon a galley with five banks of oars, to follow her that had already begun to overthrow him, and would in the end be his utter destruction. When she knew this galley afar off, she lift up a sign in the poop of her ship and so Antonius coming to it, was plucked up where Cleopatra was, howbeit he saw her not at his first coming, nor she him, but went and sat down in the prow of his ship and said never a word, clapping his head between his hands. [3.10.1–24] . . .

Then began there again a great number of merchants' ships to gather about them, and some of their friends that had escaped from this overthrow, who brought news that his army by sea was overthrown, but that they thought the army by land was yet whole. Then Antonius sent unto Canidius to return with his army into

Asia, by Macedon. Now for himself, he determined to cross over into Africa, and took one of his carracks or hulks, laden with gold and silver and other rich carriage, and gave it unto his friends; commanding them to depart and to seek to save themselves. They answered him, weeping, that they would neither do it, nor yet forsake him. [3.11.4–24] Then Antonius very courteously and lovingly did comfort them and prayed them to depart; and wrote unto Theophilus, governor of Corinth, that he would see them safe, and help to hide them in some secret place until they had made their way and peace with Cæsar. This Theophilus was the father of Hipparchus, who was had in great estimation about Antonius. He was the first of all his enfranchised bondmen that revolted from him and yielded unto Cæsar, and afterwards went and dwelt at Corinth.

And thus it stood with Antonius. Now for his army by sea, that fought before the head or foreland of Actium, they held out a long time, and nothing troubled them more than a great boisterous wind that rose full in the prows of their ships; and yet with much ado, his navy was at length overthrown, five hours within night. There were not slain above five thousand men, but yet there were three hundred ships taken, as Octavius Cæsar writeth himself in his *Commentaries*. Many plainly saw Antonius fly and yet could hardly believe it—that he, that had nineteen legions whole by land and twelve thousand horsemen upon the seaside, would so have forsaken them and have fled so cowardly, as if he had not oftentimes proved both the one and the other fortune, and that he had not been thoroughly acquainted with the divers changes and fortunes of battles. And yet his soldiers still wished for him, and ever hoped that he would come by some means or other unto them. Furthermore, they showed themselves so valiant and faithful unto him, that after they certainly knew he was fled, they kept themselves whole together seven days. In the end, Canidius, Antonius' lieutenant, flying by night and forsaking his camp, when they saw themselves thus destitute of their heads and leaders, they yielded themselves unto the stronger. [3.10.24–34]

[Alexandria]

Antonius, he forsook the city and company of his friends, and built him a house in the sea, by the Isle of Pharos, upon certain forced mounts which he caused to be cast into the sea, and dwelt there as a man that banished himself from all men's company; saying that he would lead Timon's life, because he had the like wrong offered him that was afore offered unto Timon, and that for the unthankfulness of those he had done good unto, and whom he took to be his friends, he was angry with all men, and would trust no man. . . . Canidius himself came to bring him news that he had lost all his army by land at Actium. On th'other side, he was advertised also that Herodes king of Jewry, who had also certain legions and bands with him, was revolted unto Cæsar and all the other kings in like manner; so that, saving those that were about him, he had none left him. All this notwithstanding did nothing trouble him, and it seemed that he was contented to forego all his hope and so to be rid of all his care and troubles. Thereupon he left his solitary house he had built in the sea, which he called Timoneon, and Cleopatra received him into her royal palace. He was no sooner come thither, but he straight set all the city of rioting and banqueting again, and himself to liberality and gifts. He caused the son of Julius Cæsar and Cleopatra to be enrolled (according to the manner of the Romans) amongst the number of young men; and gave Antyllus, his eldest son he had by Fulvia, the man's gown, the which was a plain gown without guard or embroidery of purple.

For these things there was kept great feasting, banqueting, and dancing in Alexandria many days together. Indeed, they did break their first order they had set down, which they called *Amimetobion* (as much to say, no life comparable), and did set up another, which they called *Synapothanumenon* (signifying the order and agreement of those that will die together), the which in exceeding sumptuousness and cost was not inferior to the first. For their friends made themselves to be enrolled in this order of those that would die together, and so made great feasts one to another; for every man, when it came to his turn, feasted their whole company and fraternity.

Cleopatra in the meantime was very careful in gathering all sorts of poisons together to destroy men. [5.2.351–53] Now, to make proof of those poisons which made men die with least pain, she tried it upon condemned men in prison. For when she saw the poisons that were sudden and vehement, and brought speedy death with grievous torments, and, in contrary manner, that such as were more mild and gentle had not that quick speed and force to make one die suddenly, she afterwards went about to prove the stinging of snakes and adders, and made some to be applied unto men in her sight, some in one sort and some in another. So when she had daily made divers and sundry proofs, she found none of all them she had proved so fit as the biting of an aspic; the which only causeth a heaviness of the head, without swounding or complaining, and bringeth a great desire also to sleep, with a little sweat in the face, and so by little and little taketh away the senses and vital powers, no living creature perceiving that the patients feel any pain. For they are so sorry when anybody waketh them and taketh them up, as those that being taken out of a sound sleep are very heavy and desirous to sleep.

This notwithstanding, they sent ambassadors unto Octavius Cæsar in Asia, Cleopatra requesting the realm of Egypt for her children, and Antonius praying that he might be suffered to live at Athens like a private man, if Cæsar would not let him remain in Egypt. And, because they had no other men of estimation about them, for that some were fled and those that remained they did not greatly trust them, they were enforced to send Euphronius, the schoolmaster of their children. [3.12.1–19] For Alexas Laodician, who was brought into Antonius' house and favor by Timagenes, and afterwards was in greater credit with him than any other Grecian (for that he had alway been one of Cleopatra's ministers to win Antonius, and to overthrow all his good determinations to use his wife Octavia well), him Antonius had sent unto Herodes king of Jewry, hoping still to keep him his friend, that he should not revolt from him. But he remained there, and betrayed Antonius. For where he should have kept Herodes from revolting from him, he persuaded him to turn to Cæsar; and trusting King Herodes, he presumed to come in Cæsar's presence. Howbeit Herodes did him no pleasure; for he was presently taken prisoner and sent in chains to his own country, and there by Cæsar's commandment put to death. Thus was Alexas in Antonius' lifetime put to death for betraying of him. [4.6.12–16]

Furthermore, Cæsar would not grant unto Antonius' requests; but for Cleopatra, he made her answer that he would deny her nothing reasonable, so that she would either put Antonius to death or drive him out of her country. [3.12.19–24; 3.13.15–19] Therewithal he sent Thyreus one of his men unto her, a very wise and discreet man, who, bringing letters of credit from a great lord unto a noble lady, and that besides greatly liked her beauty, might easily by his eloquence have persuaded her. He was longer in talk with her than any man else was, and the queen herself also did him great honor; insomuch as he made Antonius jealous of him. Whereupon Antonius caused him to be taken and well-favoredly whipped, and so sent him unto Cæsar; and bade him tell him that he made him angry with him, because he showed himself proud and disdainful towards him, and now specially when he was easy to be angered, by reason of his present misery. "To be short, if this mislike thee," said he, "thou hast Hipparchus one of my enfranchised bondmen with thee; hang him if thou wilt, or whip him at thy pleasure, that we may cry quittance." [3.12.26–36; 3.13.46–155]

From thenceforth Cleopatra, to clear herself of the suspicion he had of her, she made more of him than ever she did. For first of all, where she did solemnize the day of her birth very meanly and sparingly, fit for her present misfortune, she now in contrary manner did keep it with such solemnity that she exceeded all measure of sumptuousness and magnificence; so that the guests that were bidden to the feasts and came poor, went away rich. [3.13.158–90]

Now, things passing thus, Agrippa by divers letters sent one after another unto Cæsar, prayed him to return to Rome, because the affairs there did of necessity require his person and presence. Thereupon he did defer the war till the next year following; but when winter was done he returned again through Syria by the coast of Africa, to make wars against Antonius, and his other captains. When the city of Pelusium was taken, there ran a rumor in the city that Seleucus, by Cleopatra's consent, had surrendered the same. But to clear herself that she did not, Cleopatra brought Seleucus' wife and children unto Antonius, to be revenged of them at his pleasure. Furthermore, Cleopatra had long before made many sumptuous tombs and monuments, as well for excellency of workmanship as for height and greatness of building, joining hard to the temple of Isis. Thither she caused to be brought all the treasure and precious things she had of the ancient kings her predecessors; as gold, silver, emeralds, pearls, ebony, ivory, and cinnamon, and besides all that a marvelous number of torches, faggots, and flax. So Octavius Cæsar being afraid to lose such a treasure and mass of riches, and that this woman for spite would set it afire and burn it every whit, he always sent some one or other unto her from him, to put her in good comfort, whilst he in the meantime drew near the city with his army.

So Cæsar came and pitched his camp hard by the city, in the place where they run and manage their horses. Antonius made a sally upon him, and fought very valiantly, so that he drave Cæsar's horsemen back, fighting with his men even into their camp. [4.7] Then he came again to the palace, greatly boasting of this victory, and sweetly kissed Cleopatra, armed as he was when he came from the fight, recommending one of his men of arms unto her that had valiantly fought in this skirmish. Cleopatra to reward his manliness gave him an armor and headpiece of clean gold; howbeit the man at arms, when he had received this rich gift, stale away by night, and went to Cæsar. [4.8]

Antonius sent again to challenge Cæsar to fight with him hand to hand. [3.13.20–28] Cæsar answered him that he had many other ways to die than so. [4.1.1–6] Then Antonius, seeing there was no way more honorable for him to die than fighting valiantly, he determined to set up his rest, both by sea and land. [4.2.5–8] So, being at supper (as it is reported), he commanded his officers and household servants that waited on him at his board, that they should fill his cups full and make as much of him as they could; "For," said he, "you know not whether you shall do so much for me tomorrow, or not, or whether you shall serve another master; and it may be you shall see me no more, but a dead body." This notwithstanding, perceiving that his friends and men fell a-weeping to hear him say so, to salve that he had spoken, he added this more unto it, that he would not lead them to battle where he thought not rather safely to return with victory, than valiantly to die with honor. [4.2.10–46]

Furthermore, the selfsame night within little of midnight, when all the city was quiet, full of fear and sorrow, thinking what would be the issue and end of this war; it is said that suddenly they heard a marvelous sweet harmony of sundry sorts of instruments of music, with the cry of a multitude of people, as they had been dancing and had sung as they use in Bacchus' feasts, with movings and turnings after the manner of the satyrs; and it seemed that this dance went through the city unto the gate that opened to the enemies, and that all the troop that made this noise they heard went out of the city at that gate. Now, such as in reason sought the depth of the interpretation of this wonder, thought that it was the god unto whom Antonius bare singular devotion to counterfeit and resemble him, that did forsake them. [4.3]

The next morning by break of day he went to set those few foot-men he had, in order upon the hills adjoining unto the city; and there he stood to behold his galleys which departed from the haven, and rowed against the galleys of his enemies, and so stood still, looking what exploit his soldiers in them would do. But when by force of rowing they were come near unto them, they first saluted Cæsar's men, and then Cæsar's men re-saluted them also, and of two armies made but one; and then did all together row toward the city. When Antonius saw that his men did forsake him and yielded unto Cæsar, and that his footmen were broken and overthrown, he then fled into the city, crying out that Cleopatra had betrayed him unto them, with whom he had made war for her sake. [4.12.9–49]

[The Deaths of Antony and Cleopatra]

Then she, being afraid of his fury, fled into the tomb which she had caused to be made, and there locked the doors unto her, and shut all the springs of the locks with great bolts; and in the meantime sent unto Antonius to tell him that she was dead. [4.13] Antonius believ-ing it said unto himself: "What dost thou look for further, Antonius, sith spiteful fortune hath taken from thee the only joy thou hadst, for whom thou yet reservedst thy life?" When he had said these words, he went into a chamber and unarmed himself, and being naked said thus: "O Cleopatra, it grieveth me not that I have lost thy company, for I will not be long from thee; but I am sorry that having been so great a captain and Emperor, I am indeed condemned to be judged of less courage and noble mind than a woman." [4.14.23–54]

Now he had a man of his called Eros, whom he loved and trusted much, and whom he had long before caused to swear unto him that he should kill him when he did command him; and then he willed him to keep his promise. His man drawing his sword lift it up as though he had meant to have stricken his master; but turning his head at one side he thrust his sword into himself, and fell down dead at his master's foot. Then said Antonius, "O noble Eros, I thank thee for this, and it is valiantly done of thee, to show me what I should do to myself, which thou couldst not do for me." There-withal he took his sword and thrust it into his belly, and so fell down upon a little bed. The wound he had killed him not presently, for the blood stinted a little when he was laid, and when he came somewhat to himself again, he prayed them that were about him to dispatch him. But they all fled out of the chamber and left him crying out and tormenting himself; until at last there came a secretary unto him called Diomedes, who was commanded to bring him into the tomb or monument where Cleopatra was.

When he heard that she was alive, he very earnestly prayed his men to carry his body thither, and so he was carried in his men's arms into the entry of the monument. [4.14.118–45] Notwithstanding, Cleopatra would not open the gates, but came to the high windows and cast out certain chains and ropes, in the which Antonius was trussed, and Cleopatra her own self, with two women only which she had suffered to come with her into these monuments, triced Antonius up. They that were present to behold it said they never saw so pitiful a sight. For they plucked up poor Antonius, all bloody as he was, and drawing on with pangs of death, who holding up his hands to Cleopatra raised up himself as well as he could. It was a hard thing for these women to do, to lift him up, but Cleopatra stooping down with her head, putting to all her strength to her uttermost power, did lift him up with much ado, and never let go her hold, with the help of the women beneath that bade her be of good courage, and were as sorry to see her labor so, as she herself. [4.15.22–38]

So, when she had gotten him in after that sort, and laid him on a bed, she rent her garments upon him, clapping her breast, and scratching her face and stomach. Then she dried up his blood that had bewrayed his face, and called him her lord, her husband, and Emperor, forgetting her own misery and calamity for the pity and compassion she took of him. Antonius made her cease her lamenting and called for wine, either because he was athirst, or else for that he thought thereby to hasten his death. When he had drunk, he earnestly prayed her and persuaded her that she would seek to save her life, if she could possible, without reproach and dishonor; and that chiefly she should trust Proculeius above any man else about Cæsar. [4.15.43–50] And, as for himself, that she should not lament nor sorrow for the miserable change of his fortune at the end of his days, but rather that she should think him the more fortunate for the former triumphs and honors he had received; considering that while he lived he was the noblest and greatest prince of the world, and that now he was overcome not cowardly but valiantly, a Roman by another Roman. [4.15.53–61]

As Antonius gave the last gasp, Proculeius came that was sent from Cæsar. For after Antonius had thrust his sword in himself, as they carried him into the tombs and monuments of Cleopatra, one of his guard called Dercatæus took his sword with the which he had stricken himself, and hid it; then he secretly stole away and brought Octavius Cæsar the first news of his death and showed him his sword that was bloodied. Cæsar hearing these news straight withdrew himself into secret place of his tent, and there burst out with tears, lamenting his hard and miserable fortune that had been his friend and brother-in-law, his equal in the empire, and companion with him in sundry great exploits and battles. [5.1.4–48] Then he called for all his friends and showed them the letters Antonius had written to him, and his answers also sent him again, during their quarrel and strife, and how fiercely and proudly the other answered him to all just and reasonable matters he wrote unto him. [5.1.73–77]

After this, he sent Proculeius, and commanded him to do what he could possible to get Cleopatra alive, fearing lest otherwise all the treasure would be lost; and furthermore, he thought that if he could take Cleopatra and bring her alive to Rome, she would marvelously beautify him and set out his triumph. [5.1.61–68] But Cleopatra would never put herself into Proculeius' hands, although they spake together. For Proculeius came to the gates that were very thick and strong and surely barred, but yet there were some crannies through the which her voice might be heard; and so they without understood that Cleopatra demanded the kingdom of Egypt for her sons, and that Proculeius answered her that she should be of good cheer and not be afraid to refer all unto Cæsar. [5.2.15–35] After he had viewed the place very well, he came and reported her answer unto Cæsar. Who immediately sent Gallus to speak once again with her, and bade him purposely hold her with talk, whilst Proculeius did set up a ladder against that high window by the which Antonius was triced up, and came down into the monument with two of his men, hard by the gate where Cleopatra stood to hear what Gallus said unto her.

One of her women which was shut in her monument with her saw Proculeius by chance as he came down, and shrieked out, "O, poor Cleopatra, thou art taken." Then, when she saw Proculeius behind her as she came from the gate, she thought to have stabbed herself in with a short dagger she wore of purpose by her side. But Proculeius came suddenly upon her, and taking her by both the hands said unto her, "Cleopatra first thou shalt do thyself great wrong, and secondly unto Cæsar, to deprive him of the occasion and opportunity openly to show his bounty and mercy, and to give his enemies cause to accuse the most courteous and noble prince that ever was, and to appeach him as though he were a cruel and merciless man that were not to be trusted." So even as he spake the word, he took her dagger from her, and shook her clothes for fear of any poison hidden about her. [5.2.35–63] Afterwards Cæsar sent one of his enfranchised men called Epaphroditus, whom he straitly charged to look well unto her, and to beware in any case that she made not herself away; and for the rest, to use her with all the courtesy possible. . . .

Now touching Antonius' sons, Antyllus his eldest son by Fulvia was slain because his schoolmaster Theodorus did betray him unto the soldiers, who struck off his head. And the villain took a precious stone of great value from his neck, the which he did sew in his girdle and afterwards denied that he had it; but it was found about him, and so Cæsar trussed him up for it. For Cleopatra's children, they were very honorably kept, with their governors and train that waited on them. But for Cæsarion, who was said to be Julius Cæsar's son, his mother Cleopatra had sent him unto the Indians, through Ethiopia, with a great sum of money. But one of his governors also called Rhodon, even such another as Theodorus, persuaded him to return into his country, and told him that Cæsar sent for him to give him his mother's kingdom. So, as Cæsar was determining with himself what he should do, Arrius said unto him,

Too many Cæsars is not good,

alluding unto a certain verse of Homer that saith,

Too many lords doth not well.

Therefore Cæsar did put Cæsarion to death, after the death of his mother Cleopatra.

Many princes, great kings, and captains did crave Antonius' body of Octavius Cæsar, to give him honorable burial; but Cæsar would never take it from Cleopatra, who did sumptuously and royally bury him with her own hands, whom Cæsar suffered to take as much as she would to bestow upon his funerals. Now was she altogether overcome with sorrow and passion of mind, for she had knocked her breast so pitifully that she had martyred it, and in divers places had raised ulcers and inflammations, so that she fell into a fever withal; whereof she was very glad, hoping thereby to have good color to abstain from meat, and that so she might have died easily, without any trouble. She had a physician called Olympus, whom she made privy of her intent, to th'end he should help her to rid her out of her life, as Olympus writeth himself, who wrote a book of all these things. But Cæsar mistrusted the matter by many conjectures he had, and therefore did put her in fear and threatened her to put her children to shameful death. [5.2.123–32] With these threats, Cleopatra for fear yielded straight as she would have yielded unto strokes, and afterwards suffered herself to be cured and dieted as they listed.

Shortly after, Cæsar came himself in person to see her and to comfort her. Cleopatra being laid upon a little low bed in poor estate, when she saw Cæsar come into her chamber, she suddenly rose up, naked in her smock, and fell down at his feet marvelously disfigured, both for that she had plucked her hair from her head, as also for that she had martyred all her face with her nails; and besides her voice was small and trembling, her eyes sunk into her head with continual blubbering, and moreover they might see the most part of her stomach torn in sunder. To be short, her body was not much better than her mind; yet her good grace and comeliness and the force of her beauty was not altogether defaced. But notwithstanding this ugly and pitiful state of hers, yet she showed herself within by her outward looks and countenance. When Cæsar had made her lie down again, and sat by her bed's side, Cleopatra began to clear and excuse herself for that she had done, laying all to the fear she had of Antonius. [3.13.56–57] Cæsar, in contrary manner, reproved her in every point. Then she suddenly altered her speech and prayed him to pardon her, as though she were afraid to die, and desirous to live.

At length, she gave him a brief and memorial of all the ready money and treasure she had. But by chance there stood Seleucus by, one of her treasurers, who to seem a good servant came straight to Cæsar to disprove Cleopatra—that she had not set in all, but kept many things back of purpose. Cleopatra was in such a rage with him that she flew upon him, and took him by the hair of the head, and boxed him well favoredly. Cæsar fell a-laughing, and parted the fray. "Alas," said she, "O Cæsar, is not this a great shame and reproach, that thou having vouchsafed to take the pains to come unto me, and hast done me this honor—poor wretch and caitiff creature, brought into this pitiful and miserable estate—and that mine own servants should come now to accuse me; though it may be I have reserved some jewels and trifles meet for women, but not for me (poor soul) to set out myself withal, but meaning to give some pretty presents and gifts unto Octavia and Livia, that they making means and intercession for me to thee, thou mightest yet extend thy favor and mercy upon me?" Cæsar was glad to hear her say so, persuading himself thereby that she had yet a desire to save her life. So he made her answer that he did not only give her that to dispose of at her pleasure, which she had kept back, but further promised to use her more honorably and bountifully than she would think for, and he so took his leave of her, supposing he had deceived her; but indeed he was deceived himself. [5.2.135–90]

There was a young gentleman, Cornelius Dolabella, that was one of Cæsar's very great familiars, and besides did bear no evil will unto Cleopatra. [5.2.70–109] He sent her word secretly, as she had requested him, that Cæsar determined to take his journey through Syria, and that within three days he would send her away before with her children. [5.2.197–207] When this was told Cleopatra, she requested Cæsar that it would please him to suffer her to offer the last oblations of the dead unto the soul of Antonius. This being granted her, she was carried to the place where his tomb was, and there falling down on her knees, embracing the tomb with her women, the tears running down her cheeks, she began to speak in this sort: "O, my dear lord Antonius, not long sithence I buried thee here, being a free woman; and now I offer unto thee the funeral sprinklings and oblations, being a captive and prisoner; and yet I am forbidden and kept from tearing and murdering this captive body of mine with blows, which they carefully guard and keep only to triumph of thee; look therefore henceforth for no other honors, offerings, nor sacrifices from me, for these are the last which Cleopatra can give thee, sith now they carry her away. Whilst we lived together, nothing could sever our companies, but now at our death I fear me they will make us change our countries. For as thou being a Roman hast been buried in Egypt, even so, wretched creature, I an Egyptian shall be buried in Italy, which shall be all the good that I have received by thy country. If therefore the gods where thou art now have any power and authority—sith our gods here have forsaken us—suffer not thy true friend and lover to be carried away alive, that in me they triumph of thee; but receive me with thee and let me be buried in one self tomb with thee. For though my griefs and miseries be infinite, yet none hath grieved me more, nor that I could less bear withal, than this small time which I have been driven to live alone without thee."

Then having ended these doleful plaints and crowned the tomb with garlands and sundry nosegays and marvelous lovingly embraced the same, she commanded they should prepare her bath, and when she had bathed and washed herself, she fell to her meat and was sumptuously served. Now whilst she was at dinner there came a country man and brought her a basket. The soldiers that warded at the gates asked him straight what he had in his basket. He opened the basket and took out the leaves that covered the figs and showed them that they were figs he brought. They all of them marveled to see so goodly figs. The country man laughed to hear them, and bade them take some if they would. They believed he told them truly, and so bade him carry them in. [5.2.233–76] After Cleopatra had dined, she sent a certain table written and sealed unto Cæsar, and commanded them all to go out of the tombs where she was, but the two women; then she shut the doors to her. Cæsar, when he received this table and began to read her lamentation and petition, requesting him that he would let her be buried with Antonius, found straight what she meant and thought to have gone thither himself; howbeit he sent one before in all haste that might be, to see what it was.

Her death was very sudden. For those whom Cæsar sent unto her ran thither in all haste possible and found the soldiers standing at the gate, mistrusting nothing, nor understanding of her death. But when they had opened the doors, they found Cleopatra stark dead, laid upon a bed of gold, attired and arrayed in her royal robes, and one of her two women, which was called Iras, dead at her feet; and her other woman called Charmion, half dead, and trembling, trimming the diadem which Cleopatra wore upon her head. One of the soldiers, seeing her, angrily said unto her, "Is that well done, Charmion?" "Very well," said she again, "and meet for a princess descended from the race of so many noble kings." She said no more, but fell down dead hard by the bed. [5.2.317–25]

Some report that this aspic was brought unto her in the basket with figs, and that she had commanded them to hide it under the fig leaves, that when she should think to take out the figs the aspic should bite her before she should see her; howbeit, that when she would have taken away the leaves for the figs, she perceived it, and said, "Art thou here then?" And so, her arm being naked, she put it to the aspic to be bitten. Other say again, she kept it in a box and that she did prick and thrust it with a spindle of gold, so that the aspic being angered withal leapt out with great fury and bit her in the arm. Howbeit few can tell the troth. For they report also that she had hidden poison in a hollow razor which she carried in the hair of her head; and yet was there no mark seen of her body, or any sign discerned that she was poisoned, neither also did they find this serpent in her tomb. But it was reported only that there were seen certain fresh steps or tracks where it had gone, on the tomb side toward the sea, and specially by the door's side. Some say also that they found two little pretty bitings in her arm, scant to be discerned; the which it seemeth Cæsar himself gave credit unto, because in his triumph he carried Cleopatra's image with an aspic biting of her arm. [5.2.342–51] And thus goeth the report of her death.

Now Cæsar, though he was marvelous sorry for the death of Cleopatra, yet he wondered at her noble mind and courage, and therefore commanded she should be nobly buried and laid by Antonius [5.2.353–57]; and willed also that her two women should have honorable burial. Cleopatra died being eight and thirty year old, after she had reigned two and twenty years, and governed above fourteen of them with Antonius. And for Antonius, some say that he lived three and fifty years; and others say, six and fifty. All his statues, images, and metals were plucked down and overthrown, saving those of Cleopatra, which stood still in their places by means of Archibius one of her friends, who gave Cæsar a thousand talents that they should not be handled as those of Antonius were.

Dio Cassius (150–235 CE)

Dio Cassius Cocceianus lived and wrote a century after Plutarch. His account, written in Greek, is more pro-Augustan and censorious of Antony and Cleopatra. According to Dio, after the defeat at Actium, Cleopatra repeatedly betrayed Antony and caused her fleet to go over to *Octavius Caesar in Alexandria* (Antony and Cleopatra 4.12.9ff). *Caesar had tricked Cleopatra by sending to her an ambassador Thyrus, Thidias in Shakespeare's play, to tell her that Caesar himself was in love with her. Accordingly, in the passage presented here, after the death of Antony, Cleopatra arranged an audience with Caesar in which she tried to seduce him, reminding him that she had been the mistress of Julius Caesar, his adoptive father, and producing letters from that earlier love affair: all to no avail. Whether received or invented, Dio's story is almost certainly fabricated. It corresponds to a conventional "continence of the conqueror" narrative that had been told about Alexander the Great and Scipio Africanus and was intended to flatter Caesar. Shakespeare seems to have been aware of it, perhaps through Dio's* History *(translated into Latin in 1526) or through Samuel Daniel's retelling of it in his* Cleopatra. *Shakespeare transfers the scene back to Cleopatra's meeting with Thidias himself in 3.13, particularly in her allowing Thidias to kiss her hand where "Your Caesar's father oft / . . . Bestowed his lips" (3.13.83–85).*

from *Roman History*, Book 51[1]

Even then in such depths of calamity she remembered that she was queen, and chose rather to die with the name and dignities of a sovereign than to live as an ordinary person. It should be stated that she kept fire on hand to use upon her money and asps and other reptiles to use upon herself, and that she had tried the latter on human beings to see in what way they killed in each case. Cæsar was anxious to make himself master of her treasures, to seize her alive, and to take her back for his triumph. However, as he had given her a kind of pledge, he did not wish to appear to have acted personally as an impostor, since this would prevent him from treating her as a captive and to a certain extent subdued against her will. He therefore sent to her Gaius Proculeius, a knight, and Epaphroditus, a freedman, giving them directions what they must say and do. So they obtained an audience with Cleopatra and after some accusations of a mild type suddenly laid hold of her before any decision was reached. Then they put out of her way everything by which she could bring death upon herself and allowed her to spend some days where she was, since the embalming of Antony's body claimed her attention. After that they took her to the palace, but did not remove

[1]*Dio's Rome*, trans. Herbert Baldwin Foster (Troy, NY: Pafraets, 1906).

any of her accustomed retinue or attendants, to the end that she should still more hope to accomplish her wishes and do no harm to herself. When she expressed a desire to appear before Cæsar and converse with him, it was granted; and to beguile her still more, he promised that he would come to her himself.

She accordingly prepared a luxurious apartment and costly couch, and adorned herself further in a kind of careless fashion,—for her mourning garb mightily became her,—and seated herself upon the couch; beside her she had placed many images of his father, of all sorts, and in her bosom she had put all the letters that his father had sent her. When, after this, Cæsar entered, she hastily arose, blushing, and said: "Hail, master, Heaven has given joy to you and taken it from me. But you see with your own eyes your father in the guise in which he often visited me, and you may hear how he honored me in various ways and made me queen of the Egyptians. That you may learn what were his own words about me, take and read the missives which he sent me with his own hand."

As she spoke thus, she read aloud many endearing expressions of his. And now she would lament and caress the letters and again fall before his images and do them reverence. She kept turning her eyes toward Cæsar, and melodiously continued to bewail her fate. She spoke in melting tones, saying at one time, "Of what avail, Cæsar, are these your letters?," and at another, "But in the man before me you also are alive for me." Then again, "Would that I had died before you!," and still again, "But if I have him, I have you!"

Some such diversity both of words and of gestures did she employ, at the same time gazing at and murmuring to him sweetly. Cæsar comprehended her outbreak of passion and appeal for sympathy. Yet he did not pretend to do so, but letting his eyes rest upon the ground, he said only this: "Be of cheer, woman, and keep a good heart, for no harm shall befall you." She was distressed that he would neither look at her nor breathe a word about the kingdom or any sigh of love, and fell at his knees wailing: "Life for me, Cæsar, is neither desirable nor possible. This favor I beseech of you in memory of your father,—that since Heaven gave me to Antony after him, I may also die with my lord. Would that I had perished on the very instant after Cæsar's death! But since this present fate was my destiny, send me to Antony:

grudge me not burial with him, that as I die because of him, so in Hades also I may dwell with him."

Such words she uttered expecting to obtain commiseration: Cæsar, however, made no answer to it. Fearing, however, that she might make away with herself he exhorted her again to be of good cheer, did not remove any of her attendants, and kept a careful watch upon her, that she might add brilliance to his triumph. Suspecting this, and regarding it as worse than innumerable deaths, she began to desire really to die and begged Cæsar frequently that she might be allowed to perish in some way, and devised many plans by herself. When she could accomplish nothing, she feigned to change her mind and to repose great hope in him, as well as great hope in Livia. She said she would sail voluntarily and made ready many treasured adornments as gifts. In this way she hoped to inspire confidence that she had no designs upon herself, and so be more free from scrutiny and bring about her destruction. This also took place. The other officials and Epaphroditus, to whom she had been committed, believed that her state of mind was really as it seemed, and neglected to keep a careful watch. She, meanwhile, was making preparations to die as painlessly as possible. First she gave a sealed paper, in which she begged Cæsar to order that she be buried beside Antony, to Epaphroditus himself to deliver, pretending that it contained some other matter. Having by this excuse freed herself of his presence, she set to her task. She put on her most beauteous apparel and after choosing a most becoming pose, assumed all the royal robes and appurtenances, and so died.

No one knows clearly in what manner she perished, for there were found merely slight indentations on her arm. Some say that she applied an asp which had been brought in to her in a water-jar or among some flowers. Others declare that she had smeared a needle, with which she was wont to braid her hair, with some poison possessed of such properties that it would not injure the surface of the body at all, but if it touched the least drop of blood it caused death very quickly and painlessly. The supposition is, then, that previously it had been her custom to wear it in her hair, and on this occasion after first making a small scratch on her arm with some instrument, she dipped the needle in the blood. In this or some very similar way she perished with her two handmaidens. The eunuch, at the moment her body was taken up, presented himself voluntarily to the serpents, and after being bitten by them leaped into a coffin which had been prepared by him. Cæsar on hearing of her demise was shocked, and both viewed her body and applied drugs to it and sent for Psylli, in the hope that she might possibly revive. These Psylli, who are male, for there is no woman born in their tribe, have the power of sucking out before a person dies all the poison of every reptile and are not harmed themselves when bitten by any such creature. They are propagated from one another and they test their offspring, the latter being thrown among serpents at once or having serpents laid upon their swaddling-clothes. In such cases the poisonous creatures do not harm the child and are benumbed by its clothing. This is the nature of their function. But Cæsar, when he could not in any way resuscitate Cleopatra, felt admiration and pity for her and was himself excessively grieved, as much as if he had been deprived of all the glory of the victory.

So Antony and Cleopatra, who had been the authors of many evils to the Egyptians and to the Romans, thus fought and thus met death. They were embalmed in the same fashion and buried in the same tomb. Their spiritual qualities and the fortunes of their lives deserve a word of comment.

Antony had no superior in comprehending his duty, yet he committed many acts of folly. He was distinguished for his bravery in some cases, yet he often failed through cowardice. He was characterized equally by greatness of soul and a servile disposition of mind. He would plunder the property of others, and still relinquish his own. He pitied many without cause and chastised even a greater number unjustly. Consequently, though he rose from weakness to great strength, and from the depths of poverty to great riches, he drew no profit from either circumstance, but whereas he had hoped to hold the Roman power alone, he actually killed himself.

Cleopatra was of insatiable passion and insatiable avarice, was ambitious for renown, and most scornfully bold. By the influence of love she won dominion over the Egyptians, and hoped to attain a similar position over the Romans, but being disappointed of this she destroyed herself also. She captivated two of the men who were the greatest Romans of her day, and because of the third she committed suicide.

Three Augustan Poets: Virgil, Horace, Propertius

The victory over Antony and Cleopatra at Actium by Octavius Caesar, proclaimed Augustus Caesar four years later, was variously celebrated by the great poets who wrote under Caesar's patronage and that of his close associate Maecenas. Their poetry was part of the cultural inheritance of educated Renaissance people, including Shakespeare. The three presented here differ in their visions of the historical events and in their identifications and sympathies with the protagonists.

Virgil (70–19 BCE)

In Book 8 of Virgil's great epic poem, the Aeneid, *the hero Aeneas receives a shield on which the God Vulcan has prophetically sculpted the scene of the battle of Actium. Following the propaganda of Augustus that cast the civil war against Antony as a foreign war against Cleopatra—never mentioned by these poets by name but as the "queen" of a barbarous Egypt—Virgil depicts Actium as the victory of the West, masculinity, reason (Apollo), order, and unity against the East, femininity, irrationality (monster gods), disorder, and multiplicity. The shield goes on to portray the triumph that Augustus celebrated at Rome. Representations of rivers carried in the procession signify the pacified borders of the Roman empire and turn Augustus's victory into a triumph of civilization itself over raw nature. (The final image of the Araxes, on the border with the hostile Parthians, which had twice flooded and washed away the bridges of former conquerors, suggests the possible impermanence of Augustus's achievement and of nature's revenge.) Virgil's fiction thus transmits a view of Egypt and of Cleopatra as censorious as any voiced by Roman characters in Shakespeare's play. Even so, there is something moving in his image of another river, the sorrowing Nile, embracing the defeated Antony and Cleopatra, a euphemism for their suicides, but also a sympathetic response from the natural world.*

Aeneid 8.675–731[1]

Amid the main two mighty fleets engage,
Their brazen beaks opposed with equal rage.
Actium surveys the well-disputed prize,
Leucate's watery plain with foamy billows fries.
Young Caesar on the stern in armor bright
Here leads the Romans and their gods to fight.   900
His beamy temples shoot their flames afar,
And o'er his head is hung the Julian star.[2]
Agrippa seconds him, with prosperous gales
And with propitious gods, his foes assails.
A naval crown, that binds his manly brows
The happy fortune of the fight foreshows.
    Ranged on the line opposed, Antonius brings
Barbarian aids and troops of Eastern kings,
The Arabians near and Bactrians from afar,
Of tongues discordant, and a mingled war;   910
And rich in gaudy robes amidst the strife,
His ill fate follows him—the Egyptian wife.
Moving they fight: with oars and forky prows
The froth is gathered, and the water glows.
It seems as if the Cyclades[3] again
Were rooted up and jostled in the main,
Or floating mountains floating mountains meet,
Such is the fierce encounter of the fleet.
Fireballs are thrown, and pointed javelins fly;
The fields of Neptune take a purple dye.   920
The queen herself, amidst the loud alarms,
With cymbals tossed her fainting soldiers warms—
Fool as she was, who had not yet divined
Her cruel fate, nor saw the snakes behind.
Her country gods, the monsters of the sky,
Great Neptune, Pallas, and love's queen defy.

[1]Trans. John Dryden (1697). *Virgil's Aeneid* (London and New York: G. Routledge and Sons, 1884). The line numbers in the cited text refer to Dryden's translation.

[2]A comet that appeared after the death of Julius Caesar and was supposed to embody his deified spirit. Here it indicates Augustus as the true heir of Caesar.

[3]A Greek island chain that included Delos, an island that wandered until it was fixed by the gods.

The dog Anubis barks, but barks in vain,
No longer dares to oppose the ethereal train.
Mars in the middle of the shining shield
Is graved, and strides along the liquid field.   930
The Dirae souse[4] from heaven with swift descent
And Discord, dyed in blood, with garments rent,
Divides the press. Her steps Bellona treads,
And shakes her iron rod above their heads.
This seen, Apollo from his Actian height
Pours down his arrows, at whose winged flight
The trembling Indians and Egyptians yield,
And soft Sabaeans quit the watery field.
The fatal mistress hoists her silken sails,
And shrinking from the fight, invokes the gales.   940
Aghast she looks, and heaves her breast for breath,
Panting and pale with fear of future death.
The god had figured her as driven along
By winds and waves, and scudding through the throng.
Just opposite, sad Nilus opens wide
His arms and ample bosom to the tide,
And spreads his mantle o'er the winding coast,
In which he wraps the queen and hides the flying host.
The victor to the gods his thanks expressed,
And Rome triumphant with his presence blessed.   950
Three hundred temples in the town he placed;
With spoils and altars every temple graced.
Three shining nights and three succeeding days,
The fields resound with shouts, the streets with praise,
The domes with songs, the theaters with plays.
All altars flame: before each altar lies,
Drenched in his gore, the destined sacrifice.
Great Caesar sits sublime upon his throne,
Before Apollo's porch of Parian stone,
Accepts the presents vowed for victory,   960
And hangs the monumental crowns on high.
Vast crowds of vanquished nations march along,
Various in arms, in habit, and in tongue.

[4]Swoop.

Here Mulciber[5] assigns the proper place
For Carians and the ungirt Numidian race;
Then ranks the Thracians in the second row
With Scythians, expert in the dart and bow.
And here the tamed Euphrates humbly glides
And there the Rhine submits her swelling tides,
And proud Araxes, whom no bridge could bind.   970
The Danes's unconquered offspring march behind,
And Morini, the last of human kind.
    These figures, on the shield divinely wrought,
By Vulcan labored and by Venus wrought,
With joy and wonder fill the hero's thought.
Unknown the names, he yet admires the grace,
And bears aloft the fame and fortune of his race.

Horace (65–8 BCE)

The famous ode (1.37) by Horace in celebration of the victory at Actium shifts more dramatically in its attitude toward Cleopatra. The poem first calls for wine and celebration, now that the woman who thought to overthrow Rome in her drunken ambition and who surrounded herself with effeminate men and eunuchs is dead. One of those effeminate men presumably was Antony; recall how Antony and Cleopatra *opens on the sight of Cleopatra fanned by her eunuchs and Antony described as a "fan / To cool a gypsy's lust" (1.1.9–10). But Horace's view of Cleopatra slowly admits pity—she is the dove hunted by Caesar the hawk—and admiration as she faces suicide with regal courage and escapes being led in triumph. Moving from festive drinking, to Cleopatra's drunken thirst for power, to her imbibing the poison of the asp, this ode would later serve as a model for Andrew Marvell's "An Horatian Ode on Cromwell's Return from Ireland" (1650), where the executed King Charles I plays the role of Horace's Cleopatra, the "royal actor" as much a king as she a queen.*

[5]Vulcan.

Odes 1.37[1]

Now let the bowl with wine be crowned,
Now lighter dance the mazy round,
And let the sacred couch be stored
  With rich dainties of a priestly board.

Sooner to draw the mellow wine,
Pressed from the rich Caecubian vine,
Were impious mirth, while yet elate
  The queen breathed ruin to the Roman state.

Surrounded by a tainted train,
Wretches enervate and obscene,   10
She raved of empire—nothing less—
  Vast in her hopes, and giddy with success.

But hardly rescued from the flames,
One lonely ship her fury tames;
While Caesar with impelling oar
  Pursued her flying from the Latian shore:

Her, with Egyptian wine inspired,
With the full draught to madness fired,
Augustus sobered into tears,
  And turned her visions into real fears.   20

As darting sudden from above
The hawk attacks a tender dove:
Or sweeping huntsman drives the hare
  O'er wide Aemonia's icy deserts drear;

So Caesar through the billows pressed
To lead in chains the fatal pest:
But she nobler fate explored,
  Nor woman-like beheld the deathful sword.

[1]*The Odes, Epodes, and Carmen Seculare of Horace*, trans. Philip Francis (London:
A. Millar, 1743–46).

Nor with her navy fled dismayed,
In distant realms to seek for aid,   30
But saw unmoved her state destroyed.
  Her palace desolate, a lonely void;

With fearless hand she dared to grasp
The writhings of the wrathful asp,
And suck the poison through her veins,
  Resolved on death, and fiercer from its pains:

Thus scorning to be led the boast
Of mighty Caesar's naval host,
And armed with more than mortal spleen,
  Defrauds a triumph, and expires a queen.   40

Propertius (c. 50–c. 15 BCE)

Propertius presents the most complicated response to Antony and Cleopatra, for as a love poet, a singer of wine and women, he feels kinship with Antony. One of his poems that will go on to celebrate Augustus Caesar's victory at Actium (3.11) begins by responding to an imagined critic: Why should you blame me, the speaker says, for being unable to break free from love when there are so many examples of gods and heroes in a similar predicament? Leaving myth aside, there is the recent case of the lover of Cleopatra, whom the poem goes on to paint in the deeply misogynist terms of Augustan propaganda, terms that reappear in poem 4.6, dedicated to Apollo, the divine guarantor of the victory at Actium. Propertius's identification with Antony is similarly proclaimed in the charming poem 2.16, included here, where the poet expresses his jealousy of a rival suitor to his mistress Cynthia. This praetor (a judicial magistrate) has returned from the Dalmatian coast—the poet wishes he had drowned on the way at "Thunder's Rock"—and has showered Cynthia with gifts. The poem warns Cynthia against divine retribution for her fickleness: Jove may strike her with one of his thunderbolts, and she'll have to worry whenever it storms. Propertius praises the clemency of Augustus after Actium, but the austerity of Augustus's moral program is not for him: He gently satirizes it when he imagines the law requiring the fidelity of

Cynthia, his mistress, not *his wife. The poet persists, like Antony, in his shameful love. (See Jasper Griffin, "Propertius and Antony," Journal of Roman Studies 67 [1977].)*

Elegies 2.16[1]

A praetor from Illyria came of late,
Cynthia, thy greatest prey, my greatest care!
At Thunder's Rock why found he not his fate?
Neptune, what gifts from me had been thy share!
Now, feasts and table full, but not for me!
Now, not for me, door night-long open wide!
If wise, now reap the harvest offered thee!
Shear the crass brute! His fleece is yet his pride!
Then, spent his gifts, as wealth bids him adieu,
Ship all that's left of him to see Illyrias new!   10

Cynthia follow rods of state?
Cynthia care for honours? No!
Cynthia studies pockets' weight,
And in the scales her lovers go.
But, Venus, now my grief assist!
Let his unending lust wear out the sensualist!

So any one with gifts her love can buy?
Jove, a girl spoilt by what unworthy hire!
For gems she bids me to the ocean fly,
Ransack for gifts the citadel of Tyre.   20
Would none were rich at Rome, and he, our lord,
Could live, like Romulus, in house of straw![2]
No sweethearts then for presents were bewhored;
One maid grow gray in one home were the law!
'Tis not that thou a se'nnight sleep'st away,

---

[1]*The Elegies of Propertius*, trans. E. H. W. Meyerstein (London: Oxford University Press and Humphrey Milford, 1935).

[2]Augustus, the lord in question, dwelled in his mansion on the Palatine adjacent to an archaic brick and straw dwelling that was supposed to have belonged to Romulus, the founder of the Rome that Augustus claimed to refound. In the next lines Propertius tweaks the marital legislation of Augustus.

While thy white arms round that foul lover bend!
'Tis not that I have sinned (Confirm, I say!);
The fair have always fickleness for friend.
Shut out, a stranger's stamping at thy door;
And lo! he reigns, enskied, where I was king before!   30

Gifts! What Eriphyla found
See, by their bitter hire!
Gifts, Creusa, bridal-gowned,
Aflame with swathing fire![3]

Will no wrong e'er my tears assuage?
Still must my grief be thy sins' wage?
All these days gone, and I unable
To joy in Campus, theatre, or table!
Shame's a great matter, shame! And yet they say
Infamous loves are deaf alway.   40
Behold the chief,[4] who late with fruitless roar
Of death-doomed soldiers filled the Actian Sea!
Honourless love bade him turn ships and flee,
And seek refuge on earth's extremest shore.
Here Caesar's virtue, here his fame record!
The selfsame hand that conquered sheathed the sword!

But every garment, every emerald,
And every yellow-beaming chrysolite
  He gave to thee,
  All may I see   50
To empty airs by rapid storms recalled,
And turned to earth, to water, in thy sight!
Calmly Jove laughs at lovers' perjuries
Not alway, nor prayers deafly doth forget.
Ye have seen thunderclaps race through the skies,
And levin-bolts from heaven's dome leap down:

---

[3]Eriphyla was bribed with the gift of a necklace to send her husband Amphiaraus to the war against Thebes where he would die; Creusa was set on fire and consumed by the poisoned robe that Medea sent her as wedding gift.

[4]Antony.

No doing of the Pleiads or of wet
Orion, nor for naught falls lightning's rage!
Jove then gives perjured girls their penal wage,
Because, deceived, the god himself once cried.   60
Wherefore let no Sidonian raiment's pride
Be worth thy fear when Auster's[5] cloud-ranks frown!

[5] The south wind's.

Antony and Cleopatra on the Sixteenth- and Seventeenth-Century Stage

The dramatic potential of the story of Antony and Cleopatra was grasped from the very beginnings of Renaissance theater.

Shakespeare's *Antony and Cleopatra* (1607–8) was preceded and followed by other versions of their downfall. Cleopatra, in particular, focused some of the earliest tragedies in Italy and France: The first great modern tragedian, Giovan Battista Giraldi Cinzio, wrote a Cleopatra play in the 1540s, and Estienne Jodelle's *Cléopatre captive* of 1553 inaugurated French tragedy. These were dramas in the neoclassical style, imitating Seneca's Roman tragedies. Their plots follow the classical unities, set in one place and confined to a twenty-four-hour period. Action and violence are excluded from the stage and reported instead by messengers. A chorus comments on the events. Characters and chorus express their emotions in long speeches employing the persuasive figures of classical rhetoric and liberally sprinkled with *sententiae*, maxims ready to be detached and universalized. The use of metaphor and imagery, on the other hand, is strictly restrained. Contrary to what is sometimes said, these plays were intended not only for the page but also for the stage. Shaped for courtly and elite audiences, their aesthetic is quite foreign from Shakespeare's popular theater.

Along such classical lines, Mary Sidney, Countess of Pembroke, envisioned an alternative to or a reform of English drama when she translated the French tragedian Robert Garnier's *Marc Antoine* as *Antonius* or *The Tragedie of Antonie* in 1590. The Elizabethan poet Samuel Daniel, who wrote under Sidney's patronage, conceived his *Tragedy of Cleopatra* (1594; revised 1607) as a sequel to her play and

Renaissance humanists sought to recover and publish the portraits of famous classical figures, with more and less scholarly accuracy. These engraved portraits of
Antony and Cleopatra by the Flemish artist Théodore Galle—first published in
1598, here from a 1606 edition one year before Shakespeare's play—claim to be
based on engraved gems in the important collection of the Roman antiquarian Fulvio Orsini. By permission of Beinecke Library, Yale University.

dedicated it to her. Another writer in the Sidney circle, Fulke Greville,
wrote an *Antony and Cleopatra* but suppressed it in the wake of the

failed conspiracy of the Earl of Essex. These were all plays in the classical format. Shakespeare appears to have known Daniel's play and perhaps Sidney's *Tragedie of Antonie*; Daniel may have revised his *Cleopatra* to respond to the popularity of Shakespeare's play.

In the Restoration period, two plays on Antony and Cleopatra came out within a year of one another, Sir Charles Sedley's *Antony and Cleopatra* (1677) and John Dryden's famous *All for Love* (1678). These plays try to effect a compromise between Shakespearean practice and neoclassical protocols as these had evolved in France in the plays of Racine and Corneille. Action is now staged, and the chorus is omitted.

The following excerpts show the death scene of Cleopatra toward each play's end. They place Shakespeare's dramatically freer, more modern treatment of Antony and Cleopatra within a larger, ongoing tradition. They also suggest that from its beginning Renaissance drama chose to champion the historically defeated Antony and Cleopatra in the face of the pro-Caesar propaganda in the classical sources. It is largely through these plays, primarily, of course, through Shakespeare's, that the historical image of the two lovers has been reversed.

The English language texts are presented with modernized spelling. The translations of Giraldi Cinzio and Jodelle are my own.

Giovan Battista Giraldi Cinzio (1504–1573)

The greatest early tragedian of the Renaissance was Giovan Battista Giraldi Cinzio, who flourished at the Este ducal court in Ferrara. He is best known to Shakespeareans for his collection of short novellas, Gli ecatommiti, *which provided the plots for* Othello *and* Measure for Measure. *He was preceded in the writing of tragedy by Giangiorgio Trissino's* Sofonisba *(1515), the first modern tragedy in a vernacular language; its heroine Sophonisba, the beautiful Carthaginian-born Queen of Numidia, drinks poison in order to escape falling into the hands of the Romans during the Punic Wars in 203* BCE. *Giraldi Cinzio pays tribute to the earlier play when his Cleopatra holds up the example of this other African queen. (Shakespeare's contemporary John Marston wrote a tragedy,* Sophonisba, *in 1606, a year or so before* Antony and Cleopatra.) *Cleopatra's long soliloquy presented here—largely in the form of an address to her absent adversary—precedes her reported death to Octavius four scenes later. Her* sententia *is underscored in the printed edition of the play.*

from *Cleopatra* (1541–1543; pub. 1583)[1]

ACT 5, SCENE 2, LINES 1–97

CLEOPATRA So you think me, Octavius, so devoid of wit,
So beside myself, that I cannot understand
To what end you wish me to remain alive,
And that I cannot clearly perceive
That your promises, your flatteries
Are so many snares that you cast about me
To lead me in chains to the Capitol?
Your frauds and your simulated offers
Do not so dim the light of my mind
And I see what you do not want to show me.   10
Their minds are all too sharpened, Octavius,
Who dwell in the abyss of misery.
You want me to live, and hold my life dear,
And you would feel that you had not conquered
If you did not hold me alive in your power:
I believe you. Not because you wish
(As you have sought to convince me)
To give me a sign of your clemency,
But rather to lead me in your triumph at Rome
A slave in bondage, chains wrapped around me.   20
Do you believe, Octavius, that your face
Does not show me what you hold closed in your heart?
Your desire that I honor your triumph
And your ill will did not permit you—
Your mind, all aimed at my disgrace, did not permit you—
To look at me even once straight in the face;
You kept your eyes always fixed upon the ground.
You did not know, Octavius, how to deploy
Your wiles, that I did not discover them all,
In spite of your wishes.   30
But if you have not known how to deceive
A woman whom cruel destiny

[1]Giraldi Cinzio, *Cleopatra Tragedia*, ed. Mary Morrison and Peggy Osborn (Exeter: University of Exeter, 1985).

Placed, as if fettered, into your hands,
You'll see that a woman has known how
(To free herself from shame and opprobrium)
To deceive you, pretending to desire
To follow you to Rome, and carry out your will.
Do you think you have so prevailed
That Cleopatra has so abandoned herself
So lowered herself from her own pride   40
And from what she always was, so forgotten
The royal state in which she has lived,
That she would come as a slave to Rome
In another's power? You have but poorly
Seen into my thoughts.
I wished indeed to come to Rome
Had my Mark Antony remained alive
And a victor, to do to you, and to Octavia,
And to your Livia what you now intend
To do to Cleopatra. But Rome now   50
(Now that the fates oppose my wishes)
Will not see her, unless you take her there
Dead. For I wish now to end my life
Beneath the skies where I was born.
Sophonisba once chose rather to die
In freedom than be a slave and live.
And so do I, following her example.
If I have not known how to defend myself
From you with my forces, when I still could,
If I have not known, because of my frailty,   60
How to see to what was needful,
You'll find that I have seen in greater need,
That, having arrived to where I now am,
I have not been blind. And that if you have conquered
Egypt, you have not conquered Cleopatra.
I will know better how to die than I have lived,
And better obtain liberty with my death
Than I knew how to obtain good with my life.
If my pleasures did not let me learn
The art of living rightly, now suffering   70
Has taught me that which I need

To die a queen in my own kingdom.
Wherever I turn, I see in freedom
(In spite of you), this heaven
Under which I was born, and lived, and reigned
As queen, and Cleopatra sees this heaven
Not with shackles and chains about her,
But in her royal attire. This heaven, too,
Will receive my soul, free and released
From its bonds. I pray with all my heart   80
And pray again to the gods of Egypt
(If they have not been conquered
Along with my realm) that they so ordain
That my body be united with that of Mark Antony,
And that in their breasts (once I have performed
The funeral rites to my husband,
To my husband, no, rather to my life,
For I want to perform them now in my royal robes)
They receive my last breath in peace.
Farewell dear country mine, farewell, I leave you,   90
My people, I leave you, cherished court,
In which I lived once so happily.
Pray, all of you, for your queen a death
As peaceful as one can be. Pray that my sons,
Who should have been lords of this noble realm,
And now lie in the hands of Octavius,
Make a better end than the one I now make for myself.

Estienne Jodelle (1532–1573)

Estienne Jodelle was one of the seven poets of La Pléiade, a circle that included Ronsard and Du Bellay, who sought to revolutionize French poetry through the study of classical Greek and Latin models. He himself acted the part of Cleopatra in the presentation of Cléopatre captive *before the royal court in Reims. It was the first French neoclassical tragedy and began the tradition that would culminate in Corneille and Racine in the following century. A celebration was held following the performance in which other members of the group crowned him with the garlands of triumph. At the beginning of the play Antony is already dead and appears as a Senecan ghost; its subject is Cleopatra and her fate. The scene presented here closes the fourth act; Proculeius will report the discovery of her body in the brief Act 5. Jodelle's Cleopatra imitates the pathetic situation and speech of Plutarch's Cleopatra (see pp. 188-89) as she pays her final funeral rites over the remains of Antony.*

from *Cléopatre captive* (1553; pub. 1574)[1]

ACT 4, LINES 117–170

CLEOPATRA Antony, O dear Antony, Antony my half self
If Antony had not suffered the enmity of the heavens,
Antony, Antony, alas! of whom misfortune deprives me,
Hear the weak voice of a weak captive   120
Who with her own hands, while she was still untaken,
Placed your ashes inside this tomb:
Who, taken and captive, led to her affliction,
Enslaved and prisoner in her guarded city,
Now sacrifices to you, and not without some fear
Of making my lament go on too long in this place,
Knowing that they keep an eye on me, lest grief
Make an end in death to my unhappiness:
And so that my body, deprived of its grief,
Be reserved in the end for a Roman triumph.   130
Triumph, I say, alas! which they want me to adorn,
Triumph, I say, alas! which they will make over you.
From now on you must not expect to receive
Any further honors from me, any further offerings,
The honor I now do you will be the last honor
That Cleopatra will do her dead Antony.
And even though force and violence, while you lived,
Could not force us to set aside our alliance
And part us: nonetheless I deeply fear
That we will part, one from the other, in death,   140
And that Roman Antony will remain in Egypt,
And that I the Egyptian will die in Rome.

[1]Jodelle, *Cléopatre captive*, ed. Kathleen M. Hall (Exeter: University of Exeter, 1979).

But if the mighty gods have power in the place
Where you now dwell, pray, pray some god
Never to permit that, in carrying me off from here,
They triumph over you in my person:
Rather that your tomb, o pitiful spectacle,
Rejoin us both, two poor lovers together,
Tomb that one day Egypt will honor,
And perhaps write an epitaph to us, we two: 150
  "Here are two lovers who, happy while they lived,
Surfeited their souls with joy, honor, and revelry,
But in the end they fell beneath such misery
That the happiness of both of them was rather to die."
  Receive, receive me then before Caesar departs,
For let me be without breath than without honor:
For among all the ills, pain, grief, distress,
Sighs, regrets, cares I have suffered without number
I consider the most grievous this very brief time
That I, O Antony, feel myself apart from you.   160
CHORUS   Weeping, she goes inside the dark tomb,
The wheeling torches reveal nothing of it.
IRAS   Is there so firm a soul that would not almost fly
Its body at the pitiful hearing of such sad words?
CHARMIAN   O ashes most happy for having left this world!
Man is not happy until a tomb encloses him.
CHORUS   Is there anyone with such a desire to live
That he would not scorn such life as this?
CLEOPATRA   Let us go then, dear sisters, and let us gently take
The happy easement of our unhappy woes.   170

Mary Sidney, Countess of Pembroke (1561–1621)

Mary Sidney's brother, the great poet and writer Sir Philip Sidney, had complained about the state of English drama in his Defense of Poetry, *written around 1581 but not published until 1595, nine years after his death. He admired Thomas Sackville's and Thomas Norton's* Gorboduc *but objected that it did not observe unity of place and time. It has been suggested that Mary Sidney, Countess of Pembroke, chose to translate*

Marc Antoine *by Robert Garnier, the foremost French tragedian of the time, as a model that would point English tragedy along a new neoclassical path. Sidney was a poet-translator of remarkable gifts, whose metrical translation of the* Psalms, *completing a project begun by her brother, is her masterpiece and a major achievement of English Renaissance literature. In* The Tragedie of Antonie, *she follows Garnier's text closely, replacing the rhymed alexandrines of his French with blank verse but using rhyme when she can find it and to close verse paragraphs.*

Garnier (1545–90) dramatizes Antony's last day: his resolution to die at the end of Act 3 and his death, reported by the usual messenger, in Act 4. The last act is given over to the lamentation and funeral obsequies of Cleopatra, who indicts herself: "you, whom I destroyed, of you dear Lord, / Whom I of Empire, honor, life have spoiled." In her final speech, which ends the play, Garnier inserts in Act 5, lines 161–69—"Lived thus long . . . bury there my woe"—the words of Virgil's suicidal Dido from the Aeneid *4.653–58. He thus indicates his awareness of Virgil's alignment of these suicidal queens; the poet partly modeled the legendary Dido to reflect upon the historical Cleopatra and the erotic temptation she posed for Roman generals. Jodelle implied the connection, too, when he wrote a second tragedy,* Didon se sacrifiant *("Dido sacrificing herself"), almost as a companion piece to* Cléopatre captive. *Shakespeare also alludes to the connection when he has Antony, in a striking reversal of literary history, invoke the story of Dido and Aeneas just before he commits suicide: "Where souls do couch on flowers, we'll hand in hand, / And with our sprightly port make the ghosts gaze. / Dido and her Aeneas shall want troops, / And all the haunt be ours" (4.14.51–54). It should be noted that Dido snubs Aeneas in Virgil's underworld after the Roman leader has abandoned his African queen and consort (6.450–76); Shakespeare's Antony imagines Cleopatra and himself as a Dido and Aeneas who stay together beyond death.*

from *The Tragedie of Antonie* (1590; pub. 1592),[1] translating Robert Garnier, *Marc Antoine* (1578)

ACT 5, SCENE 1, LINES 137–208

CLEOPATRA   O Goddess thou whom Cyprus doth adore,
    Venus of Paphos, bent to work us harm
    For old Julus brood, if thou take care

---

[1] *The Tragedie of Antonie, done into English by the Countesse of Pembroke* (London: William Ponsonby, 1595).

Of Caesar, why of us tak'st thou no care?   140
Antony did descend, as well as he,
From thine own Son by long enchained line:
And might have rul'd by one and self same fate,
True Trojan blood, the stately Roman state.
　　Antony, poor Antony, my dear soul,
Now but a block, the booty of a tomb,
Thy life, thy heat is lost, thy color gone,
And hideous paleness on thy face hath seiz'd.
Thy eyes, two Suns, the lodging place of love,
Which yet for tents to warlike Mars did serve,   150
Lock'd up in lids (as fair day's cheerful light
Which darkness flies) do winking hide in night.
　　Antony by our true loves I thee beseech,
And by our hearts sweet sparks have set on fire,
Our holy marriage, and of the tender ruth
Of our dear babes, knot of our amity:
My doleful voice thy ear let entertain,
And take me with thee to the hellish plain,
Thy wife, thy friend: hear, Antony, O hear
My sobbing sighs, if here thou be, or there.   160
　　Lived thus long, the winged race of years
Ended I have as Destiny decreed,
Flourish'd and reign'd, and take just revenge
Of him who me both hated and despised.
Happy, alas too happy! if of Rome
Only the fleet had hither never come.
And now of me an Image great shall go
Under the earth to bury there my woe.
What say I? Where am I? O Cleopatra,
Poor Cleopatra, grief thy reason reaves.   170
No, no most happy in this hapless case,
To die with thee, and dying thee embrace:
My body joined with thine, my mouth with thine,
My mouth, whose moisture burning sighs have dried:
To be in one self tomb, and one self chest,
And wrapt with thee in one self sheet to rest.
　　The sharpest torment in my heart I feel
Is that I stay from thee, my heart, this while.

Die will I straight now, now straight will I die,
And straight with thee a wandering shade will be,   180
Under the Cypress trees thou haunt'st alone,
Where brooks of hell do falling seem to moan.
But yet I stay, and yet thee overlive,
That ere I die due rites I may thee give.
   A thousand sobs I from my breast will tear,
With thousand plaints thy funerals adorn:
My hair shall serve for thy oblations,
My boiling tears for thy effusions,
Mine eyes thy fire: for out them the flame
(Which burnt thy heart on me enamour'd) came.   190
   Weep my companions, weep, and from your eyes
Rain down on him of tears a brinish stream.
Mine can do no more, consumed by the coals
Which from my breast, as from a furnace, rise.
Martyr your breast with multiplied blows,
With violent hands tear off your hanging hair,
Outrage your face: alas! why should we seek
(Since now we die) our beauties more to keep?
   I spent in teares, not able more to spend,
But kiss him now, what rests me more to do?   200
Then let me kiss you, you fair eyes, my light,
Front, seat of honor, face most fierce, most fair!
O neck, O arms, O hands, O breast where death
(O mischief) comes to choke up vital breath.
A thousand kisses, thousand thousand more
Let you my mouth for honor's farewell give:
That in this office weak my limbs may grow,
Fainting on you, and forth my soul may flow.

Samuel Daniel (1562?–1619)

Samuel Daniel, a versatile writer best known for his sonnet sequence Delia *and his* Defense of Rhyme, *was the tutor of one of the sons of Mary Sidney and lived in her household at Wilton. He composed* The Tragedy of Cleopatra *as a companion piece and sequel to her* Tragedie of Antonie. *A play of considerable power as it charts Cleopatra's Stoic rejection of the world, its final act features a long speech by a messenger who was an eyewitness to her death. One detail may have caught Shakespeare's eye:*

> Well, in I went where brighter than the sun,
> Glittering in all her pompous rich array,
> Great Cleopatra sat, as if sh'had won
> Caesar, and all the world beside this day:
> Even as she was when on thy crystal streams,
> Clear Cydnos, she did show what earth could show;
> When Asia all amaz'd in wonder, deems
> Venus from heaven was come on earth below.
> Even as she went at first to meet her love,
> So goes she now again to find him. (5.2.77–86)

Compare Antony and Cleopatra *5.2.227–29: "Show me, my women, like a queen. Go fetch / My best attires. I am again for Cydnus, / To meet Mark Antony." This passage would disappear in Daniel's revised version of the play printed in 1607, a version more adapted to theatrical representation, where reported events become stage action. Why did Daniel revise his* Cleopatra? *He may have been trying to cash in on the success of Shakespeare's tragedy. The uncertain dating of* Antony and Cleopatra *makes it difficult to say. The passages here present Cleopatra's final speech in the 1594 version of Daniel's* Cleopatra *and her death scene in the 1607 revision.*

from *The Tragedy of Cleopatra* (1594)[1]

ACT 4, SCENE 2, LINES 1–118

[Cleopatra has received a letter from Dolabella revealing Caesar's plans; she realizes that Dolabella has fallen in love with her.]

CLEOPATRA   What, hath my face yet power to win a Lover?
   Can this torn remnant serve to grace me so,
   That I can Caesar's secret plots discover,
   What he intends with me and mine to do?

---

[1]*The Complete Works in Verse and Prose of Samuel Daniel,* ed. Alexander B. Grosart, Vol. 5 (London and Aylesbury: Hazell, Watson & Viney, 1885).

Why then, poor beauty, thou hast done thy last,
And best good service thou could'st do unto me;
For now the time of death reveal'd thou hast,
Which in my life dids't serve but to undo me.
    Here Dolabella, far forsooth in love,
Writes, how that Caesar means forthwith to send   10
Both me and mine, th'air of Rome to prove:
There his Triumphant Chariot to attend.
I thank the man, both for his love and letter;
The one comes fit to warn me thus before,
But for th'other I must die his debtor,
For Cleopatra now can love no more.
    But having leave, I must go take my leave
And last farewell of my dead Antony:
Whose dearly honor'd tomb must here receive
This sacrifice, the last before I die.   20
    O sacred ever-memorable stone
That hast without my tears, within my flame:
Receive th'oblation of the woefull'st moan
That ever yet from sad affliction came.
And you dear relics of my Lord and Love,
(The sweetest parcels of the faithfull'st liver,)
O let no impious hand dare to remove
You out from hence, but rest you here forever.
Let Egypt now give peace unto you dead,
That living, gave you trouble and turmoil: 30
Sleep quiet in this ever-lasting bed,
In foreign land preferr'd before your soil.
And, O, if that the sp'rits of men remain
After their bodies, and do never die,
Then hear thy ghost, thy captive spouse complain
And be attentive to her misery.
But if that laborsome mortality
Found this sweet error, only to confine
The curious search of idle vanity,
That would the depth of darkness undermine: 40
Or rather, to give rest unto the thought
Of wretched man, with th'after-coming joy

Of those conceived fields, whereon we dote,
To pacify the present world's annoy:
If it be so, why speak I then to th'air?
But 'tis not so, my Antony doth hear:
His ever-living ghost attends my prayer,
And I do know his hovering sprite is near.
And I will speak and pray, and mourn to thee.
O pure immortal soul that deign'st to hear,   50
I feel thou answer'st my credulity
With touch of comfort, finding none elsewhere.
Thou know'st these hands entomb'd thee here of late,
Free and unforced, which now must servile be,
Reserv'd for bands to grace proud Caesar's state,
Who seeks in me to triumph over thee.
O if in life we could not severed be,
Shall Death divide our bodies now asunder?
Must thine in Egypt, mine in Italy
Be kept the Monuments of Fortune's wonder?   60
If any powers be there whereas thou art,
(Sith our country gods betray our case,)
O work they may their gracious help impart,
To save thy woeful wife from such disgrace.
Do not permit she should in triumph show
The blush of her reproach, joined with thy shame:
But (rather) let that hateful tyrant know,
That thou and I had power t'avoid the same.
But what do I spend breath and idle wind,
In vain invoking a conceivèd aid?   70
Why do I not my self occasion find
To break the bounds wherein my self am stayed?
Words are for them that can complain and live,
Whose melting hearts compos'd of baser frame,
Can to their sorrows time and leisure give,
But Cleopatra may not do the same.
No, Antony, thy love requireth more:
A ling'ring death with thee deserves no merit;
I must my self force open wide a door
To let out life, and so unhouse my spirit.   80

These hands must break the prison of my soul
To come to thee, there to enjoy like state,
As doth the long-pent solitary fowl,
That hath escaped her cage, and found her mate.
This sacrifice to sacrifice my life,
Is that true incense that doth best beseem:
These rites may serve a life-desiring wife,
Who doing them, t'have done enough doth deem.
My heart blood should the purple flowers have been,
Which here upon thy tomb to thee are offered,   90
No smoke but dying breath should here been seen,
And this it had been too, had I been suffered.
But what have I save these bare hands to do it?
And these weak fingers are not iron-pointed:
They cannot pierce the flesh being put unto it,
And I of all means else am disappointed.
But yet I must a way and means seek, how
To come unto thee, whatsoe'er I do.
O, Death, art thou so hard to come by now,
That we must pray, entreat, and seek thee too?   100
But I will find thee wherefore'er thou lie,
For who can stay a mind resolv'd to die?
    And now I must go to work th'effect indeed,
I'll never send more words or sighs to thee:
I'll bring my soul my self, and that with speed,
My self will bring my soul to Antony.
Come, go my Maids, my fortunes sole attenders.
That minister to misery and sorrow:
Your Mistress you unto your freedom renders,
And will discharge your charge yet ere tomorrow.   110
    And now by this, I think the man I sent,
Is near return'd that brings me my dispatch.
God grant his cunning sort to good event,
And that his skill may well beguile my watch:
So shall I them disgrace, leave to be sorry,
Fly to my love, scape my foe, free my soul;
So shall I act the last of life with glory
Die like a Queen, and rest without control.

from *The Tragedy of Cleopatra* (1607)[1]

ACT 5, SCENE 2, LINES 67–134

CLEOPATRA   Come, rarest beast that all our Egypt breeds,
   How dearly welcome are thou now to me?
   The fairest creature that faire Nilus feeds,
   Methinks I see, in now beholding thee.   70
   Better than death, death's office thou dischargest,
   That with one gentle touch canst free our breath,
   And in a pleasing sleep our soul enlargest,
   Making ourselves not privy to our death.
   O welcome now of wonders wonder chief,
   That open canst with such an easy key
   The door of life, come gentle cunning thief,
   That from our selves so steal'st our selves away.
   And now I sacrifice these arms to death,
   That lust late dedicated to delights,   80
   Offering up my last, this last of breath,
   The complement of my loves dearest rites.
      What now, false flesh, what? and wilt thou conspire
   With Caesar too, as thou wert none of ours,
   To work my shame, and hinder my desire:
   And bend thy rebel parts against my powers?
   Wouldst thou retain in closure of thy veins
   That enemy, base life, to let my good?
   No, know there is a greater power constrains
   Than can be countercheckt with fearful blood: 90
   For in a mind that's great nothing seems great:
   And seeing death to be the last of woes,
   And life lasting disgrace, which I shall get,
   What do I lose that have but life to lose?
ERAS   See, not a yielding shrink, or touch of fear
   Consents now to bewray least sense of pain,
   But still in one same sweet unaltered cheer,
   Her honor doth her dying spirits retain.

[1]*Certaine Small Workes Heretofore Divulged by Samuel Daniel one of the Groomes of the Queenes Maiesties privie Chamber, & now againe by hm correced and augmented* (London: Simon Waterson, 1607).

CLEOPATRA   Well, now this work of mine is done, here ends
　　This act of life that part the Fates assign'd;　　　　　　　100
　　What glory of disgrace this world could lend,
　　Both have I had, and both I leave behind,
　　And Egypt, now the Theater where I
　　Have acted this, witness I die unforc'd,
　　Witness my soul parts free to Antony,
　　And now proud tyrant Caesar do thy worst.
ERAS   Come, Charmion, come, we must not only be
　　Spectators in this Scene, but Actors too.
　　Now comes our part, you know we did agree
　　The fellowship of death to undergo.　　　　　　　110
　　And though our meaner fortunes cannot claim
　　A glory by this act, they shall have fame.
CHARMION   Eras, I am prepar'd, and here is that
　　Will do the deed.
ERAS　　　　　　　　And here is of the same.
CHARMION   But, Eras, I'll begin, it is my place.
ERAS   Nay, Charmion, here I drink a death to thee.
　　I must be first.
CHARMION　　　　　Indeed thou hast prevented me.
　　Yet will I have this honor to be last
　　Which shall adorn this head, which must be seen
　　To wear that crown in death her life held fast,　　　　　120
　　That all the world may see she died a queen.
　　O see this face, the wonder of her life,
　　Retains in death a grace that graces death.
　　Color so lively, cheer so lovely rife,
　　As none would think this beauty could want breath.
　　And in this cheer th'impression of a smile
　　Doth seem to show she scorns both death and Caesar,
　　And glories that she could them so beguile.
　　And here tells death how well her death doth please her.
CAESAR'S MESSENGER   See, we are come too late, this is dispatched.　130
　　Caesar is disappointed of this grace.
　　Why how now Charmion, what, is this well done?
CHARMION   Yes, very well, and she that from the race
　　Of so great kings descends doth best become.

Fulke Greville (1554–1628)

Fulke Greville, Lord Brooke was the schoolmate and later companion of Sir Philip Sidney and was familiar with the Sidney circle after Philip's death; Samuel Daniel dedicated his finest poem, "Musophilus," to him. Greville also wrote neoclassical tragedies, which explored political themes: Mustapha, Alaham, *and an* Antony and Cleopatra. *He burned this last, as he explains in the passage presented here from his* Life of Sir Philip Sidney *(published posthumously in 1652), fearful that Antony's downfall might evoke the recent fate of the Earl of Essex, a once close friend who tried to overthrow Queen Elizabeth. There is reason to believe Greville had something to fear. Daniel was brought up before the Privy Council on account of his play* Philotas *(1605), with its transparent reflections on the Essex affair. Greville's suppressed play shows how Antony's ancient conflict with Caesar could be understood in terms of a more modern struggle between the high noble subject and an emerging absolutist monarch.*

A lost *Antony and Cleopatra,* from *Life of Sidney* (1652)[1]

Chapter 14

Lastly, concerning the tragedies themselves; they were in their first creation three; Whereof *Antony and Cleopatra,* according to their irregular passions in forsaking empire to follow sensuality, were sacrificed in the fire. The executioner, the author himself. Not that he conceived it to be a contemptible younger brother to the rest; but lest, while he seemed to look over-much upward, he might stumble into the astronomer's pit. Many members in that creature (by the opinion of those few eyes that saw it) having some childish wantonness in them apt enough to be construed or strained to a personating of vices in the present governors and government. . . . And again, in the practice of the world, seeing the like instance not poetically, but really, fashioned in the Earl of Essex then falling; and ever till then worthily beloved both of Queen, and people: This sudden descent of such a greatness, together with the quality of the actors in every scene, stirred up the author's second thoughts to be careful (in his own case) of leaving fair weather behind him.

---

[1] *The Prose Works of Fulke Greville, Lord Brooke,* ed. John Gouws (Oxford: Clarendon Press, 1986).

Sir Charles Sedley (1639–1701)

Sir Charles Sedley wrote his Antony and Cleopatra *in the rhymed couplets developed by John Dryden's heroic tragedies a year before Dryden himself turned back to Shakespearean blank verse in* All for Love. *A famous wit and favorite drinking companion of Charles II, Sedley nonetheless drifted to the nascent Whig opposition hostile to Stuart absolutism in the 1670s. His play registers this dissent in the lament that Agrippa, right-hand man of Octavius, voices for the lost liberty of the Roman republic: "Born under kings our fathers freedom fought, / And with their blood the Godlike treasure bought, / And their vile issue in chains delight, / And born to freedom for our Tyrants fight" (3.1.112–15). Even Sedley's Octavia denounces her brother's political hypocrisy.*

> CAESAR   You would not sure my love so ill repay.
>
> OCTAVIA   Your love! Your pride and endless thirst of sway.
> To gain my friends, my quarrel you pretend,
> But universal empire is your end.
> Rome's once great Senate now is but a name;
> While some with fear, and some with bribes you tame.
> Men learn at court what they must repeat,
> And for concurrence, not for council meet. (4.1.95–102)

In an age when actresses at last could act the parts of women, Sedley builds up the role and character of Octavia for a second principal actress, and he invents a romantic subplot in which she is loved by Maecenas. Keeping the classical unity of time, Sedley has Cleopatra's death take place (as in All for Love) *directly after Antony's. In keeping, too, with seventeenth-century neoclassical norms, Sedley's play adds a lowborn courtly intriguer as its treacherous villain, Cleopatra's minister Photinus. No longer a eunuch (as in Plutarch), Photinus is in love with Iras, to whom he promises the crown of Egypt, a promise that accounts for Iras's reluctance to die along with her mistress and for the extra help of Charmion. Iras stays alive just long enough for Photinus to murder her, and his own death at the hand of a soldier, Iras's brother, concludes the play.*

from *Antony and Cleopatra* (1677)[1]

ACT 5, SCENE 1, LINES 332–459:
The Deaths of Antony, Cleopatra, Iras, and Charmion

ANTONY   I die, and have but one short word to say;
  But you must swear, my Queen, you will obey.
CLEOPATRA   By all our love I will: my death command,
  And see the eager duty of my hand.
ANTONY   Your death! it is the only thing I fear:
  And Fate no other way can reach me here.
CLEOPATRA   Down from a throne to any private State:
  It is a dismal precipice to the great.
  I giddy with that horrid prospect grow;   340
  And shall fall in, unless Death help me now.
ANTONY   Heav'n, that success does to my arms deny,
  Whispers a Roman soul, and bids him die.
  Our case is different, to Caesar sue,
  Though me hate, he needs must pity you.
  Your beauty and your love were all your crime,
  And you must live my Queen.
CLEOPATRA   When you are dead—
  To be despis'd, reproach'd, in triumph led;
  A queen and slave! who would not life renounce,
  Rather than bear those distant names at once?   350
ANTONY   But you may live a queen; say you obey'd
  Through fear: and were compell'd to give me aid:
  That all your subjects private orders had
  Not to resist him, and my cause betray'd.
  Say that at last you did my death procure;
  Say any thing that may your life and crown secure.
CLEOPATRA   'Twere false and base, it rather shall be said
  I kill'd myself when I beheld you dead.
ANTONY   Me the unhappy cause of all your woe!
  Your own and your dear country's overthrow.   360
  Remember I was jealous, rash, soon moved,

---

[1]Sedley, *Antony and Cleopatra: A Tragedy* (London: Richard Tonson, 1677).

Suspected no less fiercely than I loved:
How I Thyreus kill'd, your love accused,
And to your kind defence my faith refused.
From shame and rage I soon shall be at rest,
And Death of thousand ills hath chose the best.   [*He faints.*]

CLEOPATRA   O stay! and take me with you—
ANTONY   Dearest Queen,
Let my life end before your death begin.
O Rome! thy freedom does with me expire,
And thou art lost, obtaining thy desire.   [*Dies.*]   370

CLEOPATRA   He's gone! He's gone! and I for ever lost!
The great Antonius now is but a ghost:
A wandering shadow on the Stygian coast.
I'm still a queen, though by the fate of war,
Death and these women all my subjects are;
And this unhappy Monument is all
Of the whole World, that I my own can call.

IRAS   O name not death!
Caesar men say is good, wise, mild and just;
So many virtues how can you distrust?   380

CLEOPATRA   Though his last breath advised me to submit
To Caesar, and his falling fortunes quit:
When I named death, speechless my hand he pressed
And seemed to say that I had chose the best.

IRAS   He could not be so cruel, you mistook;
Too sharply you apply his dying look.

CLEOPATRA   He does expect it, and I'll keep my word,
If there be Death in Poison, Fire, or Sword.

CHARMION   Fortune with lighter strokes strikes lighter things;
With her whole weight she crushes falling kings.   390

CLEOPATRA   We shall in triumph, Charmion, be led,
Till with our shame Rome's pride be surfeited:
Till every finger Cleopatra find
Pointing at her, who was their Queen design'd.

CHARMION   Their anger they may glut, but not their pride.
They ne'er had triumphed if men durst have died.

CLEOPATRA   Beauty, thou art a fair, but fading flow'r.
The tender prey of every coming hour:
In youth thou comet-like art gaz'd upon,

But art portentous to thy self alone.   400
Unpunished thou to few wer't ever giv'n:
Nor art a blessing, but a mark from heav'n.
Greatness most envied, when least understood:
Thou art no real, but a seeming good.
Sick at the Heart! Thou in the face look'st well,
And none but such as feel thy pangs can tell.
By thy exalted state we only gain
To be more wretched than the vulgar can.

IRAS   Think how he'll use your sons when you are dead,
And none their cause can like a mother plead.   410

CLEOPATRA   Perhaps, when I am dead, his hate may cease,
And pity take declining rage's place.
Sure in the grave all enmities take end,
And love alone can to the dead extend.
Men say that we to th'other world shall bear
The same desires and thoughts, employed as here.
The hero shall in shining arms delight,
In neighing steeds, shrill sounds and empty fight:
And lovers in eternal roses love.
If so, Antonius, we but change the scene,   420
And there pursue what we did here begin.

CHARMION   I am prepar'd to follow or to lead:
Name but the fatal path that you will tread.

CLEOPATRA   In yonder golden box three asps there lie,
Of whose least venomous bite men sleep and die:
Take one and to my naked breast apply
Its poisonous mouth—

CHARMION   Alone she shall not die.

IRAS   When Julius Caesar in the Senate fell,
Where were these thoughts? and yet he loved as well.

CLEOPATRA   He loved me not! he was ambitious he;   430
And but at looser times took thought of me.
Glory and empire filled his restless mind:
He knew not the soft pleasures of the kind.
Our joys were frighted still with fresh alarms,
And new designs still forced him from my arms.
But my Antonius loved me with his soul.
No cares of empire did his flame control.

I was his friend, the partner of his mind;
Our days were joyful, and our nights were kind:
He liv'd for me, and I will die for him.   440

[*Stings herself.*]

So, now 'tis past! I feel my eyes grow dim
I am from triumph and contempt secure,
What all must bear I earlier endure.

[*Kneels down to Antony.*]

To thy cold arms take thy unhappy Queen,
Who both thy ruin and her own has been:
Other embrace than this she'll never know,
But a pale ghost, pursue thy shade below.
Good asp, bite deep and deadly in my breast,
And give me sudden and eternal rest.   [*She dies.*]

[*Iras runs away.*]

CHARMION   Fool, from thy hasty fate thou can'st not run.   450
IRAS   Let it bite you, I'll stay till you have done:
    Alas! my life but newly is begun—
CHARMION   No: thou would'st live to shame thy family;
    But I'll take care that thou shalt nobly die.
IRAS   Good Charmion!
CHARMION   I'll hear no more: faint hearts that seek delay
    Will never want some foolish thing to say.

[*Charmion stings her, then puts to her own breast.*]

At our Queen's feet let's decently be found,
And loyal grief be thought our only wound.   [*Dies.*]

John Dryden (1631–1700)

All for Love *is the only one of these non-Shakespearean treatments of* Antony and Cleopatra *to hold the stage today. John Dryden consciously sought to imitate Shakespeare's verse—"I hope I may affirm, and without vanity, that by imitating him, I have excelled myself"—even as he artfully contracted the action to observe classical unity. As in Sedley's play, there is a villainous court-intriguer, Alexas, and the role of Octavia is augmented for a second leading lady: Sparks fly in the confrontation Dryden invents between Octavia and Cleopatra, wife and mistress, printed here. The great political conflicts of the story are reduced to domestic ones (Caesar does not appear as a character), and the play is built, in the French style of Corneille, out of the paired impulses that tear Antony into different directions: shame/heroic determination, determination/love, love/family obligation, obligation/jealousy (Antony thinks Cleopatra has returned the love of Dolabella). The death scene of Antony and Cleopatra is a worthy tribute to Shakespeare's original: Dryden points out in his Preface that "Words and phrases must of necessity receive a change in succeeding ages."*

from *All for Love or The World Well Lost* (1678)[1]

ACT 3, SCENE 1, LINES 417–467:
Octavia Meets Cleopatra

OCTAVIA   I need not ask if you are Cleopatra,
  Your haughty carriage—
CLEOPATRA   Shows I am a queen.
  Nor need I ask who you are.
OCTAVIA   A Roman;
  A name that makes and can unmake a queen.   420
CLEOPATRA   Your lord, the man who serves me, is a Roman.
OCTAVIA   He was a Roman, till he lost that name
  To be a slave of Egypt; but I come
  To free him hence.
CLEOPATRA   Peace, peace, my lover's Juno.
  When he grew weary of that household clog,
  He chose my easier bonds.
OCTAVIA   I wonder not
  Your bonds are easy. You have long been practised
  In that lascivious art. He's not the first
  For whom you spread your snares: Let Caesar witness.
CLEOPATRA   I loved not Caesar; 'twas but gratitude   430
  I paid his love: The worst your malice can
  Is but to say the greatest of mankind
  Has been my slave. The next, but far above him
  In my esteem, is he whom law calls yours,
  But whom his love made mine.

[1]*The Works of John Dryden*, Vol. 5 (London: William Miller, 1808).

OCTAVIA   I would view nearer [*Coming up closer to her.*
  That face which has so long usurped my right,
  To find the inevitable charms, that catch
  Mankind so sure, that ruined my dear lord.
CLEOPATRA   Oh, you do well to search; for had you known
  But half these charms, you had not lost his heart.   440
OCTAVIA   Far be their knowledge from a Roman lady,
  Far from a modest wife! Shame of our sex,
  Dost thou not blush to own those black endearments
  That make sin pleasing?
CLEOPATRA   You may blush, who want them.
  If bounteous nature, if indulgent heaven
  Have given me charms to please the bravest man,
  Should I not thank them? should I be ashamed,
  And not be proud? I am, that he has loved me;
  And when I love not him, heaven change this face
  For one like that.
OCTAVIA   Thou lov'st him not so well.   450
CLEOPATRA   I love him better, and deserve him more.
OCTAVIA   You do not; cannot: You have been his ruin.
  Who made him cheap at Rome but Cleopatra?
  Who made him scorned abroad but Cleopatra?
  At Actium who betrayed him? Cleopatra.
  Who made his children orphans, and poor me
  A wretched widow? Only Cleopatra.
CLEOPATRA   Yet she, who loves him best, is Cleopatra.
  If you have suffered, I have suffered more.
  You bear the specious title of a wife,   460
  To gild your cause and draw the pitying world
  To favor it. The world condemns poor me,
  For I have lost my honor, lost my fame,
  And stained the glory of my royal house,
  And all to bear the branded name of mistress.
  There wants but life, and that, too, I would lose
  For him I love.
OCTAVIA   Be't so, then; take thy wish.

                                              [*Exit with her Train.*

ACT 5, SCENE 1, LINES 362–518:
The Deaths of Antony and Cleopatra
and the End of *All for Love*

ANTONY　　. . . Sit thee down, my Cleopatra:
　　I'll make the most I can of life, to stay
　　A moment more with thee.
CLEOPATRA　　　　　　　　　How is it with you?
ANTONY　　'Tis as with a man
　　Removing in a hurry; all packed up,
　　But one dear jewel that his haste forgot;
　　And he, for that, returns upon the spur:
　　So I come back for thee.
CLEOPATRA　　Too long, you heavens, you have been cruel to me:　　370
　　Now show your mended faith, and give me back
　　His fleeting life!
ANTONY　　　　　　　It will not be, my love;
　　I keep my soul by force.
　　Say but, thou art not false.
CLEOPATRA　　　　　　　　'Tis now too late
　　To say I'm true: I'll prove it, and die with you.
　　Unknown to me, Alexas feigned my death:
　　Which, when I knew, I hasted to prevent
　　This fatal consequence. My fleet betrayed
　　Both you and me.
ANTONY　　　　　　And Dolabella—
CLEOPATRA　　　　　　　　　　Scarce
　　Esteemed before he loved; but hated now.　　380
ANTONY　　Enough: my life's not long enough for more.
　　Thou say'st, thou wilt come after: I believe thee;
　　For I can now believe what'er thou sayest,
　　That we may part more kindly.
CLEOPATRA　　　　　　　　　I will come:
　　Doubt not, my life, I'll come, and quickly too:
　　Caesar shall triumph o'er no part of thee.
ANTONY　　But grieve not, while thou stayest,
　　My last disastrous times:
　　Think we have had a clear and glorious day;

And heaven did kindly to delay the storm   390
    Just till our close of evening. Ten years' love,
    And not a moment lost, but all improved
    To the utmost joys: what ages have we lived!
    And now to die each other's; and, so dying,
    While hand in hand we walk in groves below,
    Whole troops of lovers' ghosts shall flock about us,
    And all the train be ours.
CLEOPATRA   Your words are like the notes of dying swans,
    Too sweet to last. Were there so many hours
    For your unkindness, and not one for love?   400
ANTONY   No, not a minute.—This one kiss—more worth
    Than all I leave to Caesar.   [*Dies.*
CLEOPATRA   O tell me so again,
    And take ten thousand kisses for that word.
    My lord, my lord: Speak, if you yet have being;
    Sign to me, if you can not speak, or cast
    One look. Do anything that shows you live.
IRAS   He's gone too far to hear you,
    And this you see, a lump of senseless clay,
    The leavings of a soul.
CHARMION   Remember, madam,
    He charged you not to grieve.
CLEOPATRA   And I'll obey him.   410
    I have not loved a Roman not to know
    What should become his wife—his wife, my Charmion,
    For 'tis to that high title I aspire,
    And now I'll not die less. Let dull Octavia
    Survive to mourn him dead; my nobler fate
    Shall knit our spousals with a tie too strong
    For Roman laws to break.
IRAS   Will you then die?
CLEOPATRA   Why shouldst thou make that question?
IRAS   Caesar is merciful.
CLEOPATRA   Let him be so
    To those that want his mercy; my poor lord   420
    Made no such covenant with him to spare me
    When he was dead. Yield me to Caesar's pride?
    What! to be led in triumph through the streets,

A spectacle to base plebeian eyes,
While some dejected friend of Antony's
Close in a corner, shakes his head, and mutters
A secret curse on her who ruined him?
I'll none of that.
CHARMION   Whatever you resolve
I'll follow, even to the death.
IRAS   I only feared
For you, but more should fear to live without you.   430
CLEOPATRA   Why, now, 'tis as it should be. Quick, my friends,
Dispatch; ere this, the town's in Caesar's hands.
My lord looks down concerned, and fears my stay,
Lest I should be surprised;.
Keep him not waiting for his love too long.
You, Charmion, bring my crown and richest jewels;
With them, the wreath of victory I made
(Vain augury) for him who now lies dead.
You, Iras, bring the cure of all our ills.
IRAS   The aspics, madam?
CLEOPATRA   Must I bid you twice?   440

                    [*Exeunt Charmion and Iras.*

'Tis sweet to die when they would force life on me,
To rush into the dark abode of death,
And seize him first. If he be like my love,
He is not frightful, sure.
We're now alone in secrecy and silence,
And is not this like lovers? I may kiss
These pale cold lips; Octavia does not see me.
And, oh, 'tis better far to have him thus
Than see him in her arms.

                    [*Enter Charmion and Iras.*

                    Oh welcome, welcome.
CHARMION   What must be done?
CLEOPATRA   Short ceremony, friends,   450
But yet it must be decent. First, this laurel
Shall crown my hero's head: he fell not basely
Nor left his shield behind him.—Only thou

Couldst triumph o'er thyself, and thou alone
Wert worthy so to triumph.
CHARMION   To what end
These ensigns of your pomp and royalty?
CLEOPATRA   Dull that thou art! why, 'tis to meet my love;
As when I saw him first on Cydnos' bank,
All sparkling, like a goddess: so adorned,
I'll find him once again; my second spousals   460
Shall match my first in glory. Haste, haste, both,
And dress the bride of Antony.
CHARMION   'Tis done.
CLEOPATRA   Now seat me by my lord. I claim this place;
For I must conquer Caesar, too, like him,
And win my share o' th' world.—Hail, you dear relics
Of my immortal love!
O let no impious hand remove you hence;
But rest forever here! Let Egypt give
His death that peace which it denied his life.—
Reach me the casket.
IRAS   Underneath the fruit   470
The aspic lies.
CLEOPATRA   Welcome, thou kind deceiver!

                           [*Putting aside the leaves.*

Thou best of thieves; who, with an easy key,
Dost open life, and unperceived by us,
Even steal us from ourselves; discharging so
Death's dreadful office better than himself;
Touching our limbs so gently into slumber
That death stands by, deceived by his own image,
And thinks himself but sleep.
SERAPION   The queen, where is she?   [*Within.*
The town is yielded, Caesar's at the gates.
CLEOPATRA   He comes too late to invade the rights of death.   480
Haste, bare my arm, and rouse the serpent's fury.

                  [*Holds out her arm and draws it back.*

Coward flesh,
Wouldst thou conspire with Caesar to betray me,

As thou wert none of mine? I'll force thee to't,
And not be sent by him,
But bring myself, my soul, to Antony.

> [*Turns aside, and then shows her arms bloody.*

Take hence; the work is done.

SERAPION   Break ope the door,   [*Within.*
And guard the traitor well.

CHARMION   The next is ours.

IRAS   Now, Charmion, to be worthy
Of our great queen and mistress.   [*They apply the aspics.*

CLEOPATRA   Already, death, I feel thee in my veins: 491
I go with such a will to find my lord
That we shall quickly meet.
A heavy numbness creeps through every limb,
And now 'tis at my head: My eyelids fall,
And my dear love is vanished in a mist.
Where shall I find him, where? O turn me to him,
And lay me on his breast!—Caesar, thy worst;
Now part us, if thou canst.   [*Dies.*

> [*Iras sinks down at her feet, and dies; Charmion
> stands behind her chair, as dressing her head.*

> *Enter Serapion, two Priests, Alexas bound, Egyptians.*

PRIEST   Behold, Serapion,
What havoc death has made!

SERAPION   'Twas what I feared.—   500
Charmion, is this well done?

CHARMION   Yes, 'tis well done, and like a queen, the last
Of her great race: I follow her.   [*Sinks down; dies.*

ALEXAS   'Tis true,
She has done well. Much better thus to die
Than live to make a holiday in Rome.

SERAPION   See, see how the lovers sit in state together,
As they were giving laws to half mankind!
Th'impression of a smile, left in her face,
Shows she died pleased with him for whom she lived,
And went to charm him in another world.   510

Caesar's just entering: grief has now no leisure.
Secure that villain, as our pledge of safety,
To grace the imperial triumph.—Sleep, blest pair,
Secure from human chance, long ages out,
While all the storms of fate fly o'er your tomb;
  And fame to late posterity shall tell,
    No lovers lived so great, or died so well.   *Exeunt.*

The Great Critics on Antony and Cleopatra: *Schlegel to Bradley*

Haunting the reception of *Antony and Cleopatra* has been the question of why Shakespeare's most classical play in content should also be the least classical in form. The sprawl and copiousness of the play are something of a test case for the modern criticism that praised Shakespeare precisely for being *un*classical. From August Wilhelm Schlegel at the beginning of the nineteenth century to A. C. Bradley at the beginning of the twentieth, critics used *Antony and Cleopatra* to defend a Romantic aesthetic of rulebreaking freedom and sublimity—Samuel Taylor Coleridge called it Shakespeare's "most wonderful play" and praised its "numerous momentary flashes of nature"—measured against the reasoned norms of neoclassicism. This aesthetic became identified with the play's title characters themselves, particularly with Cleopatra, in their opposition to Caesar, to his political rationality and austere personal style.

August Wilhelm Schlegel (1767–1845)

August Wilhelm Schlegel's translations into German of Shakespeare's plays, which began to appear in 1797, established Shakespeare once and for all as a European and World author. In his own Lectures on Dramatic Literature *(1809–11), translated into various European languages, into English in 1815, Schlegel recast Shakespeare for modern taste. Schlegel was happy to jettison the neoclassical (French) unities of time and place; he nevertheless found a culpable excess in the sheer historical expanse of* Antony and Cleopatra *and its numerous secondary characters.*

from *Lectures on Dramatic Literature* (1809–1811)[1]

Antony and Cleopatra may, in some measure, be considered as a continuation of *Julius Cæsar*: the two principal characters of *Antony* and *Augustus* are equally sustained in both pieces. *Antony and Cleopatra* is a play of great extent; the progress is less simple than in *Julius Cæsar*. The fullness and variety of political and warlike events, to which the union of the three divisions of the Roman world under one master necessarily gave rise, were perhaps too great to admit of being clearly exhibited in one dramatic picture. In this consists the great difficulty of the historical drama:—it must be a crowded extract, and a living development of history;—the difficulty, however, has generally been successfully overcome by Shakespeare. But now many things, which are transacted in the background, are here merely alluded to, in a manner which supposes an intimate acquaintance with the history; but a work of art should contain, within itself, every thing necessary for its being fully understood. Many persons of historical importance are merely introduced in passing; the preparatory and concurring circumstances are not sufficiently collected into masses to avoid distracting our attention. The principal personages, however, are most emphatically distinguished by lineament and colouring, and powerfully arrest the imagination. In Antony we observe a mixture of great qualities, weaknesses, and vices; violent ambition and ebullitions of magnanimity; we see him now sinking into luxurious enjoyment and then nobly ashamed of his own aberrations,—manning himself to resolutions not unworthy of himself, which are always shipwrecked against the seductions of an artful woman. It is Hercules in the chains of Omphale, drawn from the fabulous heroic ages into history, and invested with the Roman costume. The seductive arts of Cleopatra are in no respect veiled over; she is an ambiguous being made up of royal pride, female vanity, luxury, inconstancy, and true attachment. Although the mutual passion of herself and

---

[1]*Lectures on Dramatic Art and Literature by August Wilhelm Schlegel*, trans. John Black (London: George Bell, 1889).

Antony is without moral dignity, it still excites our sympathy as an insurmountable fascination:—they seem formed for each other, and Cleopatra is as remarkable for her seductive charms as Antony for the splendour of his deeds. As they die for each other, we forgive them for having lived for each other. The open and lavish character of Antony is admirably contrasted with the heartless littleness of Octavius, whom Shakspeare seems to have completely seen through, without allowing himself to be led astray by the fortune and fame of Augustus.

William Hazlitt (1778–1830)

William Hazlitt relates the multiplicity in Antony and Cleopatra *to its depiction of the "unstable, unsubstantial" nature of human greatness. This contingency is the "character" of* Antony and Cleopatra *to which the title of his* Characters of Shakespear's Plays *(1817) primarily refers. While Hazlitt analyzes the motives and manners of dramatic characters—notably Cleopatra here—he seeks to define the overall stylistic tint and effect of each Shakespearean play. His discussion follows Schlegel's polemic against neoclassical drama and its "stage puppets" and "poetical machines making set speeches" that turn into a "three hours' inaugural disputation." Writing with clarity and without condescension for a democratic public, Hazlitt defined the role of the modern journalist-critic, and he was the first great critic of live theatrical performance. His prose is unmatched for its vividness and energy, the very qualities he admired in the art, literature, acting, and sports about which he wrote.* Characters *was the first book on Shakespeare intended for a wide popular audience.*

from *Characters of Shakespear's Plays* (1817)[1]

This is a very noble play. Though not in the first class of Shakespear's productions, it stands next to them, and is, we think, the finest of his historical plays, that is, of those in which he made poetry the organ of history, and assumed a certain tone of character and sentiment, in conformity to known facts, instead of trusting to his

---

[1]Hazlitt, *Characters of Shakespear's Plays* (London: Taylor and Hessey, 1818).

observations of general nature or to the unlimited indulgence of his own fancy. What he has added to the actual story, is upon a par with it. His genius was, as it were, a match for history as well as nature, and could grapple at will with either. The play is full of that pervading comprehensive power by which the poet could always make himself master of time and circumstances. It presents a fine picture of Roman pride and Eastern magnificence: and in the struggle between the two, the empire of the world seems suspended, "like the swan's downfeather,

> That stands upon the swell at full of tide,
> And neither way inclines. [3.2.49–50]

The characters breathe, move, and live. Shakespear does not stand reasoning on what his characters would do or say, but at once *becomes* them, and speaks and acts for them. He does not present us with groups of stage-puppets of poetical machines making set speeches on human life, and acting from a calculation of problematical motives, but he brings living men and women on the scene, who speak and act from real feelings, according to the ebbs and flows of passion, without the least tincture of pedantry of logic or rhetoric. Nothing is made out by inference and analogy, by climax and antithesis, but every thing takes place just as it would have done in reality, according to the occasion.—The character of Cleopatra is a master-piece. What an extreme contrast it affords to Imogen! One would think it almost impossible for the same person to have drawn both. She is voluptuous, ostentatious, conscious, boastful of her charms, haughty, tyrannical, fickle. The luxurious pomp and gorgeous extravagance of the Egyptian queen are displayed in all their force and lustre, as well as the irregular grandeur of the soul of Mark Antony. Take only the first four lines that they speak as an example of the regal style of love-making.

> *Cleopatra.* If it be love indeed, tell me how much?
> *Antony.* There's beggary in the love that can be reckon'd.
> *Cleopatra.* I'll set a bourn how far to be belov'd.
> *Antony.* Then must thou needs find out new heav'n, new earth.
> [1.1.14–17]

The rich and poetical description of her person beginning—

The barge she sat in, like a burnish'd throne,
Burnt on the water; the poop was beaten gold,
Purple the sails, and so perfumed, that
The winds were love-sick— [2.2.200–203]

seems to prepare the way for, and almost to justify the subsequent infatuation of Antony when in the sea-fight at Actium, he leaves the battle, and "like a doating mallard" follows her flying sails.

Few things in Shakespear (and we know of nothing in any other author like them) have more of that local truth of imagination and character than the passage in which Cleopatra is represented conjecturing what were the employments of Antony in his absence— "He's speaking now, or murmuring—*Where's my serpent of old Nile?*" Or again, when she says to Antony, after the defeat at Actium, and his summoning up resolution to risk another fight—"It is my birth-day; I had thought to have held it poor; but since my lord is Antony again, I will be Cleopatra." Perhaps the finest burst of all is Antony's rage after his final defeat when he comes in, and surprises the messenger of Cæsar kissing her hand—

To let a fellow that will take rewards,
And say God quit you, be familiar with,
My play-fellow, your hand; this kingly seal,
And plighter of high hearts. [3.13.125–28]

It is no wonder that he orders him to be whipped; but his low condition is not the true reason: there is another feeling which lies deeper, though Antony's pride would not let him shew it, except by his rage; he suspects the fellow to be Cæsar's proxy.

Cleopatra's whole character is the triumph of the voluptuous, of the love of pleasure and the power of giving it, over every other consideration. Octavia is a dull foil to her, and Fulvia a shrew and shrill-tongued. What a picture do those lines give of her—

Age cannot wither her, nor custom stale
Her infinite variety. Other women cloy

The appetites they feed, but she makes hungry
Where most she satisfies. [2.2.244–47]

What a spirit and fire in her conversation with Antony's messenger who brings her the unwelcome news of his marriage with
Octavia! How all the pride of beauty and of high rank breaks out in
her promised reward to him—

————There's gold, and here
My bluest veins to kiss!— [2.5.28–29]

She had great and unpardonable faults, but the grandeur of her
death almost redeems them. She learns from the depth of despair
the strength of her affections. She keeps her queen-like state in the
last disgrace, and her sense of the pleasurable in the last moments of
her life. She tastes a luxury in death. After applying the asp, she says
with fondness—

Dost thou not see my baby at my breast,
That sucks the nurse asleep?
As sweet as balm, as soft as air, as gentle.
Oh Antony! [5.2.306–9]

It is worth while to observe that Shakespear has contrasted the
extreme magnificence of the descriptions in this play with pictures
of extreme suffering and physical horror, not less striking—partly
perhaps to place the effeminate character of Mark Antony in a
more favourable light, and at the same time to preserve a certain
balance of feeling in the mind. Cæsar says, hearing of his rival's
conduct at the court of Cleopatra,

————Antony,
Leave thy lascivious wassels. When thou once
Wert beaten from Mutina, where thou slew'st
Hirtius and Pansa, consuls, at thy heel
Did famine follow, whom thou fought'st against,
Though daintily brought up, with patience more
Than savages could suffer. Thou did'st drink

The stale of horses, and the gilded puddle
Which beast would cough at. Thy palate then did deign
The roughest berry on the rudest hedge,
Yea, like the stag, when snow the pasture sheets,
The barks of trees thou browsed'st. On the Alps,
It is reported, thou didst eat strange flesh,
Which some did die to look on: and all this,
It wounds thine honour, that I speak it now,
Was borne so like a soldier, that thy cheek
So much as lank'd not. [1.4.56–72]

The passage after Antony's defeat by Augustus, where he is
made to say—

Yes, yes; he at Philippi kept
His sword e'en like a dancer; while I struck
The lean and wrinkled Cassius, and 'twas I
That the mad Brutus ended— [3.11.35–38]

is one of those fine retrospections which shew us the winding and
eventful march of human life. The jealous attention which has been
paid to the unities both of time and place has taken away the principle of perspective in the drama, and all the interest which objects
derive from distance, from contrast, from privation, from change of
fortune, from long-cherished passion; and contrasts our view of life
from a strange and romantic dream, long, obscure, and infinite,
into a smartly contested, three hours' inaugural disputation on its
merits by the different candidates for theatrical applause.

The latter scenes of *Antony and Cleopatra* are full of the changes of
accident and passion. Success and defeat follow one another with startling rapidity. Fortune sits upon her wheel more blind and giddy than
usual. This precarious state and the approaching dissolution of his
greatness are strikingly displayed in the dialogue of Antony with Eros.

> *Antony.* Eros, thou yet behold'st me?
> *Eros.* Ay, noble lord.
> *Antony.* Sometime we see a cloud that's dragonish,
> A vapour sometime, like a bear or lion,

A towered citadel, a pendant rock,
A forked mountain, or blue promontory
With trees upon't, that nod unto the world
And mock our eyes with air. Thou hast seen these signs,
They are black vesper's pageants.
    Eros. Ay, my lord.
    Antony. That which is now a horse, even with a thought
The rack dislimns, and makes it indistinct
As water is in water.
    Eros. It does, my lord.
    Antony. My good knave, Eros, now thy captain is
Even such a body, &c. [4.14.1–13]

This is, without a doubt, one of the finest pieces of poetry in Shakespear. The splendour of the imagery, the semblance of reality, the lofty range of picturesque objects hanging over the world, their evanescent nature, the total uncertainty of what is left behind, are just like the mouldering schemes of human greatness. It is finer than Cleopatra's passionate lamentation over his fallen grandeur, because it is more dim, unstable, unsubstantial. Antony's head-strong presumption and infatuated determination to yield to Cleopatra's wishes to fight by sea instead of land, meet a merited punishment; and the extravagance of his resolutions, increasing with the desperateness of his circumstances, is well commented upon by Œnobarbus.

————I see men's judgments are
A parcel of their fortunes, and things outward
Do draw the inward quality after them
To suffer all alike. [3.13.31–34]

The repentance of Œnobarbus after his treachery to his master is the most affecting part of the play. He cannot recover from the blow which Antony's generosity gives him, and he dies broken-hearted, "a master-leaver and a fugitive."

Shakespear's genius has spread over the whole play a richness like the overflowing of the Nile.

Anna Jameson (1794–1860)

Characteristics of Women, Moral, Poetical, and Historical *(1832) by Mrs. Anna Jameson is devoted to Shakespeare's heroines. After working fifteen years as a governess and after her subsequent, unhappy marriage in 1825, which eventually led to separation, Jameson (like Hazlitt) made her living with her pen. While she was more a friend of feminists than one herself, her* Characteristics *pioneered a criticism concerned with the literary representation of women. As opposed to Hazlitt's* Characters, *Jameson's* Characteristics *is a study of literary characters, and she views Shakespeare's Cleopatra as a "dramatic portrait of astonishing beauty, spirit, and originality." Her insisting that the play's Cleopatra is identical to the equally contradictory Cleopatra of the historical record makes a polemical point about the humanity, the "consistent inconsistency," of Shakespeare's creation. Here, too, the contrast is with the neoclassical tragedy of Dryden and Racine and its more formulaic, one-dimensional characters: Witness Dryden's Cleopatra in* All for Love, *whose exchange with Octavia (included earlier, on p. 227–28) comes in for Jameson's particular censure.*

from *Characteristics of Women, Moral, Poetical, Historical* (1832)[1]

CLEOPATRA.

I cannot agree with one of the most philosophical of Shakspeare's critics, who has asserted "that the actual truth of particular events, in proportion as we are conscious of it, is a drawback on the pleasure, as well as the dignity of tragedy." If this observation applies at all, it is equally just with regard to characters: and in either case can we admit it? The reverence and the simpleness of heart with which Shakspeare has treated the received and admitted truths of history—I mean according to the imperfect knowledge of his time—is admirable; his inaccuracies are few; his general accuracy, allowing for the distinction between the narrative and the dramatic form, is acknowledged to be wonderful. He did not steal the precious material from the treasury of history, to debase its purity,—new-stamp it arbitrarily with effigies

[1]Jameson, *Characteristics of Women, Moral, Poetical and Historical* (Annapolis: J. Hughes, 1833).

and legends of his own devising, and then attempt to pass it current, like Dryden, Racine, and the rest of those poetical coiners. He only rubbed off the rust, purified and brightened it, so that history herself has been known to receive it back as sterling. [. . .]

Of all Shakspeare's female characters, Miranda and Cleopatra appear to me the most wonderful. The first, unequalled as a poetical conception; the latter miraculous as a work of art. If we could make a regular classification of his characters, these would form the two extremes of simplicity; and all his other characters would be found to fill up some shade or gradation between these two.

Great crimes, springing from high passions, grafted on high qualities, are the legitimate source of tragic poetry. But to make the extremes of littleness produce an effect like grandeur—to make the excess of frailty produce an effect like power—to heap up together all that is most unsubstantial, frivolous, vain, contemptible, and variable, till the worthlessness be lost in the magnitude, and a sense of the sublime spring from the very elements of littleness,—to do this, belonged only to Shakspeare, that worker of miracles. Cleopatra is a brilliant antithesis—a compound of contradictions—of all that we most hate, with what we most admire. The whole character is the triumph of the external over the innate, and yet, like one of her country's hieroglyphics, though she present at first view a spendid and perplexing anomaly, there is deep meaning and wondrous skill in the apparent enigma, when we come to analyze and decipher it. But how are we to arrive at the solution of this glorious riddle, whose dazzling complexity continually mocks and eludes us? What is most astonishing in the character of Cleopatra is its antithetical construction—its *consistent inconsistency*, if I may use such an expression—which renders it quite impossible to reduce it to any elementary principles. It will, perhaps, be found on the whole, that vanity and the love of power predominate; but I dare not say it *is* so, for these qualities and a hundred others mingle into each other, and shift, and change, and glance away, like the colors in a peacock's train.

In some others of Shakspeare's female characters, also remarkable for their complexity, (Portia and Juliet, for instance,) we are struck with the delightful sense of harmony in the midst of contrast, so that the idea of unity and simplicity of effect is produced in the midst of variety; but in Cleopatra, it is the absence of unity and simplicity which strikes us; the impression is that of perpetual and irreconcilable contrast. The continual approximation of whatever is most opposite in character, in situation, in sentiment, would be fatiguing, were it not so perfectly natural; the woman herself would be distracting, if she were not so enchanting.

I have not the slightest doubt that Shakspeare's Cleopatra is the real historical Cleopatra—the "Rare Egyptian"—individualized and placed before us. Her mental accomplishments, her unequalled grace, her woman's wit and woman's wiles, her irresistible allurements, her starts of irregular grandeur, her bursts of ungovernable temper, her vivacity of imagination, her petulant caprice, her fickleness and her falsehood, her tenderness and her truth, her childish susceptibility to flattery, her magnificent spirit, her royal pride, the gorgeous eastern coloring of the character; all these contradictory elements has Shakspeare seized, mingled them in their extremes, and fused them into one brilliant impersonation of classical elegance, Oriental voluptuousness, and gypsy sorcery.

What better proof can we have of the individual truth of the character than the admission that Shakspeare's Cleopatra produces exactly the same effect on us that is recorded of the real Cleopatra?— She dazzles our faculties, perplexes our judgment, bewilders and bewitches our fancy; from the beginning to the end of the drama, we are conscious of a kind of fascination against which our moral sense rebels, but from which there is no escape. The epithets applied to her perpetually by Antony and others confirm this impression: "enchanting queen!"—"witch,"—"spell,"—"great fairy,"—"cockatrice,"— "serpent of old Nile,"—"thou grave charm!"—are only a few of them; and who does not know by heart the famous quotations in which she is described with all her infinite seductions? [...]

We learn from Plutarch, that it was a favorite amusement with Antony and Cleopatra to ramble through the streets at night, and bandy ribald jests with the populace of Alexandria. From the same authority, we know that they were accustomed to live on the most familiar terms with their attendants and the companions of their revels. To these traits we must add, that with all her violence, perverseness, egotism, and caprice, Cleopatra mingled a capability for warm affections and kindly feeling, or rather what we should call in these days, a constitutional *good-nature*—and was lavishly generous to her favorites and dependents. These characteristics we find scattered through the play: they are not only faithfully rendered by

Shakspeare, but he has made the finest use of them in his delineation of manners. Hence the occasional freedom of her women
and her attendants, in the midst of their fears and flatteries,
becomes most natural and consistent; hence, too, their devoted
attachment and fidelity, proved even in death. But as illustrative of
Cleopatra's disposition, perhaps the finest and most characteristic
scene in the whole play, is that in which the messenger arrives from
Rome with the tidings of Antony's marriage with Octavia. She per-
ceives at once with quickness that all is not well, and she hastens to
anticipate the worst, that she may have the pleasure of being disappointed. Her impatience to know what she fears to learn—the vivacity with which she gradually works herself up into a state of
excitement, and at length into fury—is wrought out with a force of
truth which makes us recoil. [. . .] The pride and arrogance of the
Egyptian queen, the blandishment of the woman, the unexpected
but natural transitions of temper and feeling, the contest of various
passions, and at length,—when the wild hurricane has spent its
fury,—the melting into tears, faintness, and languishment, are portrayed with the most astonishing power, and truth, and skill in feminine nature. More wonderful still is the splendor and force of
coloring which is shed over this extraordinary scene. The mere idea
of an angry woman beating her menial presents something ridiculous or disgusting to the mind; in a queen or a tragedy heroine it is
still more indecorous; yet this scene is as far as possible from the vulgar or the comic. Cleopatra seems privileged to "touch the brink of
all we hate" with impunity. This imperial termagant, this "wrangling queen, whom every thing becomes," becomes even her fury.
We know not by what strange power it is, that in the midst of all
these unruly passions and childish caprices, the poetry of the character, and the fanciful and sparkling grace of the delineation are sustained, and still rule in the imagination; but we feel that it is so. [. . .]
But although Cleopatra talks of dying "after the high Roman
fashion," she fears what she most desires, and cannot perform with
simplicity what costs her such an effort. That extreme physical cowardice which was so strong a trait in her historical character, which
led to the defeat of Actium, which made her delay the execution of
her fatal resolve till she had "tried conclusions infinite of *easy* ways
to die," Shakspeare has rendered with the finest possible effect, and
in a manner which heightens instead of diminishing our respect and

interest. Timid by nature, she is courageous by the mere force of will, and she lashes herself up with high-sounding words into a kind of false daring. Her lively imagination suggests every incentive which can spur her on to the deed she has resolved, yet trembles to contemplate. She pictures to herself all the degradations which must attend her captivity; and let it be observed, that those which she anticipates are precisely such as a vain, luxurious, and haughty woman would especially dread, and which only true virtue and magnanimity could despise. Cleopatra could have endured the loss of freedom; but to be led in triumph through the streets of Rome is insufferable. She could stoop to Cæsar with dissembling courtesy, and meet duplicity with superior art; but "to be chastised" by the scornful or upbraiding glance of the injured Octavia—"rather a ditch in Egypt!"

She then calls for her diadem, her robes of state, and attires herself as "if again for Cydnus, to meet Mark Antony." Coquette to the last, she must make Death proud to take her, and die, phoenix-like, as she had lived, with all the pomp of preparation—luxurious in her despair.

The death of Lucretia, of Portia, of Arria, and others, who died "after the high Roman fashion," is sublime according to the Pagan ideas of virtue, and yet none of them so powerfully affect the imagination as the catastrophe of Cleopatra. The idea of this frail, timid, wayward woman, dying with heroism from the mere force of passion and will, takes us by surprise. The attic elegance of her mind, her poetical imagination, the pride of beauty and royalty predominating to the last, and the sumptuous and picturesque accompaniments with which she surrounds herself in death, carry to its extreme height that effect of contrast which prevails through her life and character. No arts, no invention could add to the real circumstances of Cleopatra's closing scene. Shakspeare has shown profound judgment and feeling in adhering closely to the classical authorities; and to say that the language and sentiments worthily fill up the outline, is the most magnificent praise that can be given. The magical play of fancy and the overpowering fascination of the character are kept up to the last; and when Cleopatra, on applying the asp, silences the lamentations of her women—

> Peace! Peace!
> Dost thou not see my baby at my breast,
> That sucks the nurse to sleep?— [5.2.305–7]

These few words—the contrast between the tender beauty of the image and the horror of the situation—produce an effect more intensely mournful than all the ranting in the world. The generous devotion of her women adds the moral charm which alone was wanting: and when Octavius hurries in too late to save his victim, and exclaims, when gazing on her—

> She looks like sleep—
> As she would catch another Antony
> In her strong toil of grace, [5.2.343–45]

the image of her beauty and her irresistible arts, triumphant even in death, is at once brought before us, and one masterly and comprehensive stroke consummates this most wonderful, most dazzling delineation.

I am not here the apologist of Cleopatra's historical character, nor of such women as resemble her: I am considering her merely as a dramatic portrait of astonishing beauty, spirit, and originality. She has furnished the subject of two Latin, sixteen French, six English, and at least, four Italian, tragedies;[2] yet Shakspeare alone has availed himself of all the interest of the story, without falsifying the character. He alone has dared to exhibit the Egyptian queen with all her greatness and all her littleness—all her frailties of temper—all her paltry arts and dissolute passions—yet preserved the dramatic propriety and poetical coloring of the character, and awakened our pity for fallen grandeur, without once beguiling us into sympathy with guilt and error. Corneille has represented Cleopatra as a model of chaste propriety, magnanimity, constancy, and every female virtue; and the effect is almost ludicrous. In our own language, we have two very fine tragedies on the story of Cleopatra: in that of Dryden, which is in truth a noble poem, and which he himself considered his master-piece, Cleopatra is a mere

---

[2]The Cleopatra of Jodelle was the first regular French tragedy; the last French tragedy on the same subject was the Cleopatra of Marmontel. For the representation of this tragedy, Vaucanson, the celebrated French mechanist, invented an automaton asp, which crawled and hissed to the life,—to the great delight of the Parisians. But it appears that neither Vaucanson's asp, nor Clairon, could save Cleopatra from a deserved fate. Of the English tragedies, one was written by the Countess of Pembroke, the sister of Sir Philip Sydney; and is, I believe, the first instance in our language of original dramatic writing by a female. [Jameson]

common-place "all-for-love" heroine, full of constancy and fine sentiments. For instance—

> My love 's so true,
> That I can neither hide it where it is,
> Nor show it where it is not. Nature meant me
> A wife—a silly, harmless, household dove;
> Fond without art, and kind without deceit.
> But fortune, that has made a mistress of me,
> Has thrust me out to the wide world, unfurnished
> Of falsehood to be happy. [*All for Love* 4.1.89–96]

Is this Antony's Cleopatra—the Cleopatra of the Cydnus? *She* never uttered any thing half so mawkish in her life. [. . .]

Dryden has committed a great mistake in bringing Octavia and her children on the scene, and in immediate contact with Cleopatra. To have thus violated the truth of history might have been excusable, but to sacrifice the truth of nature and dramatic propriety, to produce a mere stage effect, was unpardonable. In order to preserve the unity of interest, he has falsified the character of Octavia as well as that of Cleopatra: he has presented us with a regular scolding match between the rivals, in which they come sweeping up to each other from opposite sides of the stage, with their respective trains, like two pea-hens in a passion. Shakspeare would no more have brought his captivating, brilliant, but meretricious Cleopatra into immediate comparison with the noble and chaste simplicity of Octavia, than a connoisseur in art would have placed Canova's Dansatrice, beautiful as it is, beside the Athenian Melpomene, or the Vestal of the Capitol.

A. C. Bradley (1851–1935)

A. C. Bradley is one of the greatest critics of Shakespeare. His lecture on Antony and Cleopatra *(1905; published in 1909) has largely shaped twentieth-century views of the play. Bradley was an academic critic in the emerging discipline of English Literature. He held the newly created Professorship of Poetry at Oxford from 1901 to 1906, after teaching at*

the University of Liverpool and the University of Glasgow; his Shake-
spearean writings are based on classroom lectures. He opposed Antony
and Cleopatra *not to neoclassical unity, but to Shakespeare's own*
tauter, more concentrated and inherently dramatic design in the four
*great tragedies (*Hamlet, King Lear, Othello, *and* Macbeth*), which he*
had discussed in his landmark book, Shakespearean Tragedy *(1904).*
Antony and Cleopatra, *Bradley contends, though a less tragic play,*
exerts so strong a fascination that it sets its own terms. Unlike his near
academic contemporary at Trinity College, Dublin, the Anglo-Irish
critic Edward Dowden (1847–1913), Bradley does not see the play
severely or simply moralizing against the love of Antony and Cleopa-
tra. "She destroys him," Bradley laconically notes, but he argues that
the political world in which they contend with Octavius is already dis-
enchanted. It is rather in the lovers' passion that we feel "the infinity
there is in man: even while we acquiesce in their defeat, we are exulting
in their victory."

from *Oxford Lectures on Poetry* (1905; pub. 1909)[1]

SHAKESPEARE'S ANTONY AND CLEOPATRA

Coleridge's one page of general criticism on *Antony and Cleopatra*
contains some notable remarks. "Of all Shakespeare's historical
plays," he writes, "*Antony and Cleopatra* is by far the most wonderful. There is not one in which he has followed history so minutely,
and yet there are few in which he impresses the notion of angelic
strength so much—perhaps none in which he impresses it more
strongly. This is greatly owing to the manner in which the fiery
force is sustained throughout." In a later sentence he refers to the
play as "this astonishing drama." In another he describes the style:
"*feliciter audax* is the motto for its style comparatively with that of
Shakespeare's other works." And he translates this motto in the
phrase "happy valiancy of style."

Coleridge's assertion that in *Antony and Cleopatra* Shakespeare
followed history more minutely than in any other play might well
be disputed; and his statement about the style of this drama
requires some qualification in view of the results of later criticism as
to the order of Shakespeare's works. The style is less individual than

[1]Bradley, *Oxford Lectures on Poetry* (London: Macmillan and Co., 1909).

he imagined. On the whole it is common to the six or seven dramas subsequent to *Macbeth*, though in *Antony and Cleopatra*, probably the earliest of them, its development is not yet complete. And we must add that this style has certain special defects, unmentioned by Coleridge, as well as the quality which he points out in it. But it is true that here that quality is almost continuously present; and in the phrase by which he describes it, as in his other phrases, he has signalised once for all some of the most salient features of the drama.

It is curious to notice, for example, alike in books and in conversation, how often the first epithets used in reference to *Antony and Cleopatra* are "wonderful" and "astonishing." And the main source of the feeling thus expressed seems to be the "angelic strength" or "fiery force" of which Coleridge wrote. The first of these two phrases is, I think, the more entirely happy. Except perhaps towards the close, one is not so conscious of fiery force as in certain other tragedies; but one is astonished at the apparent ease with which extraordinary effects are produced, the ease, if I may paraphrase Coleridge, of an angel moving with a wave of the hand that heavy matter which men find so intractable. We feel this sovereign ease in contemplating Shakespeare's picture of the world—a vast canvas, crowded with figures, glowing with colour and a superb animation, reminding one spectator of Paul Veronese and another of Rubens. We feel it again when we observe (as we can even without consulting Plutarch) the nature of the material; how bulky it was, and, in some respects, how undramatic; and how the artist, though he could not treat history like legend or fiction, seems to push whole masses aside, and to shift and refashion the remainder, almost with the air of an architect playing (at times rather carelessly) with a child's bricks.

Something similar is felt even in the portrait of Cleopatra. Marvellous as it is, the drawing of it suggests not so much the passionate concentration or fiery force of *Macbeth*, as that sense of effortless and exultant mastery which we feel in the portraits of Mercutio and Falstaff. And surely it is a total mistake to find in this portrait any trace of the distempered mood which disturbs our pleasure in *Troilus and Cressida*. If the sonnets about the dark lady were, as need not be doubted, in some degree autobiographical, Shakespeare may well have used his personal experience both when he drew Cressida and when he drew Cleopatra. And, if he did, the story in the later play was the nearer to his own; for Antony might well have said what Troilus could never say,

> When my love swears that she is made of truth,
> I do believe her, though I know she lies. [Sonnet 138]

But in the later play, not only is the poet's vision unclouded, but his whole nature, emotional as well as intellectual, is free. The subject no more embitters or seduces him than the ambition of Macbeth. So that here too we feel the angelic strength of which Coleridge speaks. If we quarrelled with the phrase at all, it would be because we fancied we could trace in Shakespeare's attitude something of the irony of superiority; and this may not altogether suit our conception of an angel.

I have still another sentence to quote from Coleridge: "The highest praise, or rather form of praise, of this play which I can offer in my own mind, is the doubt which the perusal always occasions in me, whether the 'Antony and Cleopatra' is not, in all exhibitions of a giant power in its strength and vigour of maturity, a formidable rival of 'Macbeth,' 'Lear,' 'Hamlet,' and 'Othello.'" Now, unless the clause here about the "giant power" may be taken to restrict the rivalry to the quality of angelic strength, Coleridge's doubt seems to show a lapse in critical judgment. To regard this tragedy as a rival of the famous four, whether on the stage or in the study, is surely an error. The world certainly has not so regarded it; and, though the world's reasons for its verdicts on works of art may be worth little, its mere verdict is worth much. Here, it seems to me, that verdict must be accepted. One may notice that, in calling *Antony and Cleopatra* wonderful or astonishing, we appear to be thinking first of the artist and his activity, while in the case of the four famous tragedies it is the product of this activity, the thing presented, that first engrosses us. I know that I am stating this difference too sharply, but I believe that it is often felt; and, if this is so, the fact is significant. It implies that, although *Antony and Cleopatra* may be for us as wonderful an achievement as the greatest of Shakespeare's plays, it has not an equal value. Besides, in the attempt to rank it with them there is involved something more, and more important, than an error in valuation. There is a failure to discriminate the peculiar marks of *Antony and Cleopatra* itself, marks which, whether or no it be the equal of the earlier tragedies, make it decidedly different. If I speak first of some of these differences it is because they thus contribute to the individuality of the play, and because they seem often not to be distinctly apprehended in criticism.

1.

Why, let us begin by asking, is *Antony and Cleopatra*, though so wonderful an achievement, a play rarely acted? For a tragedy, it is not painful. Though unfit for children, it cannot be called indecent; some slight omissions, and such a flattening of the heroine's part as might confidently be expected, would leave it perfectly presentable. It is, no doubt, in the third and fourth Acts, very defective in construction. Even on the Elizabethan stage, where scene followed scene without a pause, this must have been felt; and in our theatres it would be felt much more. There, in fact, these two and forty scenes could not possibly be acted as they stand. But defective construction would not distress the bulk of an audience, if the matter presented were that of *Hamlet* or *Othello*, or *Lear* or *Macbeth*. The matter, then, must lack something which is present in those tragedies; and it is mainly owing to this difference in substance that *Antony and Cleopatra* has never attained their popularity either on the stage or off it.

Most of Shakespeare's tragedies are dramatic, in a special sense of the word as well as in its general sense, from beginning to end. The story is not merely exciting and impressive from the movement of conflicting forces towards a terrible issue, but from time to time there come situations and events which, even apart from their bearing on this issue, appeal most powerfully to the dramatic feelings—scenes of action or passion which agitate the audience with alarm, horror, painful expectation, or absorbing sympathies and antipathies. Think of the street fights in *Romeo and Juliet*, the killing of Mercutio and Tybalt, the rapture of the lovers, and their despair when Romeo is banished. Think of the ghost-scenes in the first Act of *Hamlet*, the passion of the early soliloquies, the scene between Hamlet and Ophelia, the play-scene, the sparing of the King at prayer, the killing of Polonius. Is not *Hamlet*, if you choose so to regard it, the best melodrama in the world? Think at your leisure of *Othello*, *Lear*, and *Macbeth* from the same point of view;

but consider here and now even the two tragedies which, as dealing with Roman history, are companions of *Antony and Cleopatra*. Recall in *Julius Cæsar* the first suggestion of the murder, the preparation for it in a "tempest dropping fire," the murder itself, the speech of Antony over the corpse, and the tumult of the furious crowd; in *Coriolanus* the bloody battles on the stage, the scene in which the hero attains the consulship, the scene of rage in which he is banished. And remember that in each of these seven tragedies the matter referred to is contained in the first three Acts.

In the first three Acts of our play what is there resembling this? Almost nothing. People converse, discuss, accuse one another, excuse themselves, mock, describe, drink together, arrange a marriage, meet and part; but they do not kill, do not even tremble or weep. We see hardly one violent movement; until the battle of Actium is over we witness scarcely any vehement passion; and that battle, as it is a naval action, we do not see. Even later, Enobarbus, when he dies, simply dies; he does not kill himself. We hear wonderful talk; but it is not talk, like that of Macbeth and Lady Macbeth, or that of Othello and Iago, at which we hold our breath. The scenes that we remember first are those that portray Cleopatra; Cleopatra coquetting, tormenting, beguiling her lover to stay; Cleopatra left with her women and longing for him; Cleopatra receiving the news of his marriage; Cleopatra questioning the messenger about Octavia's personal appearance. But this is to say that the scenes we remember first are the least indispensable to the plot. One at least is not essential to it at all. And this, the astonishing scene where she storms at the messenger, strikes him, and draws her dagger on him, is the one passage in the first half of the drama that contains either an explosion of passion or an exciting bodily action. Nor is this all. The first half of the play, though it forebodes tragedy, is not decisively tragic in tone. Certainly the Cleopatra scenes are not so. We read them, and we should witness them, in delighted wonder and even with amusement. The only scene that can vie with them, that of the revel on Pompey's ship, though full of menace, is in great part humorous. Enobarbus, in this part of the play, is always humorous. Even later, when the tragic tone is deepening, the whipping of Thyreus, in spite of Antony's rage, moves mirth. A play of which all this can truly be said may well be as masterly as *Othello* or *Macbeth*, and more delightful; but, in the greater part of its course, it cannot possibly excite the same emotions. It makes no attempt to do so; and to regard it as though it made this attempt is to miss its specific character and the intention of its author.

That character depends only in part on Shakespeare's fidelity to his historical authority, a fidelity which, I may remark, is often greatly exaggerated. For Shakespeare did not merely present the story of ten years as though it occupied perhaps one fifth of that time, nor did he merely invent freely, but in critical places he effected startling changes in the order and combination of events. Still it may be said that, dealing with a history so famous, he could not well make the first half of his play very exciting, moving, or tragic. And this is true so far as mere situations and events are concerned. But, if he had chosen, he might easily have heightened the tone and tension in another way. He might have made the story of Antony's attempt to break his bondage, and the story of his relapse, extremely exciting, by portraying with all his force the severity of the struggle and the magnitude of the fatal step.

And the structure of the play might seem at first to suggest this intention. At the opening, Antony is shown almost in the beginning of his infatuation; for Cleopatra is not sure of her power over him, exerts all her fascination to detain him, and plays the part of the innocent victim who has yielded to passion and must now expect to be deserted by her seducer. Alarmed and ashamed at the news of the results of his inaction, he rouses himself, tears himself away, and speeds to Italy. His very coming is enough to frighten Pompey into peace. He reconciles himself with Octavius, and, by his marriage with the good and beautiful Octavia, seems to have knit a bond of lasting amity with her brother, and to have guarded himself against the passion that threatened him with ruin. At this point his power, the world's peace, and his own peace, appear to be secured; his fortune has mounted to its apex. But soon (very much sooner than in Plutarch's story) comes the downward turn or counter-stroke. New causes of offence arise between the brothers-in-law. To remove them Octavia leaves her husband in Athens and hurries to Rome. Immediately Antony returns to Cleopatra and, surrendering himself at once and wholly to her enchantment is quickly driven to his doom.

Now Shakespeare, I say, with his matchless power of depicting an inward struggle, might have made this story, even where it could not furnish him with thrilling incidents, the source of powerful tragic emotions; and, in doing so, he would have departed from his authority merely in his conception of the hero's character. But he does no such thing till the catastrophe is near. Antony breaks away from Cleopatra without any strenuous conflict. No serious doubt of his return is permitted to agitate us. We are almost assured of it through the impression made on us by Octavius, through occasional glimpses into Antony's mind, through the absence of any doubt in Enobarbus, through scenes in Alexandria which display Cleopatra and display her irresistible. And, finally, the downward turn itself, the fatal step of Antony's return, is shown without the slightest emphasis. Nay, it is not shown, it is only reported; and not a line portrays any inward struggle preceding it. On this side also, then, the drama makes no attempt to rival the other tragedies; and it was essential to its own peculiar character and its most transcendent effects that this attempt should not be made, but that Antony's passion should be represented as a force which he could hardly even desire to resist. By the very scheme of the work, therefore, tragic impressions of any great volume or depth were reserved for the last stage of the conflict; while the main interest, down to the battle of Actium, was directed to matters exceedingly interesting and even, in the wider sense, dramatic, but not overtly either terrible or piteous: on the one hand, to the political aspect of the story; on the other, to the personal causes which helped to make the issue inevitable.

2.

The political situation and its development are simple. The story is taken up almost where it was left, years before, in *Julius Cæsar*. There Brutus and Cassius, to prevent the rule of one man, assassinate Cæsar. Their purpose is condemned to failure, not merely because they make mistakes, but because that political necessity which Napoleon identified with destiny requires the rule of one man. They spill Cæsar's blood, but his spirit walks abroad and turns their swords against their own breasts; and the world is left divided among three men, his friends and his heir. Here *Antony and Cleopatra* takes up the tale; and its business, from this point of view, is to show the reduction of these three to one. That Lepidus will not be this one was clear already in *Julius Cæsar*; it must be Octavius or Antony. Both ambitious, they are also men of such opposite tempers that they would scarcely long agree even if they wished to, and even if destiny were not stronger than they. As it is, one of them has fixed his eyes on the end, sacrifices everything for it, uses everything as a means to it. The other, though far the greater soldier and worshipped by his followers, has no such singleness of aim; nor yet is power, however desirable to him, the most desirable thing in the world. At the beginning he is risking it for love; at the end he has lost his half of the world, and lost his life, and Octavius rules alone. Whether Shakespeare had this clearly in his mind is a question neither answerable nor important; this is what came out of his mind.

Shakespeare, I think, took little interest in the character of Octavius, and he has not made it wholly clear. It is not distinct in Plutarch's "Life of Antony"; and I have not found traces that the poet studied closely the "Life of Octavius" included in North's volume. To Shakespeare he is one of those men, like Bolingbroke and Ulysses, who have plenty of "judgment" and not much "blood." Victory in the world, according to the poet, almost always goes to such men; and he makes us respect, fear and dislike them. His Octavius is very formidable. His cold determination half paralyses Antony; it is so even in *Julius Cæsar*. In *Antony and Cleopatra* Octavius is more than once in the wrong; but he never admits it; he silently pushes his rival a step backward; and, when he ceases to fear, he shows contempt. He neither enjoys war nor is great in it; at first, therefore, he is anxious about the power of Pompey, and stands in need of Antony. As soon as Antony's presence has served his turn, and he has patched up a union with him and seen him safely off to Athens, he destroys first Pompey and next Lepidus. Then, dexterously using Antony's faithlessness to Octavia and excesses in the East in order to put himself in the right, he makes for his victim with admirable celerity while he is still drunk with the joy of reunion with Cleopatra. For his ends Octavius is perfectly efficient, but he is so partly from his limitations. One phrase of his is exceedingly characteristic. When Antony in rage and desperation challenges him to single combat, Octavius calls him "the old ruffian." There is a horrid aptness in the phrase, but it disgusts us. It is shameful in this boy, as hard and smooth as polished steel, to feel at such a time nothing of the greatness of his victim and the tragedy of his victim's fall. Though the challenge of Antony is absurd, we would give much to see them sword to sword. And when Cleopatra by her death cheats the conqueror of his prize, we feel unmixed delight.

The doubtful point in the character is this. Plutarch says that Octavius was reported to love his sister dearly; and Shakespeare's Octavius several times expresses such love. When, then, he proposed the marriage with Antony (for of course it was he who spoke through Agrippa), was he honest, or was he laying a trap and, in doing so, sacrificing his sister? Did he hope the marriage would really unite him with his brother-in-law; or did he merely mean it to be a source of future differences; or did he calculate that, whether it secured peace or dissension, it would in either case bring him great advantage? Shakespeare, who was quite as intelligent as his readers, must have asked himself some such question; but he may not have cared to answer it even to himself; and, in any case, he has left the actor (at least the actor in days later than his own) to choose an answer. If I were forced to choose, I should take the view that Octavius was, at any rate, not wholly honest; partly because I think it best suits Shakespeare's usual way of conceiving a character of the kind; partly because Plutarch construed in this manner Octavius's behaviour in regard to his sister at a later time, and this hint might naturally influence the poet's way of imagining his earlier action.

Though the character of Octavius is neither attractive nor wholly clear, his figure is invested with a certain tragic dignity, because he is felt to be the Man of Destiny, the agent of forces against which the intentions of an individual would avail nothing. He is represented as having himself some feeling of this sort. His lament over Antony, his grief that their stars were irreconcilable, may well be genuine, though we should be surer if it were uttered in soliloquy. His austere words to Octavia again probably speak his true mind:

> Be you not troubled with the time, which drives
> O'er your content these strong necessities;
> But let determined things to destiny
> Hold unbewailed their way. [3.6.85–88]

In any case the feeling of fate comes through to us. It is aided by slight touches of supernatural effect; first in the Soothsayer's warning to Antony that his genius or angel is overpowered whenever he is near Octavius; then in the strangely effective scene where Antony's soldiers, in the night before his last battle, hear music in the air or under the earth:

> 'Tis the god Hercules, whom Antony loved,
> Now leaves him. [4.3.21–22]

And to the influence of this feeling in giving impressiveness to the story is added that of the immense scale and world-wide issue of the conflict. Even the distances traversed by fleets and armies enhance this effect.

And yet there seems to be something half-hearted in Shakespeare's appeal here, something even ironical in his presentation of this conflict. Its external magnitude, like Antony's magnificence in lavishing realms and gathering the kings of the East in his support, fails to uplift or dilate the imagination. The struggle in Lear's little island seems to us to have an infinitely wider scope. It is here that we are sometimes reminded of *Troilus and Cressida*, and the cold and disenchanting light that is there cast on the Trojan War. The spectacle which he portrays leaves Shakespeare quite undazzled; he even makes it appear inwardly small. The lordship of the world, we ask ourselves, what is it worth, and in what spirit do these "world-sharers" contend for it? They are no champions of their country like Henry V. The conqueror knows not even the glory of battle. Their aims, for all we see, are as personal as if they were captains of banditti; and they are followed merely from self-interest or private attachment. The scene on Pompey's galley is full of this irony. One "third part of the world" is carried drunk to bed. In the midst of this mock boon-companionship the pirate whispers to his leader to cut first the cable of his ship and then the throats of the two other Emperors; and at the moment we should not greatly care if Pompey took the advice. Later, a short scene, totally useless to the plot and purely satiric in its purport, is slipped in to show how Ventidius fears to pursue his Parthian conquests because it is not safe for Antony's lieutenant to outdo his master. A painful sense of hollowness oppresses us. We know too well what must happen in a world so splendid, so false, and so petty. We turn for relief from the political game to those who are sure to lose it; to those who love some human being better than a prize, to Eros and Charmian and Iras; to Enobarbus, whom the world corrupts, but who has a heart that can break with shame; to the lovers, who seem to us to find in death something better than their victor's life.

This presentation of the outward conflict has two results. First, it blunts our feeling of the greatness of Antony's fall from prosperity. Indeed this feeling, which we might expect to be unusually acute, is hardly so; it is less acute, for example, than the like feeling in the case of Richard II, who loses so much smaller a realm. Our deeper sympathies are focussed rather on Antony's heart, on the inward fall to which the enchantment of passion leads him, and the inward recovery which succeeds it. And the second result is this. The greatness of Antony and Cleopatra in their fall is so much heightened by contrast with the world they lose and the conqueror who wins it, that the positive element in the final tragic impression, the element of reconciliation, is strongly emphasised. The peculiar effect of the drama depends partly, as we have seen, on the absence of decidedly tragic scenes and events in its first half; but it depends quite as much on this emphasis. In any Shakespearean tragedy we watch some elect spirit colliding, partly through its error and defect, with a superhuman power which bears it down; and yet we feel that this spirit, even in the error and defect, rises by its greatness into ideal union with the power that overwhelms it. In some tragedies this latter feeling is relatively weak. In *Antony and Cleopatra* it is unusually strong; stronger, with some readers at least, than the fear and grief and pity with which they contemplate the tragic error and the advance of doom.

3.

The two aspects of the tragedy are presented together in the opening scene. Here is the first. In Cleopatra's palace one friend of Antony is describing to another, just arrived from Rome, the dotage of their great general; and, as the lovers enter, he exclaims:

> Look, where they come:
> Take but good note, and you shall see in him
> The triple pillar of the world transformed
> Into a strumpet's fool: behold and see.

With the next words the other aspect appears:

> *Cleopatra.* If it be love indeed, tell me how much.
> *Antony.* There's beggary in the love that can be reckoned.
> *Cleopatra.* I'll set a bourne how far to be beloved.
> *Antony.* Then must thou needs find out new heaven, new earth. [1.1.14–17]

And directly after, when he is provoked by reminders of the news from Rome:

> Let Rome in Tiber melt, and the wide arch
> Of the ranged empire fall! Here is my space.
> Kingdoms are clay; our dungy earth alike
> Feeds beast as man: the nobleness of life
> Is to do thus. [1.1.35–39]

Here is the tragic excess, but with it the tragic greatness, the capacity of finding in something the infinite, and of pursuing it into the jaws of death.

The two aspects are shown here with the exaggeration proper in dramatic characters. Neither the phrase "a strumpet's fool," nor the assertion "the nobleness of life is to do thus," answers to the total effect of the play. But the truths they exaggerate are equally essential; and the commoner mistake in criticism is to understate the second. It is plain that the love of Antony and Cleopatra is destructive; that in some way it clashes with the nature of things; that, while they are sitting in their paradise like gods, its walls move inward and crush them at last to death. This is no invention of moralising critics; it is in the play; and any one familiar with Shakespeare would expect beforehand to find it there. But then to forget because of it the other side, to deny the name of love to this ruinous passion, to speak as though the lovers had utterly missed the good of life, is to mutilate the tragedy and to ignore a great part of its effect upon us. For we sympathise with them in their passion; we feel in it the infinity there is in man; even while we acquiesce in their defeat we are exulting in their victory; and when they have vanished we say,

> the odds is gone,
> And there is nothing left remarkable
> Beneath the visiting moon. [**4.15.68–70**]

Though we hear nothing from Shakespeare of the cruelty of Plutarch's Antony, or of the misery caused by his boundless profusion, we do not feel the hero of the tragedy to be a man of the noblest type, like Brutus, Hamlet, or Othello. He seeks power merely for himself, and uses it for his own pleasure. He is in some respects unscrupulous; and, while it would be unjust to regard his marriage exactly as if it were one in private life, we resent his treatment of Octavia, whose character Shakespeare was obliged to leave a mere sketch, lest our feeling for the hero and heroine should be too much chilled. Yet, for all this, we sympathise warmly with Antony, are greatly drawn to him, and are inclined to regard him as a noble nature half spoiled by his time.

It is a large, open, generous, expansive nature, quite free from envy, capable of great magnanimity, even of entire devotion. Antony is unreserved, naturally straightforward, we may almost say simple. He can admit faults, accept advice and even reproof, take a jest against himself with good-humour. He is courteous (to Lepidus, for example, whom Octavius treats with cold contempt); and, though he can be exceedingly dignified, he seems to prefer a blunt though sympathetic plainness, which is one cause of the attachment of his soldiers. He has none of the faults of the brooder, the sentimentalist, or the man of principle; his nature tends to splendid action and lusty enjoyment. But he is neither a mere soldier nor a mere sensualist. He has imagination, the temper of an artist who revels in abundant and rejoicing appetites, feasts his senses on the glow and richness of life, flings himself into its mirth and revelry, yet feels the poetry in all this, and is able also to put it by and be more than content with the hardships of adventure. Such a man could never have sought a crown by a murder like Macbeth's, or, like Brutus, have killed on principle the man who loved him, or have lost the world for a Cressida.

Beside this strain of poetry he has a keen intellect, a swift perception of the lie of things, and much quickness in shaping a course to suit them. In *Julius Cæsar* he shows this after the assassination, when he appears as a dexterous politician as well as a warm-hearted friend. He admires what is fine, and can fully appreciate the nobility of Brutus; but he is sure that Brutus's ideas are moonshine, that (as he says in our play) Brutus is mad; and, since his mighty friend, who was incomparably the finest thing in the world, has perished, he sees no reason why the inheritance should not be his own. Full of sorrow, he yet uses his sorrow like an artist to work on others, and greets his success with the glee of a successful adventurer. In the earlier play he proves himself a master of eloquence, and especially of pathos; and he does so again in the later. With a few words about his fall he draws tears from his followers and even from the caustic humorist Enobarbus. Like Richard II, he sees his own fall with the eyes of a poet, but a poet much greater than the young Shakespeare, who could never have written Antony's marvellous speech about the sunset clouds. But we listen to Antony, as we do not to Richard, with entire sympathy, partly because he is never unmanly, partly because he himself is sympathetic and longs for sympathy.

The first of living soldiers, an able politician, a most persuasive orator, Antony nevertheless was not born to rule the world. He enjoys being a great man, but he has not the love of rule for rule's sake. Power for him is chiefly a means to pleasure. The pleasure he wants is so huge that he needs a huge power; but half the world, even a third of it, would suffice. He will not pocket wrongs, but he shows not the slightest wish to get rid of his fellow Triumvirs and reign alone. He never minded being subordinate to Julius Cæsar. By women he is not only attracted but governed; from the effect of Cleopatra's taunts we can see that he had been governed by Fulvia. Nor has he either the patience or the steadfastness of a born ruler. He contends fitfully, and is prone to take the step that is easiest at the moment. This is the reason why he consents to marry Octavia. It seems the shortest way out of an awkward situation. He does not intend even to try to be true to her. He will not think of the distant consequences.

A man who loved power as much as thousands of insignificant people love it, would have made a sterner struggle than Antony's against his enchantment. He can hardly be said to struggle at all. He brings himself to leave Cleopatra only because he knows he will return. In every moment of his absence, whether he wake or sleep, a siren music in his blood is singing him back to her; and to this music, however he may be occupied, the soul within his soul leans and listens. The joy of life had always culminated for him in the love of women: he could say "no" to none of them: of Octavia herself he speaks like a poet. When he meets Cleopatra he finds his Absolute. She satisfies, nay glorifies, his whole being. She intoxicates his senses. Her wiles, her taunts, her furies and meltings, her laughter and tears, bewitch him all alike. She loves what he loves, and she surpasses him. She can drink him to his bed, out-jest his practical jokes, out-act the best actress who ever amused him, out-dazzle his own magnificence. She is his play-fellow, and yet a great queen. Angling in the river, playing billiards, flourishing the sword he used at Philippi, hopping forty paces in a public street, she remains an enchantress. Her spirit is made of wind and flame, and the poet in him worships her no less than the man. He is under no illusion about her, knows all her faults, sees through her wiles, believes her capable of betraying him. It makes no difference. She is his heart's desire made perfect. To love her is what he was born for. What have the gods in heaven to say against it? To imagine heaven is to imagine her; to die is to rejoin her. To deny that this is love is the madness of morality. He gives her every atom of his heart.

She destroys him. Shakespeare, availing himself of the historic fact, portrays, on Antony's return to her, the suddenness and the depth of his descent. In spite of his own knowledge, the protests of his captains, the entreaties even of a private soldier, he fights by sea simply and solely because she wishes it. Then in mid-battle, when she flies, he deserts navy and army and his faithful thousands and follows her. "I never saw an action of such shame," cries Scarus; and we feel the dishonour of the hero keenly. Then Shakespeare begins to raise him again. First, his own overwhelming sense of shame redeems him. Next, we watch the rage of the dying lion. Then the mere sally before the final defeat—a sally dismissed by Plutarch in three lines—is magnified into a battle, in which Antony displays to us, and himself feels for the last time, the glory of his soldiership. And, throughout, the magnanimity and gentleness which shine through his desperation endear him to us. How beautiful is his affection for his followers and even for his servants, and the devotion they return! How noble his reception of the news that Enobarbus has deserted him! How touchingly significant the refusal of Eros either to kill him or survive him! How pathetic and even sublime the completeness of his love for Cleopatra! His anger is born and dies in an hour. One tear, one kiss, outweighs his ruin. He believes she has sold him to his enemy, yet he kills himself because he hears that she is dead. When, dying, he learns that she has deceived him once more, no thought of reproach crosses his mind: he simply asks to be carried to her. He knows well that she is not capable of dying because he dies, but that does not sting him; when, in his last agony, he calls for wine that he may gain a moment's strength to speak, it is to advise her for the days to come. Shakespeare borrowed from Plutarch the final speech of Antony. It is fine, but it is not miraculous. The miraculous speeches belong only to his own hero:

> I am dying, Egypt, dying; only
> I here importune death awhile, until
> Of many thousand kisses the poor last
> I lay upon thy lips; [4.15.19–22]

or the first words he utters when he hears of Cleopatra's death:

> Unarm, Eros: the long day's task is done,
> And we must sleep. [4.14.35–36]

If he meant the task of statesman and warrior, that is not what his words mean to us. They remind us of words more familiar and less great—

> No rest but the grave for the pilgrim of love.

And he is more than love's pilgrim; he is love's martyr.

4.

To reserve a fragment of an hour for Cleopatra, if it were not palpably absurd, would seem an insult. If only one could hear her own remarks upon it! But I had to choose between this absurdity and the plan of giving her the whole hour; and to that plan there was one fatal objection. She has been described (by Ten Brink) as a courtesan of genius. So brief a description must needs be incomplete, and Cleopatra never forgets, nor, if we read aright, do we forget, that she is a great queen. Still the phrase is excellent; only a public lecture is no occasion for the full analysis and illustration of the character it describes.

Shakespeare has paid Cleopatra a unique compliment. The hero dies in the fourth Act, and the whole of the fifth is devoted to the heroine.[2] In that Act she becomes unquestionably a tragic character, but, it appears to me, not till then. This, no doubt, is a heresy; but as I cannot help holding it, and as it is connected with the remarks already made on the first half of the play, I will state it more fully. Cleopatra stands in a group with Hamlet and Falstaff. We might join with them Iago if he were not decidedly their inferior in one particular quality. They are inexhaustible. You feel that, if they were alive and you spent your whole life with them, their infinite variety could never be staled by custom; they would continue every day to surprise, perplex, and delight you. Shakespeare has bestowed on each of them, though they differ so much, his own originality, his genius. He has given it most fully to Hamlet, to whom none of the chambers of experience is shut, and perhaps more of it to Cleopatra than to Falstaff. Nevertheless, if we ask whether Cleopatra, in the first four Acts, is a tragic figure like Hamlet, we surely cannot answer "yes." Naturally it does not follow that she is a comic figure like Falstaff. This would be absurd; for, even if she were ridiculous like Falstaff, she is not ridiculous to herself; she is no humorist. And yet there is a certain likeness. She shares a weakness with Falstaff—vanity; and when she displays it, as she does quite naïvely (for instance, in the second interview with the Messenger), she does become comic. Again, though like Falstaff she is irresistible and carries us away no less than the people around her, we are secretly aware, in the midst of our delight, that her empire is built on sand. And finally, as his love for the Prince gives dignity and pathos to Falstaff in his overthrow, so what raises Cleopatra at last into pure tragedy is, in part, that which some critics have denied her, her love for Antony.

Many unpleasant things can be said of Cleopatra; and the more that are said the more wonderful she appears. The exercise of sexual attraction is the element of her life; and she has developed nature into a consummate art. When she cannot exert it on the present lover she imagines its effects on him in absence. Longing for the living, she remembers with pride and joy the dead; and the past

---

[2]The point of this remark is unaffected by the fact that the play is not divided into acts and scenes in the folios. [Bradley]

which the furious Antony holds up to her as a picture of shame is, for her, glory. She cannot see an ambassador, scarcely even a messenger, without desiring to bewitch him. Her mind is saturated with this element. If she is dark, it is because the sun himself has been amorous of her. Even when death is close at hand she imagines his touch as a lover's. She embraces him that she may overtake Iras and gain Antony's first kiss in the other world.

She lives for feeling. Her feelings are, so to speak, sacred, and pain must not come near her. She has tried numberless experiments to discover the easiest way to die. Her body is exquisitely sensitive, and her emotions marvellously swift. They are really so; but she exaggerates them so much, and exhibits them so continually for effect, that some readers fancy them merely feigned. They are all-important, and everybody must attend to them. She announces to her women that she is pale, or sick and sullen; they must lead her to her chamber but must not speak to her. She is as strong and supple as a leopard, can drink down a master of revelry, can raise her lover's helpless heavy body from the ground into her tower with the aid only of two women; yet, when he is sitting apart sunk in shame, she must be supported into his presence, she cannot stand, her head droops, she will die (it is the opinion of Eros) unless he comforts her. When she hears of his marriage and has discharged her rage, she bids her women bear her away; she faints; at least she would faint, but that she remembers various questions she wants put to the Messenger about Octavia. Enobarbus has seen her die twenty times upon far poorer moment than the news that Antony is going to Rome.

Some of her feelings are violent, and, unless for a purpose, she does not dream of restraining them; her sighs and tears are winds and waters, storms and tempests. At times, as when she threatens to give Charmian bloody teeth, or hales the luckless Messenger up and down by the hair, strikes him and draws her knife on him, she resembles (if I dare say it) Doll Tearsheet sublimated. She is a mother; but the threat of Octavius to destroy her children if she takes her own life passes by her like the wind (a point where Shakespeare contradicts Plutarch). She ruins a great man, but shows no sense of the tragedy of his ruin. The anguish of spirit that appears in his language to his servants is beyond her; she has to ask Enobarbus what he means. Can we feel sure that she would not have sacrificed him if she could have saved herself by doing so? It is not even certain that she did not attempt it. Antony himself believes that she did—that the fleet went over to Octavius by her orders. That she and her people deny the charge proves nothing. The best we can say is that, if it were true, Shakespeare would have made that clear. She is willing also to survive her lover. Her first thought, to follow him after the high Roman fashion, is too great for her. She would live on if she could, and would cheat her victor too of the best part of her fortune. The thing that drives her to die is the certainty that she will be carried to Rome to grace his triumph. That alone decides her.

The marvellous thing is that the knowledge of all this makes hardly more difference to us than it did to Antony. It seems to us perfectly natural, nay, in a sense perfectly right, that her lover should be her slave; that her women should adore her and die with her; that Enobarbus, who foresaw what must happen, and who opposes her wishes and braves her anger, should talk of her with rapture and feel no bitterness against her; that Dolabella, after a minute's conversation, should betray to her his master's intention and enable her to frustrate it. And when Octavius shows himself proof against her fascination, instead of admiring him we turn from him with disgust and think him a disgrace to his species. Why? It is not that we consider him bound to fall in love with her. Enobarbus did not; Dolabella did not; we ourselves do not. The feeling she inspires was felt then, and is felt now, by women no less than men, and would have been shared by Octavia herself. Doubtless she wrought magic on the senses, but she had not extraordinary beauty, like Helen's, such beauty as seems divine. Plutarch says so. The man who wrote the sonnets to the dark lady would have known it for himself. He goes out of his way to add to her age, and tells us of her wrinkles and the waning of her lip. But Enobarbus, in his very mockery, calls her a wonderful piece of work. Dolabella interrupts her with the cry, "Most sovereign creature," and we echo it. And yet Octavius, face to face with her and listening to her voice, can think only how best to trap her and drag her to public dishonour in the streets of Rome. We forgive him only for his words when he sees her dead:

> She looks like sleep,
> As she would catch another Antony
> In her strong toil of grace. [5.2.343–45]

And the words, I confess, sound to me more like Shakespeare's than his.

That which makes her wonderful and sovereign laughs at definition, but she herself came nearest naming it when, in the final speech (a passage surpassed in poetry, if at all, only by the final speech of Othello), she cries,

> I am fire and air; my other elements
> I give to baser life. [5.3.286–87]

The fire and air which at death break from union with those other elements, transfigured them during her life, and still convert into engines of enchantment the very things for which she is condemned. I can refer only to one. She loves Antony. We should marvel at her less and love her more if she loved him more—loved him well enough to follow him at once to death; but it is to blunder strangely to doubt that she loved him, or that her glorious description of him (though it was also meant to work on Dolabella) came from her heart. Only the spirit of fire and air within her refuses to be trammelled or extinguished; burns its way through the obstacles of fortune and even through the resistance of her love and grief; and would lead her undaunted to fresh life and the conquest of new worlds. It is this which makes her "strong toil of grace" unbreakable; speaks in her brows' bent and every tone and movement; glorifies the arts and the rages which in another would merely disgust or amuse us; and, in the final scenes of her life, flames into such brilliance that we watch her entranced as she struggles for freedom, and thrilled with triumph as, conquered, she puts her conqueror to scorn and goes to meet her lover in the splendour that crowned and robed her long ago, when her barge burnt on the water like a burnished throne, and she floated to Cydnus on the enamoured stream to take him captive for ever.

Why is it that, although we close the book in a triumph which is more than reconciliation, this is mingled, as we look back on the story, with a sadness so peculiar, almost the sadness of disenchantment? Is it that, when the glow has faded, Cleopatra's ecstasy comes to appear, I would not say factitious, but an effort strained and prodigious as well as glorious, not, like Othello's last speech, the final expression of character, of thoughts and emotions which have dominated a whole life? Perhaps this is so, but there is something more, something that sounds paradoxical: we are saddened by the very fact that the catastrophe saddens us so little; it pains us that we should feel so much triumph and pleasure. In *Romeo and Juliet, Hamlet, Othello*, though in a sense we accept the deaths of hero and heroine, we feel a keen sorrow. We look back, think how noble or beautiful they were, wish that fate had opposed to them a weaker enemy, dream possibly of the life they might have led. Here we can hardly do this. With all our admiration and sympathy for the lovers we do not wish them to gain the world. It is better for the world's sake, and not less for their own, that they should fail and die. At the very first they came before us, unlike those others, unlike Coriolanus and even Macbeth, in a glory already tarnished, half-ruined by their past. Indeed one source of strange and most unusual effect in their story is that this marvellous passion comes to adepts in the experience and art of passion, who might be expected to have worn its charm away. Its splendour dazzles us; but, when the splendour vanishes, we do not mourn, as we mourn for the love of Romeo or Othello, that a thing so bright and good should die. And the fact that we mourn so little saddens us.

A comparison of Shakespearean tragedies seems to prove that the tragic emotions are stirred in the fullest possible measure only when such beauty or nobility of character is displayed as commands unreserved admiration or love; or when, in default of this, the forces which move the agents, and the conflict which results from these forces, attain a terrifying and overwhelming power. The four most famous tragedies satisfy one or both of these conditions; *Antony and Cleopatra*, though a great tragedy, satisfies neither of them completely. But to say this is not to criticise it. It does not attempt to satisfy these conditions, and then fail in the attempt. It attempts something different, and succeeds as triumphantly as *Othello* itself. In doing so it gives us what no other tragedy can give, and it leaves us, no less than any other, lost in astonishment at the powers which created it.

Further Reading

Criticism on *Antony and Cleopatra*

Anthologies

Bloom, Harold, ed. *William Shakespeare's Antony and Cleopatra.* Chelsea House, 1988.

Brown, John Russell, ed. *"Antony and Cleopatra": A Casebook.* Revised edition. Macmillan, 1991.

Deats, Sarah Munson, ed. *Antony and Cleopatra: New Critical Essays.* Routledge, 2005.

Drakakis, John, ed. *Antony and Cleopatra.* St. Martin's Press, 1994.

Individual Studies

Adelman, Janet. *The Common Liar: An Essay on "Antony and Cleopatra."* Yale Univ. Press, 1973.

Archer, John Michael. "Antiquity and Degeneration: The Representation of Egypt and Shakespeare's *Antony and Cleopatra.*" *Genre* 27 (1994): 1–27.

Bamber, Linda. "*Antony and Cleopatra.*" In *Comic Women, Tragic Men: A Study of Gender and Genre in Shakespeare.* Stanford Univ. Press, 1982.

Barton, Anne. "'Nature's Piece 'gainst fancy': The Divided Catastrophe in *Antony and Cleopatra.*" In *Essays, Mainly Shakespearean.* Cambridge Univ. Press, 1994.

Bono, Barbara. *Literary Transvaluation from Virgilian Epic to Shakespearean Tragicomedy.* Univ. of California Press, 1984.

Braden, Gordon. "Plutarch, Shakespeare and the Alpha Males." In *Shakespeare and the Classics*, ed. Charles Martindale. Cambridge Univ. Press, 2004.

Colie, Rosalie. "*Antony and Cleopatra*: The Significance of Style." In *Shakespeare's Living Art*. Princeton, 1974.

Danby, John. "*Antony and Cleopatra*: A Shakespearian Adjustment." In *Poets on Fortune's Hill*. Faber and Faber, 1952.

Garber, Marjorie. "*Antony and Cleopatra*." In *Shakespeare After All*. Pantheon Books, 2004.

Greene, Thomas M. "Pressures of Context in *Antony and Cleopatra*." In *Poetry, Signs, and Magic*. Univ. of Delaware Press, 2005.

Kahn, Coppélia. *Roman Shakespeare: Warriors, Wounds, and Women*. Routledge, 1997.

Knight, G. Wilson. *The Imperial Theme*. Oxford Univ. Press, 1931.

Lamb, Margaret. *"Antony and Cleopatra" on the English Stage*. Associated Univ. Presses, 1980.

Mack, Maynard. "The Stillness and the Dance: *Antony and Cleopatra*." In *Everybody's Shakespeare*. Univ. of Nebraska Press, 1993.

Miola, Robert S. *Shakespeare's Rome*. Cambridge Univ. Press, 1983.

Quint, David. "The Tragedy of Nobility on the Seventeenth-Century Stage." *Modern Language Quarterly* 67 (2006): 7–29.

Snyder, Susan. "Patterns of Motion in *Antony and Cleopatra*." *Shakespeare Survey* 33 (1980): 113–22.

Tanner, Tony. "*Antony and Cleopatra*: Boundaries and Excess." *Hebrew University Studies in Literature and the Arts* 5 (1987): 78–104.

Traversi, Derek. *Shakespeare: The Roman Plays*. Stanford Univ. Press, 1963.

Van Doren, Mark. "*Antony and Cleopatra*." In *Shakespeare*. Henry Holt, 1939.

Williamson, Marilyn L. *Infinite Variety: Antony and Cleopatra in Renaissance Drama and Earlier Tradition*. Lawrence Verry, Inc., 1974.

On the Historical Antony and Cleopatra and the Image of Cleopatra in Subsequent History

Chauveau, Michel. *Cleopatra: Beyond the Myth*. Cornell Univ. Press, 2002.

Grant, Michael. *Cleopatra*. Weidenfeld and Nicolson, 1972.

Griffin, Jasper. "Propertius and Antony." *Journal of Roman Studies* 67 (1977): 17–26.

Hamer, Mary. *Signs of Cleopatra: History, Politics, Representation*. Routledge, 1992.

Kleiner, Diana E. E. *Cleopatra and Rome*. Harvard Univ. Press, 2005.

Rowell, Henry Thompson. *Rome in the Augustan Age*. Univ. of Oklahoma Press, 1962.

Syme, Ronald. *The Roman Revolution*. Clarendon Press, 1939.

Tarn, W. W., and Charlesworth, M. P. *Octavian, Antony and Cleopatra*. Cambridge Univ. Press, 1965.

Walker, Susan, and Higgs, Peter, eds. *Cleopatra of Egypt: From History to Myth*. Princeton Univ. Press, 2001.